The Hesterville Bible Trial

The Hesterville Bible Trial

a novel
including appendix
with full trial transcript

Yaakov Yosef Reinman

SHUFRA
institute press

dedicated to the memory
of my good friend
Rabbi Pinchas Stolper זצ"ל
who encouraged me to
write this book

I would like to express my deepest gratitude to

Mrs. Cherna Moskowitz

and the

Irving I Moskowitz Foundation

for their generous support for this project

in its earliest stages.

Preface

**The Genesis and Evolution of
"The Hesterville Bible Trial"**

The idea for this book was born in 2005, not in my head but in the head of my good friend Rabbi Pinchas Stolper זצ"ל, to whose memory this book is dedicated. Actually, I did not know Rabbi Stolper when he first approached me. He had served for many years as executive vice president of the Orthodox Union and national director of the National Council of Synagogue Youth. After he retired, he moved to Lakewood, New Jersey, where I live, and turned his full attention to the study of biblical archaeology. Rabbi Stolper was looking for someone to write a book to defend classical Judaism against the minimalists who claim the Old Testament is a fraud.

Several years earlier, I had co-authored a book called "One People, Two Worlds: A Reform Rabbi and an Orthodox Rabbi Explore the Issues that Divide Them" with Ammiel Hirsch, a prominent Reform rabbi. It was essentially an exchange of emails, a ferocious battle in cyberspace that pitted our ideologies against each other.

Although there are undoubtedly many paths to God, Orthodox Judaism believes that the Jewish path requires strict observance of the Torah's commandments. Therefore, the Orthodox rabbinate eschews dialogue or debate with the liberal streams so as to avoid the impression that there are other legitimate Jewish paths. When the suggestion of writing a book with a Reform rabbi was presented to me, I asked several venerable rabbis if such a project would violate the general rule since I am technically not a practicing member of the rabbinate; I am a Talmudic scholar, an academic, and hold no official rabbinic position. Because there is so much misinformation about Orthodoxy in the liberal communities, these rabbis encouraged me to take on the project.

The book, which was published by Random House, caused quite a media sensation. It also triggered serious blowback in the Orthodox community, which generated even more media attention. Considering that my works on Talmudic civil law are studied in yeshivos worldwide and have even entered the Torah canon, many rabbis disagreed with the premise that I do not represent the rabbinate. Some were also uncomfortable with exposing the rank and file of the Orthodox community to heretical views. Unwilling to risk a controversy that might damage the reputation of my scholarly works, I said my mea culpas and dropped out of a scheduled seventeen-city book tour. Over time, it fortunately became clear that I had weathered the storm.

Among the subjects discussed in the book were biblical archaeology and the documentary hypothesis. These were not my fields of special expertise, but with the help of others, I was able to mount a strong defense of the authenticity of the Old Testament. Having read "One People, Two Worlds," Rabbi Stolper was convinced I was the writer he was seeking.

At first, I demurred. Even though I had some qualifications for writing such a book, the scope of this project was too daunting. It would require an inordinate amount of research. There had to be others better qualified than I was. Rabbi Stolper asked that I at least give it some serious thought. He claimed that my studies of Talmudic civil law showed my analytic skills and that my Torah commentaries showed a deep knowledge and understanding of the texts. He promised to provide me with the books of the leading professors on both sides of the argument and any other source materials I felt I would need. It was important that it be done, and he didn't have anyone else. In the meantime, he argued, thousands of college kids were being turned away from their religion.

At our next meeting, I had already looked through some of the books he had given me, and I thought I might be able to counter some of their arguments effectively. The problem, I told Rabbi Stolper, was that I didn't think any book I wrote would have any appreciable effect. On the one side was almost the entire academic establishment that accepted the views of the Bible critics and archaeological minimalists as dogma, and who was on the other side? A Talmudic scholar from Lakewood. I would be dismissed, and nothing I said would be taken seriously.

The only way forward, I suggested, was to circumvent academia and make the case directly to the public. My thought was to write a legal thriller, a novel that somehow involved a Bible trial. I would present both sides of the argument and let the readers decide for themselves. The book would inevitably be slanted toward one side of the argument. I could not deny the influence of bias, but then again, there was bias on both sides. I did resolve to make a good faith effort to present both sides fairly and honestly. All the witnesses in the trial would present the views of prominent professors and the respective sides of the argument. Hopefully, the truth will speak for itself.

The goal of this book was not to prove or disprove the veracity of prophecy or divine intervention in a supernatural manner. It was to establish the historical period during which the Old Testament was written. Was it written more or less during the time it claimed to have been written, which would lend credence to its narrative, or was it written a thousand years later, which would indeed expose it as a hoax? It would be a battle of science against science.

There was one problem, however. The controversy that surrounded "One People, Two Worlds" was partially triggered by the exposure of readers to heretical views. Would this book spark the same sort of controversy?

In January 2005, Rabbi Stolper and I flew to Jerusalem to present the question to Rabbi Yosef Sholom Elyashiv, the leading Torah sage in the world. If he said we could not present both sides in a trial format, I would step away from the project.

Rabbi Elyashiv was open to the idea and even enthusiastic. He did insist that we should not leave the issue as a teiku, an unresolved question. The trial had to end with a positive verdict, to which we, of course, agreed. The rabbi gave us his warm blessings, and we returned to the States. The meeting is memorialized in a letter from Rabbi Stolper addressed to me dated September 19, 2010.

"I am writing this letter to you for the record," he wrote. "In January 2005, I asked you to write a book countering the heretical writings of the minimalist archaeologists and biblical critics who contend that the Bible is a myth. These professors exert a powerful influence on the hundreds of thousands of young Jewish people who attend colleges and universities all over the world, and it is important to challenge and disprove their claims. You suggested that the most effective way of reaching the largest readership would be to write a gripping novel, titled The Bible Trial, centered on a trial in which the authenticity of the Bible is examined and verified.

"Because such a book would require the presentation of arguments for both sides of the issue, you suggested that we travel to Eretz Israel to ask for the advice and endorsement of Rabbi Yosef Shalom Elyashiv, the leading Torah sage of our generation. We met in his home. Also in attendance at that meeting were Rabbi Yosef Wallis, Rabbi Shalom Serebrenik and Rabbi Daniel Nasi of Arachim, your son Rabbi Berel Reinman and Aryeh Elyashiv, the rabbi's grandson.

"We explained the purpose of our project to Rabbi Elyashiv, and his response was positive and encouraging. He had one condition: that the trial come to a clean and unequivocal resolution ("men ken nisht lazen mit a teiku"), to which we, of course, agreed. Rabbi Elyashiv then gave us his blessing for the success of our project.

"It seems that the project is finally nearing completion. May the Master of the Universe grant that all the years of effort we both have invested in it should bear fruit and result in a true sanctification of His holy Name."

A copy of the original letter is attached here. I have to admit that the thought of not having a verdict, as if to say the answer is obvious, did cross my mind, but the rabbi disabused me of it.

DAVID DOV FOUNDATION, INC.
RABBI PINCHAS STOLPER
603 TWIN OAKS DRIVE
LAKEWOOD · NEW JERSEY 08701
732-370-6078 FAX: 732 370-6079
PINCHASSTOLPER@AOL.COM

בס"ד

September 19, 2010

To: Rabbi Yaakov Yosef Reinman שליט"א,

I am writing this letter to you for the record.

In January, 2005, I asked you to write a book countering the heretical writings of the minimalist archaeologists and biblical critics who contend that the Bible is myth. These professors exert a powerful influence on the hundreds of thousands of young Jewish people who attend colleges and universities all over the world, and it is important to challenge and disprove their claims. You suggested that the most effective way of reaching a largest readership would be to write a gripping novel, titled *The Bible Trial*, centered on a trial in which the authenticity of the Bible is examined and verified.

Because such a book would require the presentation of arguments for both sides of the issue, you suggested that we travel to Eretz Yisrael to ask for the advice and *haskamah* of Harav Yosef Shalom Elyashiv, the *gadol hador*. We met in his home. Also in attendance at that meeting were Rav Yosef Wallis, Rav Shalom Srebrenik and Rav Daniel Nasi of Arachim, your son Rav Berel Reinman and Aryeh Elyashiv, the *rav's* grandson.

We explained the purpose of our project to Rav Elyashiv, and his response was positive and encouraging. He had one condition: that the trial come to a clear and unequivocal resolution ("*men ken nisht lazen mit a teiku*"), to which we, of course, agreed.

Rav Elyashiv then gave us his *berachah* for the success of our project.

It seems that the project is finally nearing completion. May the Ribono Shel Olam grant that all the years of effort we both have invested in it should bear fruit and result in a true *kiddush Hashem*.

בברכה ואהבה

פינחס אויר

Sincerely yours,

Rabbi Pinchas Stolper

My first attempt at the book did not give adequate attention to the backstory. I had always studied the Bible on its own internal merits, seeking to derive new meaning and interpretations from the nuances of the text and the narrative. But now, I was suddenly deep into the study of the Bible in the context of the external evidence of ancient history and archaeology. Any proficiency with the subject I had gained while writing "One People, Two Worlds" was inadequate for this new project. I put all my efforts into the book and spent most of the next year writing the entire trial without even touching the backstory.

Towards the end of the year, I concocted a story about a teacher who is fired for using the Bible as a historical resource and a lawyer with a dark secret who is blackmailed into taking the case. The story was derivative and mediocre, but no worse than many stories you would find in the library. I also felt it would be important to get an endorsement from a prominent professor in the academic community who supported my view. I decided to approach Dr. Kenneth Kitchen, a leading scholar, whose books featured strongly in the trial.

"I would like to make you an offer that, unfortunately, you can refuse," I wrote. "The debate regarding the reliability of the Old Testament rages among scholars in the academic community. As far as the general public is concerned, only the most erudite people are informed about the issues involved. Most others are under the impression that science has exposed the Bible as a fraud without any real understanding of why that should be so. How can that impression be combatted? Certainly not by more scholarly books.

"I have just completed a novel – it's actually a bit of a thriller, with murders and mayhem – that incorporates a trial in which the Bible is the de facto defendant. The book has been distributed to a variety of test readers who found it to be a page turner. Most of them also found themselves engrossed in the testimony regarding the Bible, although some readers admitted to skimming but not skipping those parts.

"A certain Dr. Kenneth A. Kitchen figures prominently in the trial. He is described as one of the pre-eminent scholars in the world and his excellent works – Ancient Orient and Old Testament and On the Reliability of the Old Testament – are quoted extensively. It would be extremely helpful for the project if you would review the book. I would also be honored if you penned a few reasonably complimentary words for the jacket."

Dr. Kitchen's gracious response arrived a few weeks later.

"Thank you for your kind and eloquent letter from earlier last month," he wrote, "with a tempting invitation to read over (and do a 'blurb' for) your novel on the Trial of the Scripture. Your enterprise sounds like a useful and stimulating endeavor, and I wish it well. Over the intervening weeks to now, I've had to weigh carefully what my response should be. At the end of the day, with all factors considered in the context of how I must live and work, and with great reluctance, I find myself compelled to decline your otherwise tempting invitation. The inescapable fact is that I am not just up to eyes, but well over my head with attempting to cope with existing work that is both physically massive (e.g., front line projects in A-4 format that run from 3 to 7 volumes each in mere length), never mind the intensity of detailed work essential to carrying them through.

"Basic and massive foundations very urgently need to be laid, of a kind that most people (it seems) are too lazy, or too impatient to undertake (or to tiresomely equip themselves to do), and such work then falls to a too-small handful of people like me who are at least prepared to try and fill huge gaps that should have been tackled ages ago – but for which task, the present time offers a maximum of good "raw material" information that can now be used to best effect. Once this is fully marshalled, properly understood and then applied to the background study of the OT/Hebrew Bible, results begin to emerge that are of the first importance in indicating the solid reality of the latter's contents.

"Thus, I warmly agree with you that we equally need good presentations with a wide and vividly intelligible popular appeal and clean message deriving from the biblical and external facts alike and together: and therefore, I wish every success with your enterprise ("novel" in both senses of the word!). On my part, I have a new-style popular concept in mind, too (not a novel); but it has its place in a queue of work, and must await its appropriate turn (to which I yearn to reach … but not today …)."

A copy of his original letter is attached here. It contains much intriguing information about his own, unexplained project for popular consumption. Seventeen years have passed since then, and that project, to the best of my knowledge, has not yet seen the light of day. I hope that someday it will. In any case, although he was very supportive of my project, he simply could not manage.

Nonetheless, I'm not one to take no for an answer so easily. "Thank you for your most gracious letter of January 9," I wrote back to him. "I deeply appreciate your having given my request such serious consideration, as evidenced by your thinking about it for weeks and responding with such a long and thoughtful letter. As you surely expected, I would not let the matter rest so easily. One of the virtues I admire so much in your work is your tenacity, and I must tell you that I am also tenacious in my own work.

"I recognize that your heavy schedule makes it difficult for you to commit to reading a thriller. Therefore, I would like to suggest another option. The trial itself takes up only a fraction of the whole book. I have stripped it out and saved it as a separate file. I would like to send you this minibook, which you can read over a cup of tea. I think you will find this section serious and scholarly, only the names of the witnesses are fictional. You might even find some illuminating original insights which I have provided from my own biblical studies.

J. Reinman, Esq.,.
59 Steven Lane,
Lakewood, NJ,
08701
U. S. A.

School of Archaeology, Classics & Egyptology,
14 Abercromby Square,
University of Liverpool,
LIVERPOOL, England,
L69 7WZ, Gt Britain/UK.
9th January, 2006.

Dear Mr Reinman,

Thank you for your kind and eloquent letter from earlier last month, with its tempting invitation to read over (and do 'blurb' for) your novel on the 'trial' of Scripture.

Your enterprise sounds like a useful and stimulating endeavour, and I wish it well. Over the intervening weeks to now, I've had to weigh carefully what my response should be. At the end of the day, with all factors considered in the context of how I must live & work, and with great reluctance, I find myself compelled to decline your otherwise tempting invitation. The inescapable fact is that I'm not just up to my eyes, but well over my head with attempting to cope with existing work that is both physically massive (*e.g.*, front-line projects in A-4 format that run from 3 to 7 volumes each in mere length), never mind the intensity of detailed work essential to carrying them through. Basic and massive foundations very urgently need to be laid, of a kind that most people (it seems) are too lazy, or too impatient to undertake (or to tiresomely equip themselves to do), and such work then falls to a too-small handful of people like me who are at least prepared to try & fill huge gaps that should have been tackled ages ago - but for which task, the present time offers a maximum of good "raw material" information that can now be used to best effect. Once this is fully marshalled, properly understood and then applied to the background study of the OT/Hebrew Bible, results begin to emerge that are of the first importance in indicating the solid reality of the latter's contents.

Thus, I warmly agree with you that we equally need good presentations with a wide and vividly intelligible popular appeal and clear message deriving from the biblical and external facts alike & together; and therefore I wish every success with your enterprise ("novel" in both senses of the word!). On my part, I have a new-style popular concept in mind, too [not a novel]; but it has its place in a queue of work, and must await its appropriate turn (which I yearn to reach ... but not today...).

With every warmest best wish (and for this new year of 2006 (- my! Nearly 1/2 a month's gone already, as I type this!!!), am

Yours sincerely,

Kenneth A. Kitchen

"I have taken the liberty of sending you the manuscripts – the full novel and the excerpted transcript – under separate cover. If you feel that even this is too much for you, you do not even have to open the package. Just drop me a note to that effect. In any case, I wish you the best of luck in all your endeavors. May God bless you and your work."

Two weeks later, I got my reply. It came with four pages of useful comments and suggestions. In addition, he sent me a blurb for the jacket.

"Very many thanks for your kind and kindly letter of 15th January," he wrote, "along with the packet (Bible Trial, total text and excerpt) of 17th, all of which I safely received at the Department last Tuesday 24th Jan., just a week ago. At that very busy juncture, I could but read the letter and file it all. To have junked it all would have been an unpardonably rude response – no way! As (for me) Saturdays are separate from the main workdays Mon-Fri, and reserved for alternative tasks to my taste. I took out Sat. 28th between breakfast and evening dinner, just to sit down and quietly go through the full text of The Bible Trial, with 'air-breaks' for elevenses, lunch and afternoon tea. A very good and engrossing read!

"I will end any fears you may have as to my reaction. I enjoyed the whole read! That the pre-classical ancient Near East, (outside the Tanakh) is not your habitual haunt makes your achievement here all the more creditable. Congratulations on a good (and strategic) job well-executed. So – I am happy to enclose a 'blurb', hopefully that you and the publisher may find acceptable.

"Being me, I made sundry rough-notes as I went along. On Mon and Tues (today), I got these typed off and enclosed these too. I hope you may find these observations of some use; they are intended to remove possible rough edges an opponent might fasten on, and to strengthen your hand (they have no negative intention). Just at one point at least, I would be very grateful that you tone somewhat the fulsome praise heaped on my bemused old heart (p. 322, lines 11-12 – in the context in which I serve, it is I judge a bit "over the top", and would be grateful for modification as suggested in my note thereto).

"There are many clearly made points that I especially relish e.g. the clear statement of that most basic fact that NO other book was ever in preclassical antiquity composed by a "scissors & paste" process and J and E items all 'mixed up' between documents (when, frequently, they are merely what one may term elegant variation): and the point about the utterly uncritical indoctrination of one generation of students after another down through time from the 1880s until now. (the bad old German habit, when students could only say "mein Professor sagt", 'Oh but my Prof. says', and nothing else counted!). And so much else!

"I have much work to finish because 40 years of compulsory "overreach" in my good and demanding university pushed so much research unhelpfully to one side till I could "retire". So I must work on quietly until the research-publication 'mountain' is cleared up. I can only rarely have assistance, especially as so much has to come out of my own thinking and studying and cannot be farmed out anyway. So, in trust, I just press on quietly, till it shall be done, if the good Lord so wills!"

A copy of the original letter is attached here. In the transcription, I have preserved all Dr. Kitchen's exclamation points, parentheses, textual idiosyncrasies and British punctuation. I am very grateful that he could not bring himself to toss the package and spent his free time reading the book and writing copious comments.

So now I was all ready to move ahead. I had obtained the blessing of the leading rabbi of our times and the endorsement of the leading orientologist of our times. But finding a publisher turned out to be difficult.

Over the next few years, different agents represented the book, and although a few editors nibbled no one pulled the

THE UNIVERSITY
of LIVERPOOL

31st January, 2006.

School of Archaeology,
Classics and Egyptology

Department of Archaeology

Faculty of Arts

14 Abercromby Square
Liverpool
L69 7WZ

Telephone: 0151 794 2467
Answerphone: 0151 794 2467
Facsimile: 0151 794 2226
Secretary's email: winkerpa@liverpool.ac.uk

Dr. Joseph Reinman.
59, Steven Lane.
LAKEWOOD.
NJ.
08701.
USA.

Dear Dr. Reinman.

Very many thanks for your kind and kindly letter of 15th January, which - along with the packet (*Bible on Trial*, total text & excerpt) of 17th - all of which I safely received at the Dept., last Tuesday, 24th Jan. , just a week ago. At that very busy juncture. I could but read the letter & file it all. To have junked it all, would have been an unpardonably rude response - no way! As (for me) Saturdays are separate from the main workdays Mon-Fri. & reserved for alternative tasks to my taste. I took out Sat., 28th, between breakfast and evening dinner, just to sit down and quietly go through the full text of *The Bible Trial*, with 'air-breaks' for elevenses, lunch, & afternoon tea. A very good, & engrossing, read!

I will end any fears you may have as to my reaction: I thoroughly enjoyed the whole read. That the pre-classical ancient Near East (outside the Tanak) is not your habitual haunt makes your achievement here all the more creditable. Congratulations on a good (and strategic) job well executed!

So - I am happy to enclose a 'blurb', hopefully that you and the publisher may find acceptable.

Being me, I made sundry rough-notes as I went along. On Mon. & Tues (today). I got these typed-off & enclose these too. I hope you may find these observations of some use; they are intended to remove possible rough edges an opponent might fasten on, and to strengthen your hand (they have no negative intention). Just at one point at least, I would be very grateful that you tone down somewhat the fulsome praise heaped upon my bemused old head (p. 322, lines 11-12 - in the context in which I serve, it is I judge a bit "over the top", and would be grateful for modification as suggested in my note thereto).

There are so many clearly-made points that I especially relish - *e.g.*, the clear statement of that most basic fact that NO other book was ever in preclassical antiquity composed by a "scissors-&-paste" process: and J and E items all 'mixed up' between documents (when, frequently, they are merely what one may term 'elegant variation'): and the point about the utterly uncritical indoctrination of one generation of students after another down through time from the 1880s till now (the bad old German habit, when students could only say "mein Professor sagt", 'Oh but my Prof. says', and nothing else counted!) And so much else!

I have much work to finish, because 40 years' compulsory "overteach" in my good but demanding university pushed so much research unhelpfully to one side till I could "retire". So I must work on quietly until this research/publication 'mountain' is cleared up. I can only rarely have assistance, esp. as so much has to come out of my own thinking & studying and cannot be farmed out anyway. So, in trust, I just press on quietly, till it shall be done, if the good Lord so wills! With every warmest wish to you in everything. I am

Yours as ever,

Kenneth A. Kitchen

trigger. One editor wrote that the trial was brilliant but not the story, that it was clear where the author's heart lay. She was right. The story did not have its own life. It was there to fill in the gaps of the trial, which is not the way to write a story. It was not organic. The combination of the trial and the back-story was, therefore, incongruous. It was not surprising that it was turned down.

I was encouraged, however, by the comments of some of the secular editors who turned it down. They considered the book fair to both sides. One of them also said he had to admit the book made him think. But he turned it down anyway.

Nonetheless, I did not lose heart. I kept editing and polishing the story, making revisions and additions, but it was all to no avail. Finally, I decided to discard the original back story and write a new story set against a background that I knew intimately. I am a skilled writer of pretty good fiction under the name Avner Gold. So, I put aside the trial and focused entirely on a story about a Jewish family that is deeply affected by events in Hesterville, a town reminiscent of Charlottesville that experiences a white supremacist riot. Then I blended the trial into the second half of the book. I also greatly reduced the volume of the trial that appeared in the story and instead added an appendix featuring the full transcript.

I sent the book to Nancy Rosenberg of AAABooks Un-limited, an agent in the Chicago area who had represented me some years ago. She made a tremendous effort to place the book with a publisher. Under her guidance, I prepared a sixty-page proposal; one editor commented that she had never seen such a complete proposal. We did not, however, get any offers. I think I understand the reasons. I believe Dr. Kitchen hit the nail on the head in his blurb for the jacket which begins, "Here's today's most novel novel . . ." This book is indeed a new kind of novel, a work of popular scholarship in the guise of a thriller, a hybrid of fiction and non-fiction that, although interesting, absorbing and informative, does not fit comfortably into either genre. Publication of such a book would be a risk, and the publishing industry these days is very risk averse.

After nearly twenty years, I realized I had to find a different route. I was building a website (www.rabbireinman.com) to showcase a series of lectures called "Destiny: A Jewish View of World History," and I decided to publish "Hesterville" through Shufra Institute, sell it through Amazon and serialize it on the website. Besides the traffic driven to the website by the history series, I also have over 7,000 connections on LinkedIn and many hundreds of correspondents. I will also generate traffic through social media marketing. This is the new world. I believe my book will do fine. Better than fine. I hope you enjoy it.

• • •

This book is dedicated to the memory of my good friend and colleague Rabbi Pinchas Stolper. He urged me to write it, helped me with the research and encouraged me at every step of the way. It saddens me that he has not lived to hold a copy in his hands. I will be forever grateful to him. I also want to thank Mrs. Cherna Moskowitz of Miami Beach, Florida, for her enthusiastic support for all of Rabbi Stolper's projects, including this one.

My thanks to my wonderful agent Nancy Rosenfeld of AAA Books Unlimited, to my editor Dr. Lisa Lipschutz, to my graphic artist Bracha Royde and to my wife, Zvia, my family and all my friends who read the manuscript and offered comments and criticism.

Most of all, I want to express my gratitude to the Almighty for everything He has done for me throughout my life. I hope this book will advance the quest for truth and bring honor to His holy Name.

Yaakov Yosef Reinman
October 25, 2023

Chapter One

The sun was sinking toward the Hudson River as I walked home from my law offices on Lexington Avenue. It was a chilly night in April, perfect for taking my wife out to a leisurely meal and a glass of French wine in one of our excellent Manhattan restaurants. The last thing I wanted was to go to a family Passover Seder in Brooklyn.

It's not that I have a particular issue with Passover Seders, even in Brooklyn, except that they almost always start too late and last too long. My problem is with my family. I don't like them, except for my grandson. And my father, of course.

My brother Bernard is ten years younger, two inches shorter and sixty pounds heavier than I am. He is also much richer, and I'm far from a pauper myself. Of course, I have nothing against rich people. Some of my best friends are rich people, including me. I just don't like when they're loud and smug and ignorant, like my brother Bernie. I also don't like Beatrice, his wife, and their nosy, noisy kids.

My brother Alex is fifty-three years old and a total contradiction. On the one hand, he's a firebrand progressive, a pot-smoking flower child living in a Greenwich Village bachelor pad, and at the same time, he manages one of the most predatory hedge funds on Wall Street. It's true that he sends money to displaced people in Africa and visits all the art galleries, but he impresses me as a closet philistine, a supercilious fraud.

And then there's my sister Sylvia, fifty years old, a neurologist who practices and teaches in Columbia Presbyterian Hospital near the George Washington Bridge. You'd think she'd be a person of substance, but believe me, she's not. She knows her neurology, but otherwise, she's an airhead. She's married to Edoardo Alfieri, an Italian immigrant eight years younger than she is. He's a wild-eyed, mustachioed violinist in the string section of the Jersey City Philharmonic Orchestra who dreams of making it to the New York Philharmonic but never will. They live in a six-bedroom house in upscale Montclair, New Jersey, with three cats, a butler, a maid and no children. You cannot have an intelligent conversation with either of them about anything other than neurological disorders and violins. I don't even know if they converse with each other. Edoardo's English is awful, and Sylvia speaks no Italian.

I suppose they're harmless, and we're all grateful to them for taking in my father, Maury Taylor, after my mother died. He is ninety-two years old, full of pep and vigor, in pretty good health. I don't think he's much of a burden on Sylvia and Edoardo, because I'm sure they don't converse much. He has his own room with a separate entrance, he takes care of his own expenses, and George, his assistant, drives him wherever he wants to go.

That's my family. Except, of course, for Margaret, my daughter, but that's a long and sordid story, perhaps for a different time. She has resented me since she was young.

As they say, you can pick your friends, but you can't pick your family. I would not have picked any of them for friends, but I could tolerate them for one night. Truthfully, my reluctance to go to the Seder was mostly because of Margaret, but at least I'd see David, my favorite and only grandchild.

When I got home, June was already dressed and ready to go. She prepared a snack for us while I showered and dressed. As I was struggling with my cufflinks, I heard June call me.

"Adrian! Come! I'm in the den. You have to see this! Hurry!"

I left my cuffs unfastened and went to the den. She was sitting on the edge of the sofa, her eyes glued to the screen.

"Aren't you worried that we're going to be late?" I asked.

She turned and gave me a wry look. "Me? You think I'm eager to go to this thing? I dread it. I'm only going because of you." She paused and smiled. "And because of Maury." Of all my family, whom she barely tolerates, June loves my father. Her sentiments are returned.

"Can you help me with my cufflinks?"

"Put them into your pocket, Adrian. I'll help you after we watch this. The commercial is almost over. Sit down! It's live!" June likes exclamation points.

I sat on the sofa next to her and looked at the screen. There was a wild demonstration on Freret Street in New Orleans in front of the Tulane University quad. I recognized the place. Tulane is my father's alma mater. The camera panned the raucous demonstrators. They didn't look like college students. They were men and women in their twenties, thirties and forties. Hundreds of them. Many of them carried placards. They looked like people who most probably did not have college degrees. They were screaming and waving their fists in the air. And they were all white.

In the foreground, a reporter was describing the event.

"Good evening. My name is Sheldon Friedman. We are here on this quiet street in New Orleans, but it's not so quiet this evening. A group called the Waco-Ridge Coalition is protesting the proposed appointment of Jeremy Muhammad as the new president of Tulane. Mr. Muhammad is African-American. The student population right now is over seventy percent white, less than ten percent African-American and about five percent Hispanic. Plus some Asian-Americans and international students. The nomination of Mr. Muhammad signals an attempt to achieve a more balanced demographic."

"Hey you!"

The reporter turned to see who had shouted at him. It was a burly man in his late thirties, sunburned, with a headband, an uncombed beard and long hair. His shirt was sleeveless, and his arms were heavily tattooed. The man approached the reporter and glared into his eyes.

"Hey, pinko Jew reporter, what are you telling the public? Are you telling them the truth or more pinko lies?"

"Would you like to speak on camera, sir?"

"Damn right, I would."

"I'm sure our viewers would like to hear you. Who are you, sir?"

"I'm Jimmy Joe Darby, leader of the Waco-Ridge Coalition." He said it as if he expected everyone to know his name. If he led a few more demonstrations like this, I thought, he might very well get his wish.

The reporter had obviously not heard of the organization or its leader.

"What is the Waco-Ridge Coalition?"

"It's a group of patriotic Americans organized to defend ourselves, our families and our American values from the pinko Jew nigger federal government and the corruption of our society. We honor the fallen at Waco and Ruby Ridge. We will avenge them."

"And why are you demonstrating?"

"We don't want that nigger Ayrab getting in. He should go back where he came from. He's a damn Muslim."

"Mr. Darby, I think you're misinformed. He's a Southern Baptist, a graduate of Tulane. His grandfather was a Black Muslim back in the Sixties. He's a descendant of slaves. His people have been here hundreds of years. To where should he go back?"

"Let him go to Africa. Or the Ninth Ward. Tulane is the crown jewel of Southern colleges. The Harvard of the South. They should be getting rid of their nigger students, not looking for more. And all those Jews! Why the hell do they have so many Jews?"

Darby was right that a substantial part of the student body was Jewish, far more than the Jewish percentage of the American population. Back in the day when the Ivy League colleges in the North had quotas for Jewish applicants, many who were rejected headed for Tulane. Their children and grandchildren followed in their footsteps, as children usually do, especially when it comes to the elite universities.

"I can't answer your questions, Mr. Darby," said the reporter. "I'm only here to report. How many members are there in the Coalition?"

" I'm not gonna tell you exactly, but it's thousands. And there are many more thousands in other groups like ours. And people who support us without actually being members. You won't believe how many. Millions!"

"What do you mean by support?"

"They believe in what we're doing. Some of them give us money. You look at my folks here, and you think we're a bunch of rednecks. But you don't know what's going on. Plenty of people in fancy suits in high places are behind us. There's gonna be a reckoning. We're ready."

"Are you armed?"

"You better believe it."

"Who are the other groups? Are their leaders well-known?"

Darby sneered. "You mean better known than me?"

"I'm only trying to get information for our viewers."

"Sure, why not? It's about time your viewers heard about us. They'll be hearing plenty more soon. We're tired of biding our time. There's Quincy Montague and the Bunker Hill Brigade. Darron Vandewegh and the July Fourth Faction. Knute Hatwick and the Euro-American Alliance. These are our allies. But there are plenty of other groups."

"Do you coordinate with your allies?"

"Yeah. We work together. We're all on the same page."

The reporter took a deep breath.

"Well, Mr. Darby, I can't say I wish you good luck, but I thank you for speaking to our viewers. We want them to be informed."

Darby grunted and walked away, seemingly satisfied. The reporter turned to the camera. He tried to make a final comment, but overwhelmed, he could think of nothing appropriate to say; he didn't want to end this remarkable interview with inanities.

"This is Sheldon Friedman," he said in a tight voice, eloquent in his failure to comment. "We're reporting to you from Tulane University in New Orleans, Louisiana. Good night, and God bless."

Chapter Two

The cab dropped us off at Margaret's house in the Park Slope section of Brooklyn. It was almost nine o'clock. We were sure we'd come in middle of the Seder, if not towards the end, but we couldn't tear ourselves away from the screen for long after the interview was over, switching from channel to channel to catch the reactions of the national media and the politicians.

The media, even Fox News, were outraged, as were most of the politicians. Some of them insisted we should not take the demonstrators seriously. The more we talk about them, the stronger they'd become. One politician suggested that we listen to well-meaning people on both sides. Both sides? Were there two sides? We sat in the cab in silence until our destination. Everything we could have said was said, even though it was unsaid.

The maid opened the door and took our jackets. No one was in the dining room. The settings on the table were untouched. Everyone was clustered around the big screen in the living room. No one was talking.

Margaret saw us first and stood up.

"Good evening, Dad, June," she said sweetly. "Glad you could make it." The words were friendly, but they were not.

We followed her and found seats on a couch. My father waved.

"I was waiting for you, boychik," he said. He likes to use Yiddish dialect. He says it reminds him of his father, but he speaks a very sophisticated English when he wants.

"You really shouldn't have," I said. "I'm sorry I kept you waiting."

"Pah!" He waved my apology away. "Don't be sorry. I didn't really wait for you. You were just the excuse. I wanted to watch that *sheigetz* in New Orleans. But God waits all year to see us at the Seder. We couldn't keep God waiting, could we? But how could we start the Seder without my eldest son, our own Congressman, the pride of our family?"

I saw Bernie and Alex wince. I guess they don't see me as the pride of our family. Sylvia was oblivious, as usual.

"So we waited for you, Congressman," said my father, "and we watched."

"Former Congressman. Well, that's why we were late. We were watching at home."

"What do you say, former Congressman?" he asked. I don't like it when he calls me that, but if I complain, he'll just do it more. I guess he means no harm. "Are there really tens of thousands of heavily armed roughnecks with heavily tattooed arms out in the wild hills of America? What's your opinion as a Congressman?"

"Not only in the hills, I'm afraid. I don't know if it's hundreds, thousands or tens of thousands. There are too many of them, and they have too many weapons."

He sighed and stood up, taking my hand for support. "It's time to start the Seder. We're late, so we'll have to cut a few corners."

The women lit candles. We drank the four cups of red wine, not all at once, we ate some matzah and read selections from the Passover Haggadah. Twenty-five minutes later, we were ready for dinner.

There is one paragraph in the Haggadah about how the Jewish people face annihilation in every generation and how

God always saves us. I suppose that means that he saves the Jewish people as a whole, but as individuals, we're on our own.

My father read the paragraph aloud with great emotion as the family listened transfixed.

"My dear children," he said when he finished the reading, "I'm no spring chicken. Ninety-two years old my last birthday, and I don't know if I'll see another one. I --"

Benny interrupted him. "Aw c'mon, Pop. You still got a lot of mileage left on you."

"Listen, I know you're gonna miss me, but get used to it. I'm gonna die. Maybe tomorrow. Maybe a year. Maybe five. So I might as well say my piece now. We're not safe. We live among our enemies, and we don't even know who they are. I don't think there'll be laws against us, like in Germany, but only because it'd be unconstitutional. The Constitution is holy to the American people. It protects them from each other, and incidentally, it protects us from them. If things look bad, go somewhere else. Don't worry about your property. Worry about yourselves."

Alex exchanged glances with his girlfriend. "Don't you think you're being a little alarmist, Pop?"

"Not a little. A lot. The alarm is ringing. Listen to it!"

"Is this all about what happened at Tulane? They're just a bunch of kooks. You shouldn't take them too seriously."

"They're not kooks. They're haters, and they're organizing on a large scale. Didn't you hear the guy? I don't know if they have thousands of members or only hundreds, but believe me, it's serious."

Sylvia took a sip of wine. "I hope you're wrong, Pop. But thanks for caring." Edoardo nodded in agreement.

"Where should we go?" said Max, one of Bernie's boys, his eyes wide with concern. "Should we move to Israel?"

"That's not very safe either, honey. No one's going anywhere now. I'm just telling your parents to keep their eyes open."

Beatrice was sitting next to Max. She took his hand and

patted it, then she whispered in his ear and kissed him.

"You're scaring Max, Grandpa," she said. "Did you have to do this in front of him on Passover night?"

"A little fright doesn't hurt, but enough of this. Let's eat!"

I didn't get involved in the conversation, but I understood my father's concern. He was a refugee. My grandfather, Harry Schneiderman, was born in Galicia, Poland, in 1895. His family fled to Germany during the First World War and settled in Berlin. He married my grandmother, Malka Kagan, who was also a refugee, and they opened a shoe store. My father was born in 1928. The store prospered. Life was good.

When the Nazis became a factor with their rallies, marches and violent rhetoric, my grandparents bought diamonds and made sure all the passports were in order, but they kept their store open. When the Nazis came to power, my grandparents still hoped for the best, but the situation for the Jews deteriorated from day to day. My father was beaten up in school when he was seven years old, and then he was prevented from going to school altogether. My grandfather put extra locks on the doors, and he applied for visas for the United States. The shoe store was destroyed in 1938 during Kristallnacht, and two months later, the family was in New York; had they stayed longer, they probably would have been deported and murdered.

Whether or not my father was right to be concerned, I understood him completely. Maybe it was not quite *déjà vu*, but it was deeply disturbing nonetheless. For me as well.

Chapter Three

Margaret brought us our coats and said good night. June went to powder her nose before we left, and Margaret turned to go. I could see she didn't want to have the conversation we were about to have. I wondered why. What had happened? Should I be worried?

"Not so fast, Margaret," I said. "Talk to me."

"I don't have time. I have to clean up."

"It can wait a few minutes. Where's David? Why isn't he here?'

"He couldn't make it."

"Did something happen?"

"Don't worry. He's okay. Sort of."

I was suddenly alarmed. "What do you mean?"

She gave me a hard look. "When was the last time you talked to him?"

"I'm not sure. A few months. Where is he? What happened?"

"Your precious grandson has found religion. He's dropped out of college and joined Chabad."

I was stunned. "Are you serious?"

"I'm absolutely serious. Your grandson has become a Chassid."

"But why?" I was still trying to get used to the idea.

"I guess he's found God. At least, he thinks so. He doesn't believe that God lives in this house as well."

"What do you mean? David doesn't live at home anymore?"

"No."

"Why not?"

"We're not kosher enough for him. He wanted to bring in his own food and eat in his room."

"Well, considering the situation, that seems like a good idea."

"Not to me. I put my foot down. I said that if he can't eat in my kitchen he should find somewhere else to live."

"So you threw him out of the house."

"I told him the door was open whenever he came to his senses."

"I can't believe it."

"Believe it."

"Where did he go?"

"He said he's moving to Crown Heights."

"How long ago was this?"

"Two months ago." She paused. "I'm sure you blame me."

"Why would I do that?"

"Don't give me your sarcasm. I did what I had to do. I couldn't let David become a Chassidic fanatic. I had to be firm. He'll come back. Mark my words, he'll be back. That life is not for him."

"So you haven't spoken to him in two months."

"That's right. As I understand, you haven't either. What's your excuse?"

"I just got busy. I didn't throw him out. If I knew what was going on, I would've called him every day."

"What good would that have done? Do you think you could've changed his mind? I don't think so. Not even his precious grandfather could budge him. It was like an evil spell had come over him."

"I don't know if I could've changed his mind, but I could've given him my support. I could have shown him that I love him no matter what."

"So you would've given him money?"

"If he needed it."

"You would have reinforced his bad behavior." Margaret is a professor of psychology. She speaks like that. I don't envy her students.

Just then, June came back.

"What bad behavior?" she asked.

"Not important," said Margaret. "Have a safe trip back."

June gave Margaret a peck on the cheek, and we left. You may have noticed that I didn't kiss Margaret good night. I haven't kissed her in years.

As soon as we got into the car, I told June about my conversation with Margaret, as close to verbatim as I could. She patted my hand and said nothing. June never says anything just for the sake of responding. I knew that she felt my hurt. That was all I needed from her right then.

I took out my cell phone and opened my list of favorites. I clicked on David and put the phone to my ear. After six rings, I got voice mail.

"Hey, you've reached David. Please leave a message."

The sound of his voice sparked a feeling of intense love in my heart. David was the apple of my eye, as the saying goes. When he was growing up, we were as close as grandfather and grandson could be. By the time he was ten, he could draw a rough map of the world and identify most of the major cities. He read a lot of history and well-researched historical fiction. He was a whiz at math. You could have a fairly deep conversation with him about politics and science.

When Helen, my first wife, was in the advanced stages of multiple sclerosis, David was my greatest emotional support. He was my rock. We formed an incredibly deep bond. There's nothing I wouldn't have done for him, but he gave me his love without expecting anything in return.

When Margaret told me that my precious grandson had found religion, as I mentioned before, there was an extensive subtext to it. I believe she was jealous of my relationship with David, considering that her own relationship with me when she was growing up was quite rocky to say the least. I don't know whose fault that was. She always blamed me. Since I was the adult, she used to say, the blame was always mine. Perhaps she was right, but I guess I didn't have the wisdom, the patience and the sensitivity to handle her properly.

After she married, things got better between us. Not because my very rich and very compliant son-in-law, Gerald Goldfield, was such a good influence. He was no influence at all; she overpowered him. Nonetheless, I suppose that once she had her own lavish home, she resented me less. That is, until David and I bonded in a way she and I never did. When Helen became ill and gave up her job as a paralegal, Margaret and David spent a lot of time in our home. I guess it took a deadly illness to bring a thaw to our relationship.

After Helen died, the thaw did not last long. During the last few years of my wife's illness, I was essentially alone. I met June six months after Helen passed away, and we married a few months later. Helen had told me many times that she wanted me to remarry. She even suggested some of the widows we knew, but I stopped her there.

June, my second wife, was a dermatologist from Brookline, Massachusetts. She came from a fine family. He father was a Harvard ophthalmologist and her mother an administrator in the Boston College School of Nursing. Nice people. Her first husband, an army doctor, was killed in Iraq. June was an intelligent person of excellent character with a subtle sense of humor. We really hit it off. I was sure Helen would have been pleased. She wanted me to be happy.

Margaret, however, did not exactly welcome June with open arms, but she understood that I needed to remarry. Relations between Margaret and June were cordial but not close, and that suited everyone.

Two years after June and I married, I endowed a wing of

Monteverde Children's Hospital in Helen's honor; it was a cause near and dear to her heart. Because of my prominence as a Congressman and an author, the endowment was reported in the newspapers. A nosy reporter discovered that I had left my estate to the hospital and my brownstone to June. Margaret and Gerald were wealthy, extremely wealthy. She didn't need my money, so I thought I'd put it to good use after I am gone.

Margaret could not accept what I had done. She considered it a betrayal of the worst sort. Our thawed relationship began to freeze up again. Things got much worse at David's bar-mitzvah. When Margaret got up to make a toast, she mentioned just about everyone at the party, but she did not mention me or June, a glaring omission. June told me to forget it, that it didn't deserve my emotional energy, but I was furious.

Since then, our relationship has been frosty. We only met at family gatherings. She did not invite us to her home, and she declined our invitations. But to her credit, she did not prevent me from taking David out for pizza and a ballgame from time to time. And of course, I was able to spend time with David at family gatherings. We were very close.

In recent years, however, we did not see each other as often as I would have liked. He was in college, and he had a girlfriend. We conversed at social events. We didn't go to ballgames as in the past, but we spoke on the phone once in a while. Our relationship adapted to an adult level, and it was good. It was more than good. It was wonderful.

I was looking forward to seeing David at the Passover Seder. It would have been the highlight of my evening. Besides, of course, seeing my dear father presiding at the head of the Seder table. And now, he wasn't even answering his phone. What was he doing in Crown Heights? Why wasn't he answering his phone?

I was worried.

Chapter Four

Crown Heights runs from Prospect Park and the main branch of the Brooklyn Public Library in Grand Army Plaza all the way to Brownville, bisected end to end by Eastern Parkway. Margaret lives in Park Slope, which is the next neighborhood over. I'd never been to Crown Heights or even given it much thought. My capable secretary, however, researched it and told me what to expect.

Crown Heights used to be an old middle-class neighborhood well represented by all stripes of Jewish people. In the post-War era, the Chabad-Lubavitch sect of Chassidim grew rapidly until it became the dominant group. Chabad is an evangelistic movement with branches in hundreds of cities and towns, but the world headquarters is in Crown Heights, as are its elite yeshivos.

Demographics changed. Many Jewish families and institutions moved away, and for the most part, black families took their place. Chabad, however, did not budge. The leader of the movement, the Lubavitcher Rebbe, insisted that the community stay with their black neighbors, and stay they did. The community flourished in an expanding cluster around the main synagogue at 770 Eastern Parkway. The Lubavitchers call it 770 and view the old brownstone as a holy temple with mystical dimensions. The Chabad synagogue in Jerusalem is a faithful replica of 770.

If David had joined Chabad and gone to Crown Heights, it was reasonable to assume he would still be there. I didn't think they send new recruits into the field. I was hoping I would find him there.

The next morning, after I came to my office, I called for my driver to take me to Crown Heights at noon. I don't have a steady driver. I always walk to my office and take cabs when I have to go somewhere in the city. My car stays in the garage most of the time. When I need it, a limousine service provides me with a driver for as long as I need it. My favorite is Pedro Bolivar, and I asked for him. While I waited for Pedro to pick up my car, I went through my messages and made sure everything in the office was running smoothly. In the meantime, I kept dialing David's number but with no response.

Pedro was wearing chauffeur's livery that day; he was probably coming from another assignment. He opened the passenger side door, and I got in.

"*Buenos dias, Señor Taylor*," he said. "*Como esta?*" He knew I liked to converse in Spanish, but I wasn't in the mood.

"*Desculpame, Señor Bolivar, pero no puedo hoy. Estoy occupado. Hablamos inglés, por favor.*"

"*Como quiere, patron.* Where are we going?"

"Crown Heights."

"They told me. What's the address?"

"I don't know."

He shrugged and put the car in gear. "You're the boss."

"Do you know your way around Crown Heights?"

"Sure."

"Let's start with the old synagogue. Do you know where it is?"

"Sure. 770.'"

"That's right. Go there first."

We took the FDR Drive down to the Manhattan Bridge into Brooklyn, and fifteen minutes later we were cruising down Eastern Parkway. It's a beautiful street with pedestrian islands between the six-lane road and the service roads. The corner of Eastern Parkway and Nostrand Avenue was a bustling hub of black businesses. After we crossed New York Avenue in the service road, the sidewalks were thronged with Chassidic men in prayer shawls and black fedoras. We pulled up at 770 on the corner of Eastern Parkway and Kingston Avenue. I told Pedro to keep his phone on and climbed out.

I made my way up the stairs and entered a vestibule redolent with the musty smell of old books and prayer shawls. The door on the right opened into a small synagogue. A few men sat in front of open books, humming and rocking back and forth.

"Excuse me," I said. "Can anyone help me?"

A red-bearded young fellow in white shirtsleeves and the signature black fedora jumped to his feet.

"How can I help? Are you looking for someone?"

"I'm looking for my grandson. Is this the Chabad synagogue?"

"It used to be a long time ago. The synagogue is downstairs."

"What's up here?"

"Offices."

"Maybe there's someone in the office who can help me find my grandson. They must have a register."

"The office is closed. It's Passover, Mr. … I didn't catch your name." He extended his hand. "My name is Zapadnik. Zalman Zapadnik. Pleased to meet you."

I had no choice. I shook his hand and gave my name. "Adrian Taylor. "

His eyes widened. "Hey, I recognize you. You're the Congressman."

"Well, not anymore." It makes me uncomfortable when people call me Congressman. It was just a youthful indiscretion. I wanted to accomplish something for society and thought I might do so in Congress. Two terms of sniping and frustration, and all I have to show for it are four years wasted and a bombastic title whose emptiness makes me cringe.

"Let me take you downstairs," said Zalman. "We'll find someone who can help you find your grandson."

We descended a claustrophobic creaky stairway, reeking with age, which could accommodate only one traffic direction at a time. We emerged into a large auditorium near a row of sinks. I smelled chlorine in the air and assumed a ritual bath was not too far away. A broad staircase to the left led to street level. Ahead was a cavernous room with wall-to-wall tables and benches packed with noisy young and older men dressed like my guide Zalman and with the same body language. Almost all of them were gesticulating and talking at once. I couldn't hear myself think.

Zalman brought me to a heavyset man with a stringy gray beard and a forehead covered with perspiration.

"Mendel, this gentleman is looking for his grandson," said Zalman.

Mendel looked at me, and his eyebrows rose. "Aren't you the Congressman?"

"I should've put on dark glasses and a mustache," I said.

"You're welcome here," said Mendel. He stuck out his hand. "Mendel Futerman. How can I help you?"

"I believe my grandson is here."

"What's his name?"

"David Goldfield. I've been calling him all last night and today, and he doesn't answer his phone."

"I see. Do you know that observant Jews are not supposed to speak on the phone on Shabbos or the festivals? It's Passover today. Is your grandson observant?"

"I don't know. I heard that he joined Chabad two months ago."

"Are you sure?"

"Pretty sure."

"And you've come to take him away?"

"No, of course not. He's an adult. He makes his own decisions. I just want to make sure he's okay. I missed him at the

Seder last night."

"I see. Well, if he's a beginner, he's probably at the yeshivah in Morristown, New Jersey. I can make some inquiries for you after the holiday. We'll find him."

"Do all beginners go to Morristown?"

"No, there are other yeshivos for beginners, but Morristown is the biggest and the best. If he really joined Chabad, chances are he's there."

"Are there any yeshivos in Crown Heights?"

"A couple, but your best bet is Morristown."

"Knowing my grandson, I think he'd want to stay in Crown Heights at the center of things. Where are the yeshivos in the neighborhood?"

"Maybe he should try Magen Menachem," offered Zalman.

"Why not?" said Mendel. He turned to me. "If your grandson isn't there, they'll direct you to the other yeshivos. There are just a few."

"Great. I'll start there. Could you give me the address?"

"I'll take you there," said Zalman.

"I don't want to impose," I said. "Just give me directions."

"It's no imposition. I'll be glad to take you there."

"All right, I accept your offer. You're very kind. We'll go in my car. I have a driver outside. You can direct him. He'll drive you back when we get there."

"It's a beautiful day, Mr. Taylor. Let's walk."

"I don't want to take too much of your time. Let's just go by car. My driver is right outside. You'll be back here in a few minutes."

Zalman exchanged glances with Mendel. "Well, you see, Mr. Taylor, we're not supposed to ride in a car on the holiday."

"Oh, I see. On second thought, let's walk. Is it far?"

"No, about ten minutes."

"Perfect."

We walked to the corner and turned up Kingston Avenue. All the shops were closed and secured. The street had a generally shabby look, but the people seemed cheery and purposeful. The women and the children were well-dressed, while the men all looked like Zalman and Mendel. We walked five blocks until we came to Montgomery Street and turned right. Halfway up the block, we stopped in front of an old-fashioned two-family house, which was a duplicate of its neighbors. There were two exterior doors side by side, one for the ground level apartment and one for the upstairs.

A small sign with Hebrew lettering was pasted to the door of the ground level apartment. I'd long forgotten how to read Hebrew, but I assumed this was Magen Menachem. There was a big picture of the Lubavitcher Rebbe in the window. We had reached our destination. I didn't need Zalman's help anymore, so I thanked him and wished him a happy Passover.

The door was open, as you would expect in a yeshivah. A middle-aged rabbi with a short brown beard streaked with gray sat at a table with four young fellows in jeans and colorful tee shirts, obviously beginners.

"Can I help you?" said the rabbi. He extended his hand. "I'm Rabbi Sholom Ber Gutmacher."

I shook his hand. "Pleased to meet you, Rabbi Gutmacher. I'm Adrian Taylor. I'm looking for my grandson. I was told he might be here."

"What's his name?"

"David Goldfield. Do you know him?"

"Certainly. He's one of my students."

"Is he here?"

"No, I'm afraid he's not."

"Do you know where he is?"

"He's in Katmandu."

"Katmandu? Are you sure? Katmandu?"

"Yes, I'm sure. Katmandu is the capital of Nepal."

"I know where Katmandu is, but what's he doing there? And why doesn't he answer my phone calls?"

"He may not have service up in the Himalaya Mountains.

When did you call him?"

"Last night. Today." Again, I realized the inanity of my question. "Of course, it's Passover. He can't pick up the phone."

"That's right."

"So why is he there?"

"He's helping Chabad of Nepal conduct the Passover Seder. They have a couple of thousand Israelis for the Seder every year. They need all the help they can get."

Chapter Five

David returned from Nepal a week after Passover. He heard I'd been looking for him, and he called to tell me he was fine. I invited him for dinner. I promised to get him something from a kosher restaurant. He chuckled and said I shouldn't bother. He'd bring a sandwich.

I almost didn't recognize him when he came to the door. He had a scraggly beard and a crumpled black fedora. I hugged him and kissed him on the cheek, and he responded with equal warmth.

David joined us for dinner. June had gone to a kosher restaurant and brought back an assortment of cold foods, properly wrapped and sealed so that David could eat without any concerns. We feasted on kosher sandwiches, salads and cold Heinekens, and we talked about his experiences in Katmandu. Then June went to her study to make calls and do paperwork, and we were left alone.

"So what's going on, David?" I asked.

"About what?"

"Columbia, law school, your girlfriend, Chabad, your mother, anything you care to talk about. We haven't had a real conversation in a while. If you don't want to talk, you don't have to say anything. But whatever you need, I'm there for you. No judgments."

"I know, Grandpa, and I appreciate it." He sighed. "I'm going through a time of change. All those things you mentioned are connected. It all starts in one place ..."

He waited for me to complete his sentence, and I did. "Your mother?"

"Well, of course. I mean, I love her and all that. She's my mother. I'm not one of those people that hates his mother, but sometimes, I find her insufferable. It's her way or the highway. So I guess I chose the highway."

"So this whole Chabad thing is just an act of rebellion?" I said with some relief. "Just an extreme act to help you break away from her grip?"

He grinned. "You sound relieved. Let me complete that question for you. You are basically asking me if I intend to return to normalcy after I establish my independence."

It was my turn to chuckle. "I suppose. Look, David, I'm ready to support you no matter what you do. And if you need financial support, just ask and it's yours. It's just that … Chabad? That's uncharted territory."

"I believe you've contributed to some of their campaigns."

"Sure, why not? It was only money. I'm sure they do good things for the Jewish people. But you're my grandson. My only grandchild. I don't know if I'm ready to contribute you to their movement. Not that anyone is asking my permission. Or even opinion."

"I'm not asking your permission, Grandpa, but I wouldn't mind hearing your opinion. I have to admit that my move was a breakaway to a certain extent, but it was really much more than that."

"I'm listening."

"It had something to do with your great-grandfather's *tefillin*, the ones you gave me for my bar-mitzvah."

For those unfamiliar with the term, *tefillin* are small black leather boxes containing tiny parchment scrolls inscribed with biblical passages; they're called phylacteries in English, although that term is probably even more unfamiliar. Accord-

ing to Jewish tradition, you strap on these leather boxes before morning prayers, one onto your head, near your brain,
and another onto your left arm, near your heart. And then
you pray.

My grandfather, Harry Schneiderman, had his own pair
of *tefillin*, and he also had a pair he inherited from his father, Abraham Schneiderman, whose name I carry; my name
just morphed into Adrian Taylor. Although not observant,
my grandfather feared God, so he gave a lot of money to the
Beliatzer Rebbe for his Chassidic institutions. He thought it
would buy him a ticket to Heaven, and who knows? Perhaps
it did. He was a good man.

One month before my bar-mitzvah, my grandfather handed me his father's *tefillin* and told me how precious they were.
Then he took me to the Beliatzer Rebbe to help me put them
on for the first time. Actually, that was a very significant event
for me. On that day, I also became a confirmed skeptic. You
see, my grandfather told me that the Rebbe was a holy man,
that all he had to do was glance at my forehead and he'd see all
my sins. I was terrified, but when we met the Rebbe, he gave
me a gracious smile and shook my hand warmly. I immediately knew that he hadn't seen a thing. I strapped on the *tefillin* a few times, but then I put them away in a drawer. Until I
gave them to David for his bar-mitzvah. Apparently, they had
had a weird effect on him.

"My great-grandfather's *tefillin*," I echoed.

"Yeah. When I put them on at my bar-mitzvah, I felt …
something, I don't know, connected to my past? I mean, these
were worn by my grandfather's grandfather's father well over
a hundred years earlier. That's like … five generations? Those
tefillin were carried halfway around the world, from Poland to
Germany to the United States, and all so that I, David Goldfield, could wear them on my little head. Pretty cool, don't
you think?"

"I suppose."

"And then - and this is really strange - I thought about those little holy scrolls, actually tiny Torah scrolls, and it made me feel special. Even holy? Does that make sense? I can't describe the feeling, but it was way cool."

I was surprised. "Are you saying that you've been putting on *tefillin* since your bar-mitzvah?"

"Nah. I put them on a few times, and then I put them away. I thought I'd save them for my son or grandson, just like you did."

"So what happened?"

"A few months ago, there was a Mitzvah Tank parked just outside the campus. You know what that is?"

"No."

"It's a Chabad van with religious books and articles inside, usually manned by a couple of Chabad guys who offer them to anyone that looks Jewish. 'Have you put on *tefillin* today?' the guy asked me. Actually, I hadn't put on *tefillin* in years, but what the heck? I let him put the *tefillin* on me, and I read the blessings from a prayer book. You should have heard my Hebrew. It was awful, but I managed to get through it. And you know? It was really nice. It brought back the old feelings I'd almost forgotten."

"So you decided to join Chabad? Just because of that?"

"No. I passed the same spot the next day, and the Mitzvah Tank was still there. I let the guy put *tefillin* on me again, and we got to talking. His name was Zalman, used to be Sheldon, and he'd been in Chabad for two years. He invited me to Crown Heights for the Sabbath, and I accepted. I guess I wasn't in such a good place. My mother was driving me crazy, and I wasn't getting along with my girlfriend; maybe the first led to the second. Or maybe I just don't understand Korean girls. What should I say? I wasn't happy. I thought about calling you, but like I said, I needed to work things out on my own."

"So you went to Crown heights."

He nodded. "Yeah, I did."

"And how was it?"

"Great. I met many interesting, intelligent people. We drank vodka, sang old Chabad songs and talked until late at night. They asked me if I'd like to come to a yeshivah in Crown Heights for a while, you know, take a break from school and spend some time studying Jewish traditions and Chabad mysticism, discover who I really was and my purpose in life. Spend some time in 770. Hey, that sounded good, especially the mysticism part; I'd be like the Beatles in India. It wouldn't cost anything. I could eat and sleep in the yeshivah. So I said okay. I'd try it for a couple of months."

"And how was it?"

"Great. I'm really enjoying it. I mean, these Lubavitchers live with inspiration. They're on a mission to establish outposts of Judaism all over the world, and they're incredible. There are Chabad Houses in just about every corner of the world, about five thousand. Even in Botswana! Just in case Jewish businesspeople pass through there."

"Are they trying to convert the locals?"

"No, they just reach out to Jews."

"And convince them to join Chabad?"

"Not at all. They just want to establish Jewish awareness."

"And how do they measure success?"

"Just by giving Jews a Jewish experience even once in their lifetimes. Like we did in Katmandu. We made a Seder for over two thousand Israelis. A dozen of us flew to Katmandu to help the local Chabad guy. The next day, almost all those people were gone. But we gave them a real Seder. It was extremely satisfying. What effect would that have in the future? Hard to tell. But in the moment, it was a great success. It made me feel good. It made me feel useful."

"What about your girlfriend?"

"That relationship wasn't going anywhere. I told her I needed a break. She didn't seem too upset."

"So are you a Chabad guy? I see that you're kosher. Is that a permanent commitment?"

"Not yet. As long as I'm in Chabad, I feel I should be kosher. But for the time being, I'm still learning and exploring. I don't have to make a decision right away."

"And your mother?"

"She is adamant against my joining Chabad. She won't let me into the house until I leave Chabad. Which just makes me want to stay in Chabad even more."

"I understand. Who knows? Maybe you'll marry a nice Lubavitch girl and give me many religious grandchildren."

He gave me a long look. "Would that be so bad?"

I shook my head. "It would not. You're a smart young man, David. Just take your time and do what's best for you. Do what will make you happy. You only live once, so you might as well be happy. Anything you need, you know I'm here."

"I know, Grandpa, but I'm fine. My trust fund kicks in next year, so I'll always have the basics. Where do I want to invest my efforts beyond that? I'm not sure yet, but I don't think it'll be about becoming rich."

"Good for you, David. Good for you. Now tell me about Katmandu. I want to hear every detail."

David began by portraying the city, its people, its culture, its streets, its sights and smells. He was like an artist painting the scene for me with his words until I could almost smell the vegetables in the stalls of the markets. He had just begun to describe the tremendous logistical effort that went into preparations for the Seder when my cellphone rang. It was June.

"Adrian! Turn on the television!" she said. "There's news! It's about those militia guys from New Orleans. I'll be out right away."

David and I went into the den to watch the news on the big screen. June joined us a minute later. We spun the channels until we found a program that began at ten o'clock.

"Good evening, we have late breaking news," said the announcer. "Behind us you see the Grand Medallion Hotel outside Youngstown, Ohio, which has been the scene of a political conference this evening. In a statement released to the press, Frederick Farragut, former senator from South Carolina, has announced the formation of a new political party called the American Identity Party. The party was formed by the merger of four militia organizations – the Bunker Hill Brigade, the July Fourth Faction, the Euro-American Alliance and the Waco-Ridge Coalition, which was recently in the news when hundreds of its members demonstrated at Tulane University and nearly caused a riot.

"Senator Farragut declared that the new party will field full slates of candidates for national and statewide offices. He also announced that he will serve as the chairman of the party and that Dr. Sanford Johns, professor of philosophy at Mazarin University in Little Rock, Arkansas, and founder of the Church of Natural Humanism, will serve as vice chairman. Our own Charles Robinson will interview Dr. Johns for this station tomorrow evening at eleven. The interview will also be posted on our website.

"Reaction in Washington has been guarded. Lawmakers declined to comment until polling data determine the extent of this new party's support among the general population."

Chapter Six

The next evening, David came by again. He had picked up a large pizza, some bagels and a container of cream cheese in a kosher café on Lexington Avenue, and we dined on hot pizza and cold Diet Coke. After dinner, June went back to her study, and David and I watched a ball game. At eleven o'clock, we were all staring at the screen.

Charles Robinson was a rotund black man in his fifties with a bald head and big black glasses. His warm smile disarmed his subjects, even if they were prepared for it, and often left them defenseless against his probing questions. His audience cut across all lines.

Dr. Sanford Johns was not much thinner than Robinson, but he was much less bald. His hairline was receded a few inches, but from there, it was a thick bush of white hair covering his ears and the nape of his neck. His eyes were pale blue, and his half glasses gave him a pedantic look. The two men sat across from each other at a small round table.

"Good evening, Dr. Johns," said Robinson. "Thank you for coming."

"Thank you for having me."

"You are the founder and head of the Church of Natural Humanism. Where is this church located?"

"Little Rock, Arkansas."

"That's the headquarters?"

"Yes."

"Where are the other branches?"

"They're in the future."

"I see," said Robinson. "I'd like to get into the idea of Natural Humanism, but first I'd like to ask you a preliminary question. You call your organization a church, so is Natural Humanism a religion?"

"Of course."

"And you are the … high priest, shall we say?"

"Hmm. I like the sound of that. The answer is yes."

"So tell me, Dr. Johns, do you believe in God?"

"Of course. There is no doubt that God exists."

"Do you mean the argument from design?"

Johns gave him a disdainful look. "Come on. That's not conclusive proof. The existence of God is a mathematical certainty based on the concept of infinity."

"That is very interesting. Can you explain?"

"Of course. Infinity is not a humongous number. If it was, you could say infinity plus one, and you'd have a number larger than infinity. No, infinity is a concept. When we say that the number one divided by zero is infinity, it does not mean that the number one is stuffed chock full of zeros. It means that there is no limit to how many times zero can be added to zero, because you never get closer to one. It's infinite, literally, without finish. That's the meaning of infinity. Is that clear?"

"Absolutely."

"It follows that there cannot be an infinite number of pebbles at any point in time. Pebbles accumulate, and if you had the time and the inclination you could count all of them. In fact, the terms infinite and number are mutually exclusive. This is one of Aristotle's most basic propositions. The existence of an infinite number of finite entities is impossible. There cannot be an infinite number of things. Is that clear?"

"It is."

"So! The universe exists. Where did it come from? There

are only two options. One, it was created *ex nihilo*, from nothing. In order for this to have happened, there has to be a God. Two, it was always there in one form or another. But wait a minute! Time is composed of finite entities, years, hours, seconds, whichever way you care to slice it. Therefore, there cannot be infinite time. Going forward, time may be infinite, because new time is constantly being created, and there is no limit to how long that process can continue. But going backward? There's no new time being created going backward. Therefore, if you say the universe was always there, you're saying it existed in infinite time. That can't be. Let me say it again. Time cannot be infinite going backward into the past. Which leaves us with only one viable option. God created the universe. So that's the answer to your question, Mr. Robinson. Yes, I believe in God."

"I would have to give that some thought, Dr. Johns, but right now, I can't see a flaw in your argument. Very well, we've established that you believe in God. What does God expect from us? Are you a Christian church?"

"Absolutely not. Turn the other cheek? Love your enemy? Preposterous. It's a corruption of the natural human condition. We're a natural religion."

Robinson pulled off his glasses and rubbed his nose.

"I see," he said. "Do you have a sacred text, Dr. Johns?"

"No. Nature is our sacred text."

"Do you believe in revelation? Has God spoken to you?"

"Absolutely not. God has never spoken to me. Nor has He ever spoken to anyone else. God does not speak to people."

"So how is your religion practiced? Is there a particular day of the week when you have services in your church? And what are the services like?"

"We have no particular day, but we get together at least once a month. We talk about the incredible universe God has created; sometimes, we have video presentations. We talk about Natural Humanism. We know that just as God is all-powerful, He's also all-aware. He hears our words, indeed our very thoughts."

"Do you pray to Him?"

"Not in the sense of asking Him to intervene on our behalf, because He doesn't intervene. He has set the world in motion, and it goes on its own. He did a good engineering job, and it doesn't need any help to keep running smoothly. We pray in the sense that we express admiration of His glory. We ask for nothing in return. God has given us the tools to take care of ourselves. Sink or swim. It's up to us."

"But what if you're not strong enough to stand up to your opponents?"

"And not clever enough to make alliances?" said Johns.

"Yes."

"Then we sink. Life is a competition for survival. If we're not strong enough, we don't survive."

"Might makes right."

Johns nodded. "Might makes right, but not necessarily physical prowess. Intellect, cleverness and cunning are higher forms of might."

"So, what exactly does God expect from people, Dr. Johns? How has He communicated His expectations to you? And what is Natural Humanism?"

"God created a gorgeous, complex world full of all kinds of animals. He didn't tell the animals what to do. All He expects from the animals is that they do their best to survive. That's what it's all about. Survival! Eating, drinking, mating. That's all animals care about. They also like to take pleasure from the world, but it's all about survival."

"And you see human beings as glorified animals," said Robinson.

"Exactly! Human beings, not lions, are kings of the natural world. Our species is endowed with survival tools more pow-erful than those of any other species on the face of the earth. We have intellect. We have weapons. We have technology. Of all the animals, we are best equipped to survive. The threat to our survival is not from other species. It's from other members of our own species."

"Where are you going with this, Dr. Johns?"

"You asked what God wants from us. He wants us to take our cues from the natural world. He wants us to fight for our survival against our enemies with the same vigor and savagery that a lion fights to defend his lioness and cubs. In a pride of lions, the males fight to defend the group and its territory. But that's it! They will not fight to defend a different pride of lions unless it helps them defend their own. That is what we have to do. We have to be strong and vigilant for all threats to our survival."

"You would not come to the aid of a different group of human beings under attack?"

"Absolutely not. Why should we? It would be unnatural."

"What about simple human kindness?"

"Human kindness is limited to us and our group. Not to strangers. If we've done nothing to cause their misfortune, why should we expend our time, effort and money to help them? It's unnatural. It's a corruption of nature. All it does is weaken us and put us at risk."

"You're talking about paganism."

"Exactly! We're neo-pagans. We live by natural law, but we don't believe in silly deities, just in the one true God."

"And the Bible?"

"It's a fraud. All of it. The Old Testament. The New Testament. The Quran. All works of fiction. Come on, you know that, don't you, Mr. Robinson? Any college undergraduate knows it. Biblical criticism and modern archaeology have proved that the Bible was written a thousand years after it claims to have been written. It's all a myth concocted by the Jews to give them an advantage over other peoples."

"You don't believe in Jesus?"

"Did Jesus ever exist? I don't know. But if he believed the

myths of the Old Testament, then he couldn't have been much to write home about."

"So you don't believe in any moral code?"

"The only morality is survival. I believe we should work hard, be loyal to our families and our comrades, brave and strong on the battlefield, honest with our companions. That all falls under the heading of survival. Natural Humanism is about survival. Physical and racial survival."

"Do states and nations have a role under Natural Humanism?"

"We have no loyalty to other members of our species. Only to our own group, not to strangers. But if there's a broader threat, it makes sense to ally ourselves with other groups like ours."

"Can you be more specific, Dr. Johns? How does your church align with the American Identity Party? Are you facing a threat?"

"Damn sure, we are. Jews, blacks, Hispanics, Africans, Indians, Chinese, Cambodians, Vietnamese, Filipinos, Arabs, and who knows what others, they're all overrunning America. White people have to get together and drive them back before it's too late and we're strangers in our own country."

"Are you suggesting that over a hundred million people be expelled from the United States? Do you intend to exterminate them if they refuse to go?"

Johns ran his fingers through his hair

"Come on, Mr. Robinson," he said. "Do you think we're savages? They can all stay if they get the proper documentation, but their citizenship will be revoked. Only white people will be allowed to vote. Only our representatives will pass the laws and rule the country. The rest will be guest workers, always subject to the revocation of their guest visas. If they behave and obey, they can enjoy decent lives in our country. That is the salient point. Our country, our territory, not theirs."

"Are you advocating for the end of democracy in the United States?"

"God forbid. We would still be a democracy. Just as ancient Athens was a democracy, even though only Greeks, a minority of the population, were allowed to vote."

Robinson had a disturbed look on his face. He had obviously not been prepared for the radical paganism of Johns and his followers. Johns, on the other hand, looked pleased. He had presented his views articulately in front of a television audience of many millions. Some would accept his point of view, but most would reject it. That was fine. Movements did not arise full-blown. He had succeeded in planting seeds. He was satisfied. It was written all over his face.

"This is fascinating, Dr. Johns," said Robinson. "We have to break for messages from our sponsors, but please stay with us. We'll be back before you know it."

June, David and I looked at each other in disbelief. For a few long moments, no one said anything. What could we say?

June finally broke the silence. "Do we have to take this seriously, Adrian? Could this really happen?"

David said nothing, but the same question was in his eyes.

"I don't know," I said. "I think that most whites sympathize with his frustrations, if not with his solutions."

"Are we considered white?" asked David.

"Not really. We're Jewish. To these people, we're aliens of the same color. No, these people are decidedly not our friends."

"So who are our friends?" asked June.

"We don't have too many," I said. "Strange as it may seem, the devout Christians, who've persecuted us for two thousand years, may turn out to be our strongest allies. In order to defend their ideology, they have to defend the Old Testament, and that gives us legitimacy."

"Maybe we should convert some of our money into diamonds," said June. "Like your father was saying at the Seder."

"Maybe. But it's a little premature. Let's not go overboard just because some radical fringe group raises its head. We have plenty of time."

"We may have plenty of time to leave," said June, "but it's never too early to be prepared."

"Maybe. I think they'll fail. Most people do not see themselves as animals in the wild."

Chapter Seven

Three minutes later, Charles Robinson and his guest were back. The first part of the interview had run for a long time, and now the second part was about to begin. The two men seemed more relaxed. On the table in front of each of them there was a mug of what I assumed was either coffee or tea.

"Dr. Johns, thank you for giving us so much of your time," said Robinson.

"Thank you for giving me the opportunity to speak to your viewers. I wonder why you've done it. You clearly don't approve of my views."

"That's very perceptive of you. I think they're abhorrent, dehumanizing. But the role of my program is to inform and educate. I believe the formation of the American Identity Party and its association with the Church of Natural Humanism poses a serious threat to American society, especially because you provide an educated ideological voice. I believe that the more you are allowed to operate under the cloak of darkness, the greater the danger you pose. I'm not afraid that millions of my viewers will flock to your banner. They're too intelligent for that. I want them to know about the goals of your movement and make sure they are never realized."

Johns shrugged. "Fair enough. But you'd be surprised by the extent of our support, not only from the grass roots, but also from people at the highest levels of society, people with deep pockets."

"I'm not saying you're not dangerous, Dr. Johns, just misguided. People are more than glorified animals. In any case, let's move on. This is an interview, not a debate."

"By all means. You have more questions?"

"I do."

"Fire away."

"Let's talk about social services. Are you in favor of Medicare?"

"Not as it's constituted. If people want Medicare, they should squirrel away after-tax money all their working lives in special accounts. Those accounts would be used for their medical care when they retire. The rest of society should not have to pay the medical bills of some decrepit old folks."

"I see. How about food stamps for disabled people?"

"Against it. If they can't survive on their own or with the help of their friends and family, they should just be allowed to expire. Again, I point you to the natural world. The old and the sick go off to die."

"What about women? Are you in favor of women's rights?"

"Absolutely. Women should have the vote, just like men. They should have the bulk of the responsibility of child rearing, as we find in the natural world. The females protect and care for the children, and the males forage for food. Otherwise, they are equal, depending on their physical and intellectual strength, as I explained before."

"What about gay rights?"

"Gay and other alternate lifestyles are unnatural. They do not appear in the natural world, and if they do, they are extremely rare. I don't think we should discriminate against gays. They should be allowed the right to vote, but considering that they weaken the species and reduce procreation, the majority heterosexuals should not allow them to promote their lifestyles in the schools and by pride parades."

"Do you think gayness is a choice? Or does it occur naturally?"

"Are you asking if I think there is a gay gene, Mr. Robinson?"

"Yes, that's what I'm asking."

"I don't really think it's a choice for most gays, but there is no gay gene. Gayness is a condition caused by environmental factors, sometimes at a very early age. Something happens that subconsciously causes people to channel their sexuality in the direction of their own gender, such as in prisons. I don't blame the gays for being gay, but they should not promote gayness to the rest of society. The promotion itself can cause gayness."

"How can you be so sure that there is no gay gene?"

"Evolutionary biology proves it. The survival of the fittest. All evolutionary biologists agree that the definition of the fittest is those most capable of passing on their genes to the next generation. Therefore, I would think that gays are the least fit and that they should have been eliminated by evolution. And yet, they're still here in pretty much the same percentages as always. That tells me that environmental factors cause their condition."

"I think many scientists would dispute that assumption, but let me just clarify. You would not revoke their citizenship?"

"I would not, nor would I criminalize gay behavior. I would just restrict them from actively promoting their lifestyles."

"It sounds like you're a Darwinist. Is that compatible with your belief in creation? Did God create the species?"

"God created the primordial world and set it into motion by a process of evolution. Everything developed on its own."

"So did God know that human beings would emerge?"

"Of course. Human beings are the crowning achievement of the creation process. God is very smart. He knew what would result."

"But how could He know what mutations would emerge randomly?"

"Look, you said that I sound like a Darwinist, but really, I'm not. I don't believe that random mutations are responsible for all the variety of life on earth. We can talk about this until we're blue in the face, but we have to admit that Darwinism is a theory, not a fact proven scientifically by experimentation and prediction. The mathematics is problematic."

"So if you're not a Darwinian, what are you?"

"I'm a Lamarckian. Are you familiar with the name, Mr. Robinson?"

"Yes, I am. His ideas were discredited."

"Well, I beg to differ. For the benefit of your viewers, Jean-Baptiste Lamarck was a French scientist who lived about fifty years before Darwin. He suggested that certain acquired characteristics could sometimes be passed down. His ideas were rejected because there was no genetic mechanism for it. But they didn't know about DNA in the eighteen hundreds. Now we know that the DNA of a human being and the DNA of a chimpanzee are ninety percent identical. The differences depend on which switches are turned on and which are turned off. It's possible that external stimuli cause switches to be turned on or off, resulting in permanent hereditary changes. This is more logical than Darwinism, at least to me."

"So what is your point?"

"God can compute from the very beginning what changes will be coming through Lamarckian evolution even though He is not directly involved with the world. The pinnacle of evolution is the human being, as I said before. But we are still part of the animal kingdom, and we are completely on our own. It's all about survival. Anything goes."

"I understand what you're saying, Dr. Johns. As I said before, I completely disagree, but I'm not here to debate you." Robinson took off his glasses and polished them. "One final question. Most of the members of the American Identity Party and those you hope to recruit in the future were raised as Christians. They self-identify as Christians. Will you be able to wean them away from Christianity and get them to join the Church of Natural Humanism?"

"It won't be as hard as you think, Mr. Robinson. They were only Christian in name. I assure you that our members, angry, frustrated and heavily armed, are not inclined to turn the other cheek. Every single member of the American Identity Party has already taken the pledge of Natural Humanism. And for every one of them, there are a hundred more ready to do the same. The time has come."

Chapter Eight

We didn't talk much after the interview was over. What was there to say? The shock had to wear off before we could have a normal conversation about it. June whispered good-night and went off to bed, and I called a cab to take David back to Crown Heights. Afterward, I sat alone in the den and played parts of the interview over and over in my mind.

My eyes started to close, and I rose to go to bed. Halfway there, I found myself going to the computer and accessing Charles Robinson's website. The interview was posted online, and I opened it. I went through it carefully, stopping and going back many times. It was chilling, especially because Johns made his points in dispassionate academic arguments.

The leaders of the new party had recognized that they could not achieve their goals within the framework of Judeo-Christian values. They had to go back to a kind of enlightened paganism, and this they had accomplished by forming an alliance with the Church of Natural Humanism, which was a more appealing name than the Church of Neo-Paganism, although it was essentially the same. At the Seder, my father had maintained that we were protected by the Constitution. There was one problem, however. The Constitution was indeed ironclad in a Christian society, but not in a pagan world that only recognized the natural law of the wild.

I fell asleep on my folded arms in front of my computer and awoke with cramps in my neck and back. I stumbled to bed and slept fitfully until morning. I had a cup of coffee and went to work. I was not hungry.

Two unfamiliar men were waiting in the easy chairs outside my office. One of them looked like an older Jewish man. He had a receding hairline, and gold-rimmed bifocals sat on his long thin nose. His suit was of a heavy gray material with slightly frayed cuffs and dust embedded in the collar. His cuticles were black. The other was a middle-aged Latino wearing freshly pressed slacks and a white shirt open at the neck. His hands were soft and manicured. They both looked anxious but did not attempt to speak to me, and I gave them no more than a slight bow of my head.

I went into my office, made myself a strong coffee and took two Advil. The wall between my office and the waiting area was all glass, and I could see my secretary talking to the two men. They had obviously come without appointments and were waiting for me. My secretary gave me a little time to get settled before she came into my office.

"Good morning, Mr. Taylor," she said; I had long before disabused her of calling me Congressman. "These two gentlemen want to speak with you. They're here from Pennsylvania. I told them they had to make an appointment, but they said it was urgent. They insisted on waiting until you came and letting you decide."

I was about to refuse, but then I relented, more out of curiosity than kindness. "Very well," I said. "Bring them in."

My secretary showed them to the chairs in front of my desk and offered them coffee. They declined politely.

"Good morning, gentlemen," I said. "Would you kindly introduce yourselves and state your business."

The Jewish man turned to his Latino companion. "Can I speak for both of us? You know, just the basics."

"Sure. Go ahead."

"My name is Morris Ackerman," he said to me, speaking with a blue-collar drawl. "This is my friend and next-door neighbor Henry Cortez. Actually, Hernando Cortez, like the Spanish guy who conquered Mexico. We're from Hesterville, Pennsylvania. That's a small town not far from Scranton. Henry owns a pharmacy on Columbus Avenue, that's the main street of Hesterville, and I own the gas station on the corner. I'm Jewish, and my friend is Mexican. We were both born in the United States and are proud Americans." He paused.

"I'm sure you are," I said. "So, what brings you here?"

"You tell him, Henry, okay?"

"Of course, Morris," said Cortez. "Last Fourth of July, I hung a big American flag outside my pharmacy. Next to it I hung a smaller Mexican flag. My friend Morris also hung a big, beautiful American flag in his gas station and next to it a smaller Israeli flag. After some people complained, the Hesterville township committee passed an ordinance forbidding the display of flags of other countries on the Fourth of July. The ordinance carries heavy fines for the first offense and heavier fines for subsequent offenses. We feel this is a violation of our civil rights. The Fourth of July is in a couple of months, and we want to fly our flags."

Before they came into the office, I had speculated about what they might want with me, but this was completely unexpected. I steepled my fingers and closed my eyes as I considered the legal aspects of the case. I had to admit that it was quite intriguing.

"We both do well," said Ackerman when I opened my eyes. "We can pay your fees."

I smiled. "I'm relieved. I was afraid you might want me to do it pro bono. We'll talk about fees later. So let me ask you a few background questions. Mr. Ackerman, you were born here, and your parents?"

"My parents were both in Auschwitz. They came over in 1947."

"You were born in Hesterville?"

He shook his head. "Wilkes-Barre. We moved here when I was six."

"Tell me about your education."

"Well, I graduated high school but didn't go to college like my friend here. I went to vocational school, because I wanted to be a mechanic. I like working with my hands. I was sent to Vietnam in 1972. I was stationed in Danang and served as an aircraft mechanic. When I got back, I got a job at the gas station, and when I came into some money, I bought it."

"Thank you, Mr. Ackerman. And you, Mr. Cortez, what is your story? You were also born here. When did your parents come?"

Cortez smiled. "My parents were also born here, as were my grandparents and great-grandparents. My father's great-grandparents emigrated right after the Civil War from Taxco, a town in Guerrero, a state in central Mexico. They came with money and did very well here. My grandparents moved to Hesterville. My father went to Yale and became a medical doctor. I graduated from the University of Pennsylvania with a doctorate in pharmacology. I had offers from Squibb and Eli Lilly, but I preferred my own pharmacy."

"All right. Why did you display the Mexican flag?"

"My family has been here for many generations. They didn't come over on the *Mayflower*, but we've probably been here longer than most other groups. Except for the blacks. I'm as American as they come, but ethnically, I'm Mexican. The people of Mexico are my kinfolk. My family celebrates Cinco de Mayo, when my people defeated the armies of the French Empire. The flag does not show loyalty to the government of Mexico. It's loyalty to my kinfolk."

"Same for me," said Ackerman. "The Israeli flag is a symbol of my Jewishness. It has a big blue Magen David in the middle. The people of Israel are my brothers and sisters, and I love them all. The flag does not show loyalty to the Israeli government. In fact, I have issues with some of their policies. It's not safe to be at war, even if you think you're strong."

"I understand what you're saying. At first glance, I'm inclined to agree with you, but first glances are notoriously unreliable. Why did you come here without an appointment? And why me? Don't they have lawyers in Pennsylvania?"

"Oh, come on, Congressman," said Cortez. I winced but made no comment. "This is going to be a sticky case, and you're a famous constitutional lawyer, in a class by yourself. We thought it would be hard to get an appointment, so we showed up unannounced. We figured that if we came all the way from Pennsylvania, you'd hear us out."

"Fair enough. It would be inexcusably rude just to send you away. All right, tell me about Hesterville. What are the demographics?"

"We're a multiethnic, fairly prosperous community," said Cortez. "And we generally get along well with each other. We have a large Jewish population. Several hundred families. There's a big Reform temple and a small Chabad House. No kosher restaurants, but you can get kosher food in Walmart or from the Chabad House. The Latino population is diverse. The largest group is Mexican, but we also have people from Ecuador, Chile, Honduras and Colombia. Most of us are Catholics or Pentecostals."

"Do you have representation on the township committee?"

Cortez shook his head. "We do, but our people were never interested in getting into local politics. There are three minority members and six whites."

"How long have you been displaying the Mexican and Israeli flags?"

He shrugged. "I'm not sure. Twelve, fifteen years."

"Do you know the white members of the committee?"

"We do. They're nice people. But people were complaining."

"And no one complained till now?"

"No, not that I know."

"Do you know what changed?"

"I don't, but I can take a guess."

"So take a guess."

"The Vandewegh family lives in Hesterville. Darron Vandewegh and members of his July Fourth Faction have been coming around the last few months on their motorcycles. They must have been among the complainers. No one wants trouble."

"Do you want trouble?"

"Absolutely not," said Ackerman, who had been largely silent. "But where do you draw the line? We have a right to free speech. Hanging the flags is not unpatriotic. Not in the least bit."

"I understand," I said. "And what would you like me to do?"

"You know, stop them before the Fourth of July," said Ackerman. "I don't know exactly how. Get injunctions, things like that."

"All right," I said. "Let me give this some thought. I'll see what I can do. I may have to go down to Hesterville to speak with the committee."

"We'll arrange it," said Cortez, "We'll arrange a car for you, and we'll pay your hourly from the moment you leave your office until you return."

Chapter Nine

Four days later, I was on my way to Hesterville in a Lincoln Town Car from a Manhattan limousine service. Ackerman had decided that to send a car from Hesterville would require two round trips, while a car from New York would only have to make one round trip.

I invited David to join me for the day. It would be good experience if he should ever return to law school, and even if he didn't. Best of all, we would get to spend the day together. I ordered a lot of food from the kosher café on Lexington Avenue. Like it or not, David was making me a kosher eater. I didn't mind. The food was excellent, and for the time being, I could get along without shrimp and lobster.

The trip to Hesterville took about two and a half hours. My staff had done research on the dynamics of the town, and David and I discussed the various approaches we could take with the committee. We also discussed the legal aspects of the case. David had a natural talent for the law.

Ackerman and Cortez met us outside the Municipal Building, an elegant white structure with Corinthian columns and a pitched roof. It was located on Columbus Avenue, ten blocks from Ackerman's garage and Cortez's pharmacy. The building was surrounded by a vast municipal parking lot, which served the municipality as well as the local merchants. My clients wore suits and ties. Ackerman's cuticles were free of black grease.

The entire township committee had not appeared for the meeting. The mayor, who was chairman of the committee, and three members were waiting for us in a conference room on the second floor. The long table was clear of everything except for a decanter of water and a tray of glasses.

The mayor met us at the door. He was a youngish man with red hair and freckles. Ambition glittered in his brown eyes. The others, a Latina, a black woman and a white man, were standing near the table.

"Congressman, what an honor!" gushed the mayor. "I'm Gordon Meadows, mayor of Hesterville, and these are my colleagues. Eva Ramirez, Jennifer Holt and Bob Flintlock. Come, please sit down."

"Excellent," I said. "Let's get started. I have to inform you that we will be recording this meeting. So please consider your words carefully."

"Good idea," said the mayor.

He took a seat at the center of the table, with the two women to his left and Flintlock to his right. Flintlock. What a name. I sat at the center on the other side, facing the mayor, with David to my left and Ackerman and Cortez to my right. David took out his cellphone, pressed the record button and placed it on the table.

"Let me reiterate, Congressman," said the mayor with a quick glance at his phone, "how pleased I am to meet you. You are my role model." He chuckled. "Not that I can ever expect to accomplish as much as you have, but I would love to run for Congress someday. I read your books cover to cover. More than once. Brilliant."

"Thank you." He was making me uncomfortable. I imagined him holding a stiff drink and chewing my ear off at a party, and I shuddered inwardly.

He was not finished. "I particularly like *The Imperial Quadrant*. It gave me a deep insight into history."

"Mr. Meadows, perhaps we can talk about this later. The rest of us here probably haven't read my books, except for my grandson."

"I mention it for a reason, Congressman. Please give me two minutes to tell the rest of us the thesis of the book." He didn't wait to get my consent. He just pushed ahead. "In his book, the Congressman suggested that world history takes place in an area he calls the expanding Imperial Quadrant. Everything that happens within the Quadrant dominates the world at large. Everything that happens outside the Quadrant, although important, is only local history. It does not drive world history as a whole."

"What do you mean?" asked Jennifer Holt. She was a thin woman with intense features and a Caribbean accent. "And why is this important right now for this meeting? The Congressman has come a long way. Let's get down to business."

"Hold your horses, madam," said the mayor. "You'll see my point soon enough. The Quadrant began in Egypt, Mesopotamia and Persia. Then it spread west to include the entire Mediterranean basin. Then it spread north to include all of Europe from the Atlantic to the Ural Mountains. Then it spread west to include North America. The Quadrant projects its hard power over the entire world by invasions and colonization and its soft power by cultural influence. Countries outside the Quadrant never invade or colonize the Quadrant. The world idolizes the cultures of the Quadrant, but the Quadrant is ignorant of the cultures outside the Quadrant. Did I present your thesis correctly, Congressman?"

"More or less," I said. "So what is your point?"

"I'd like to reframe your thesis in racial terms," he said. "The Quadrant is the home of the white race. In other words, the white race dominates all other races. Didn't that occur to you?"

"That was not my argument, but you could make such an argument if you include brown people such as Egyptians, Arabs and Persians in the white race. And how is this relevant to this meeting? Are you saying that you are a white supremacist?"

The mayor bridled. "I am not, sir. Perish the thought! However … however … we all agree that racial tensions are rising in the United States. The white race has made many glorious contributions to civilization in science and the arts of which we are justifiably proud. White supremacy taps into the worst and darkest sides of the white race, the frustrated losers of society, but it's a real and growing force. We don't want racial conflicts spilling over into our beautiful Hesterville."

"I think I see where you're going," I said, "but could you spell it out more clearly?"

"Sure thing, Congressman. Mr. Ackerman and Mr. Cortez are among our finest residents. We all get along very well here in Hesterville, Jews, Hispanics, African-Americans, Asians, Caucasians. We get along just fine. Why should we be a lightning rod for white supremacists?"

"You mean by displaying ethnic flags."

"Yes, that's exactly what I mean. This just enrages them. Especially on the Fourth of July."

"And you know this because Vandewegh told it to you?"

"Yes. We have no quarrel with Mr. Ackerman and Mr. Cortez. We know they're good patriotic Americans. We just don't want any trouble."

"Mr. Meadows, either way there's trouble," I said. "If you prevent my clients from exercising their right of free speech, that is a violation of the Constitution. If you do not prevent them, you're afraid of Vandewegh and his followers. It's a Sophie's Choice. So what do you do?"

"What do you suggest we do, Congressman?" said Jennifer Holt.

"What would Martin Luther King do in such a situation? What would Rosa Parks do? They would stand on principle. They would do the right thing. They would not allow themselves to be intimidated. If you give in to bullies, you are just encouraging bad behavior." Shades of Margaret.

"So, what are you suggesting?" said Eva Ramirez. "You think we should face them down, and they will go away. They have hundreds of thugs with automatic weapons, and we have a small lightly armed police force. I think we shouldn't make a stand here. Let someone else face them down. There will be plenty of opportunities."

"I understand what you're saying, Ms. Ramirez," I said.

"Mrs. Ramirez," she corrected. "I'm not into the Ms. Ramirez thing."

"I understand. It's just that I didn't know your marital status, so Ms. Ramirez was the safest. We cannot control what the township committee does. But we can advise you of our plan of action."

I was waiting for Flintlock to say something, but he just sat there stone-faced.

"I've consulted with my clients," I continued, "and they feel strongly about this. They've been displaying their ethnic flags for fifteen years. Why should they have to stop doing so because of the intimidation of white supremacists?"

I turned to Jennifer Holt.

"And what if the African American residents of Hesterville decided to display some kind of tribute to their African heritage? That wouldn't sit well with Vandewegh and his buddies. Should your people be prevented from displaying pride in their ethnicity? Should they be prevented from honoring their rich history?"

She pursed her lips and stared at me for a moment or two.

"I hear you loud and clear, Congressman," she said. "But I'm still inclined to err on the side of safety. I'd like to ask your clients to reconsider."

I looked at Ackerman and Cortez. They both shook their heads.

"My clients insist on their Constitutional rights."

The mayor held up his hand. "Let's just all take a deep

breath," he said. "Let me suggest a compromise. I can't offer this on my own, but I'm confident that I can get the committee to go along with it."

"We're listening."

"What if we withdrew the ordinance? Wipe it off the books. And then Mr. Ackerman and Mr. Cortez would voluntarily refrain from displaying their flags. No one would violate their rights."

"Let me consult with my clients."

We stepped into the hall and spoke in low tones. David did not join us.

"What do you say?" I asked.

They both shook their heads again.

"It's a matter of principle," said Cortez.

"Do you want to think about it?"

"Nah," said Ackerman. "Let's go to court."

We returned to the conference room and took our seats.

"I've consulted with my clients," I said, "and we've decided to go to court."

The mayor shrugged. "You do what you gotta do," he said. "We'll see you in court." The others mumbled their assent. Even stone-faced Flintlock.

"Well, I guess this meeting is over," said the mayor. "It was a pleasure meeting you, Congressman."

"It does seem that we've reached an impasse," I said. "Before we go, however, I'd like to discuss the consequences of a highly publicized lawsuit."

The mayor raised his eyebrows. "Do you think this will go public? I haven't spoken to any reporters. Have you?"

"No, we haven't. But when we file suit, it will be in the public record. It's bound to be picked up by court reporters, especially if I'm associated with it. I'm sure the lawsuit will get extensive coverage."

"What can we do? We'll just have to bite the bullet."

"Not only a bullet. You'll also have to bite hefty legal fees. It could run into the millions."

The mayor gritted his teeth. "We'll cross that bridge when we come to it. We have some money, and we can raise some more."

"From like-minded people, of course."

"People who value safety," he said.

"No doubt. One final point. According to my staff, Hesterville's economy is heavily dependent on tourism. Poconorama Amusement Park nearby brings lots of tourists, who also enjoy your charming hotels and restaurants. Imagine what tourists would do if they thought Hesterville was under the control of white supremacists. Do you think all the ethnics in the New York-Pennsylvania area would still come? Or would they go instead to Six Flags in New Jersey or Hershey Park a little farther west? Hesterville competes very nicely, but it's not the only option."

"Are you threatening us, Congressman?"

"Heaven forbid. I would never threaten you, even if our conversation was not being recorded. I'm just pointing out the natural consequences of a lawsuit, something you might not have thought through yourselves. I suggest you reconsider. At least, give it some thought. We will wait ten days before we file suit. I really hope to hear from you before then."

We shook hands all around and left. Both sides understood that there was no malice on either side. It was just a clash of interests, idealism in conflict with pragmatism. Their job was to do what they considered best for the residents their town, and mine was to follow the instructions of my clients. It was their right to sue, and I was the attorney who would help them exercise that right.

Before we left Hesterville, David asked the driver to take us to the Chabad House, which was just three blocks away at the corner of Columbus Avenue and Jamestown Road. It was early afternoon, and the rabbi was out. His wife welcomed us at the door. We chatted for a while. She described their activities in providing services for the local Jewish residents, and for Jewish tourists eight months out of the year. Things were peaceful in Hesterville. It was a good place.

Chapter Ten

The story broke in the Scranton papers two days later. By the following day, the national media picked it up. The New York Times ran a report on the front page below the fold. CNN, MSNBC and Fox all sent reporters to Hesterville.

I don't know how it got out. Perhaps a family member of one of my clients had leaked it. Perhaps the mayor had leaked it in a preemptive attempt to win public support, but I doubted it. The source didn't really matter. The information was correct. The cat was out of the bag.

On Friday, a cavalcade of over one hundred motorcycles roared through the streets of Hesterville in a show of force. The riders all had long hair tied back with bandanas, wraparound sunglasses and black leather jackets with July Fourth Faction emblazoned on their backs. Vandewegh was sending a clear message to the committee. All the news channels ran footage of the invasion. It was frightening.

Governor Ronald Cimarron of Pennsylvania, a rising star in the Republican Party, made a public appeal for calm. "Everyone has to take a step back. There are good people on both sides." I don't think he realized how unfortunate his choice of words was. I know Ron Cimarron. He's a good and decent man. He was just trying to tamp down the tension.

Frederick Farragut, chairman of the American Identity

Party, was not as conciliatory. "It's an outrage," he declared to a reporter from Fox News. "Why do these people have to hang foreign flags on the Fourth of July, the most patriotic day of the year? Real Americans wouldn't do that. The committee did the right thing. Whoever doesn't like it can go back where they came from. This is America!" The reporter was visibly uncomfortable, but he did his job.

Darby and Vandewegh also spoke to reporters, although they received less coverage than Farragut. Dr. Johns maintained a low profile; he was an ideologue, not a warrior.

My phone also rang numerous times, both in the office and at home, but I only took calls from people I knew well, including a few journalists to whom I spoke on background. I did not want the case to be tried in the media. What was happening already fulfilled my prediction to the mayor of Hesterville. It was more than enough. I was not about to add fuel to the fire.

The motorcyclists cruised the streets of Hesterville and visited its bars for several hours. Then they left, and peace returned to the town.

The next few days were uneventful. On Saturday, a week later, I received a call from the mayor of Hesterville.

"How are you doing, Congressman?" he said. "Things got a little hot there, but it's all calmed down."

"I'm glad to hear it."

"The full township committee met last night. We discussed our problem from all sides, and we've come to the conclusion that we don't want a lawsuit that will be on the news every day. You're right. The summer season is coming up, and all those Jewish families from Brooklyn and Lakewood will stop coming. Same for the African Americans and the Hispanics. We may get some whites and Asians, but it will be a disaster. So we voted to withdraw the ordinance. Ackerman and Cortez can display their damn flags."

"You're doing the right thing. You're standing up for

the Constitution."

"Yeah. That too. If we're going to do this, we might as well put on the white hats of the good guys. Anyway, you can withdraw your lawsuit."

"I didn't file it yet."

"Yeah." He sounded dejected. "Look, Congressman, no hard feelings. As you said, our interests collided without malice on either side."

"You're very gracious, Mr. Meadows. It's much appreciated. I wish you lots of luck in your political career. You have to know when to hold 'em and when to fold 'em. You did the right thing. Be well."

I breathed a sigh of relief. I didn't want to try that lawsuit. It was bound to get ugly. I didn't know what the future would bring, but I hoped for the best. Vandewegh had tried to intimidate the committee, and he had failed. It didn't matter if the committee had acted from principle or from economic self-interest. The result was the same. They had faced down the white supremacists, and that was a good thing. It would give encouragement to others who faced similar challenges.

My optimism was short-lived. The news that the ordinance had been withdrawn and the lawsuit dropped triggered a storm of angry protest from the American Identity Party and its confederates.

"The foreigners are taking over our country," declared Farragut at a news conference. "Who can forget Iwo Jima where American boys gave their lives for the American flag? Our flag is the banner of our national pride. It's the symbol of our America. How can we let it be contaminated by other flags flying beside it? The township committee of Hesterville has caved to pressure from Jews, blacks and Hispanics. Let them go wave their flags in their own countries. This is America!" He raised his fist. "Our America for our Americans!"

The talking heads came down on the side of free speech, even on Fox News, but they voiced reservations. Tensions were running high. There was a great outcry in the country against illegal immigration. Why fan the flames at such a combustible time?

Dr. Sanford Johns also weighed in on the discussion with a press conference. "The American Identity Party is fully justified by natural law," he declared, "in protesting against the actions of the township committee of Hesterville. The white race, which is the dominant group in America, has the right to protect its territory from the invasion of peoples of different colors, races and nationalities. It's true that this America is a nation of immigrants, but the white race was the first group of immigrants. We established America as white territory, and we have to defend it as such. Everyone has to respect the American flag. We cannot allow other flags in our America. It is only natural law."

"What about the blacks?" asked a reporter. "Weren't they here from the beginning? And what about the Native Americans? Weren't they here before everyone else? Isn't this their territory?"

"You mean the Indians? It was once their territory, but it isn't any more. They were defeated, and now they're insignificant. A relic of history. As for the blacks, they didn't come as immigrants. They came as slaves. This was never their territory, and it isn't now. The white race laid claim to it first, and we will not allow other races to take the territory from us. We will defend it. It is natural law."

It was very disturbing. These racists and supremacist ideas were seeping into the mainstream consciousness. I was convinced that most white people of good will and good character would not buy into the American Identity Party platform and the creed of the Church of Natural Humanism. But maybe on some level, they would become uneasy with the presence of other races. Maybe on some level, they would feel a little threatened. No good could come of it.

Things calmed down for a while, because the media lost

interest. But ominous rumblings continued on the more extremist-minded stations and websites. The American Identity Party was increasingly militant and vocal. Nothing was happening, but it felt like the calm before the storm.

The storm was not long in coming. Farragut called a news conference at his headquarters. He promised an important newsworthy announcement. The media attended in force, as they were supposed to do. It was not up to them to decide which news to report and which to suppress. The people had a right to be informed, and it was the responsibility of the media to report with a minimum of bias. I watched the press conference live on television, as I was sure thousands of others were doing as well.

Farragut stood on the podium, flanked by Johns. Darby, Vandewegh, Montague, Hatwick and three others I did not recognize were lined up across the stage behind him. Who were these new players? They looked like clones of the others. Had more groups joined the American Identity Party? Was that the important announcement? I was about to find out.

"Thank you for coming," Farragut began. "We need the media to accomplish the goals of the American Identity Party, and we welcome your presence. All we ask is that you report with fairness. Leave the opinions for commentators and op-ed pages. Journalists should stick to journalism."

He paused for a moment, then he squared his shoulders.

"I called you here to announce that the American Identity Party will be holding a peaceful demonstration in the parking lot in front of the Hesterville Municipal Building on Sunday, the Fourth of July. We have already obtained permits. We also have the right to exercise our freedom of speech. We will be joined by three more patriotic groups that have associated themselves with the Party in the last few days, and we also invite all other patriotic Americans to join us in expressing our ... displeasure. We demand that the committee reinstate the flag protection rule and enforce it to the fullest extent of the law. We invite the media to report on the demonstration, as I'm sure you will, and we ask you to be impartial, to listen to the voices on both sides."

He adjusted his tie.

"We will not be taking questions at this time," he said. "You can ask your questions at the demonstration."

It was a double bombshell. He had shown the public that he was gathering strength with each passing day. If three more groups had already joined the American Identity Party, how many more would follow suit? And he had organized a demonstration that promised to be anything but peaceful. A tame rally would not hold the media's attention for long. There was also bound to be a large turnout of angry counter-demonstrators. Clashes were almost inevitable. The Fourth of July fireworks would dominate the news for days. If not weeks.

Chapter Eleven

On Sunday, the family got together for a barbecue at my brother Bernie's house in Passaic, New Jersey, to celebrate my father's ninety-third birthday. June called David to invite him to come with us. She promised to bring food he could eat in addition to fruit and soft drinks. He might not have attended if June had not invited him to come with us. But he agreed to come. It made me happy.

David took the subway from Crown Heights and knocked on our door before noon. He looked distracted. I asked him if everything was all right, and he assured me that it was. Still, I could see he was holding something back. Then I realized that this birthday party would be the first occasion Margaret and David attended together since she had expelled him from his home. Undoubtedly, David was concerned about meeting his mother. It would be awkward, to say the least.

Bernie lived in a large suburban mansion that stood on a full acre. The lawn was beautifully landscaped. The entire house was fronted with flower beds bursting with a dazzling display of vivid color and numerous Japanese maples. The branches of the oaks and the elms were heavy with verdant foliage. A marble fountain gurgled in the summer heat.

The rest of the family was already there when we arrived. We could hear the sounds of music and conversation from the patio as we headed around back, and as we drew closer, we smelled the roasting meat. I glanced at David to see his reaction. He gave me a crooked grin and shrugged his shoulders, as if to say that he did not expect his great uncle to make his home kosher to accommodate him.

Bernie greeted us with a broad smile. He slapped me on the back, shook David's hand and nodded at June. He led us onto the patio. The smell of roasting meat was overpowering. The children were playing in the kidney-shaped pool, and groups of friends and family were conversing on the patio near my father. He was sitting at a table under an umbrella. He had a beer in one hand and a hot dog in the other. The piano melodies of Lang Lang played in the background.

I bent over him and kissed his cheek. "Well, how's the birthday boy? It looks like you made it to another birthday. We were worried on Passover."

"Nah, I didn't think I'd die before my next birthday, but a person never knows. One day, you're here, and the next day you wake up and discover that you're dead. And how are you doing, boychik? You see, I didn't call you Congressman. I just thought it." He chuckled. Then he put back his serious face. "You've been making some noise in the news lately. Listen, you did the right thing."

"Thank you for seeing that."

"You know, of course, that there's going to be trouble, especially on the Fourth of July. Well, don't worry about it. You're not responsible. The American Identity Party is determined to make a lot of noise. If not Hesterville, it would have been somewhere else. You did right to stand up to them. It's your job to protect the Constitutional rights of your clients, and you did that very well. Leave the rest to God."

"You sound like Grandpa Harry. Since when do you talk about God?"

"You're right. My father was kind of religious. He kept kosher in the house. I don't know if it would have been kosher enough for David, but he did the best he could. He went to shul every week. He even closed his store on Saturday morning. He was terrified of God, and he did his best to appease Him."

"And you're not terrified of God?"

"Nah. Why would he want to hurt me? Did I ever hurt anyone?"

"I guess not. You're safe, Pop."

"I'm safe from God but not from those AIP crazies. Don't forget what I said on Passover. Watch your back."

June came over with David. She kissed my father, wished him a happy birthday and went to get some food.

"Come here, boychik'l," my father said to David. "Give your great grandfather a hug. We missed you on Passover."

"Happy birthday," said David. "I missed you, too, but I was away."

"I know. In Nepal. Your grandfather told me. Did you like it?"

"I enjoyed what I was doing."

"Making a Seder for all those Israeli backpackers. That was nice. Did you get a chance to climb Mount Everest?"

David smiled. "Not this time. Maybe next."

June came back with a plate of ribs and offered me some. I shook my head. "I think I'll share David's food, if he can spare some."

"Aw c'mon, Grandpa," he said. "You don't have to do that. You love ribs, and those look really good. Why should you deprive yourself?"

"I don't know," I said. I really didn't know. I had just said it on impulse. "Maybe it's just a way of showing you how much I love you."

"Well, I love you, too, David," said June, "but I'm going to eat these ribs anyway."

Just then, Margaret came out of the house. She sat down next to us.

"Hello, Dad," she said. "Hello, June." She looked at her son. "David."

"Hello, Mother. How are you?"

"Oh, I'm just fine. We miss you, David. Your room is ready, and your bed is made. You can come home anytime you choose."

"With no conditions?"

"Just one. Be normal."

"I think I am normal."

"Well, that's a matter of opinion. I hear you live in Crown Heights."

"How do you know? Did Grandpa tell you?"

"I did not," I interjected. "In fact, I haven't spoken to your mother since Passover. I've been busy."

"So have I," Margaret said with a toss of her head. "You and your precious grandfather are famous. I read all about both of you in the news." She stood up. "I have to go take care of something. Catch you later."

No one spoke for a little while. My father broke the silence.

"Well, that wasn't too painful, David. I was expecting a scene."

"Believe me," he said, "it was painful. But what can you do?"

"Exactly. What can you do? You know what you can do? Nothing! So be happy and do what you want."

David and I took our food to a small table near the back fence of the property, far from the noise and smells. David offered to get me some ribs, but I refused. I enjoyed showing him solidarity and love more than I would have enjoyed the ribs. I could always take June out for ribs tomorrow.

"What's on your mind, David," I said. "You're holding something back."

"True."

"Do you want to tell me? You don't have to, you know."

"No, I very much want to tell you. I was just waiting for a good opportunity. I didn't want to talk in front of June. Maybe now is a good time."

"Okay. I'm listening."

"You know about the July Fourth demonstration in Hesterville?"

"Who doesn't?"

"Lots of people are going to be there for the other side. You know, to demonstrate against them. There are bound to be hundreds of Jewish college students among them, almost all of them non-observant. We were talking about it in Crown Heights. The rabbis were saying that this would be a great opportunity to reach out to these kids and give them a taste of Judaism."

"How's that?"

"You know, by helping them put on *tefillin* or giving them candles for the Sabbath. Many of them have never had such an experience."

I was skeptical. "Sounds dangerous. Why don't the rabbis just do this on college campuses?"

"They do. But they figured that when Jewish kids come to demonstrate against the AIP, they'll be more receptive to their ancient heritage."

"You mean, if you persecute me for being Jewish, I might as well learn something about Judaism?"

"Something like that."

"How do they propose to do this? Just flag down people in the street?"

"No, they'll bring a Mitzvah Tank from Crown Heights to Hesterville and park it in front of the Chabad House. They'll offer food and cold drinks, and they'll offer *tefillin* and candles. And literature for those who are interested."

"And you want to go there?" I knew the dreaded answer, but I asked anyway.

"I volunteered. I told them I was familiar with Hesterville, that I knew my way around. They accepted my offer. I'm looking forward to being there on the Fourth of July. I'm excited."

"I'm against it," I said. "If you're asking my advice or approval, I'm against it. It's too risky."

"It would mean a lot to me if you supported me. I believe I'll be doing something important, something really meaningful. Be happy for me."

"I still think it's much too risky," I insisted.

"People take risks to do meaningful things. What about Doctors Without Borders? But I'm telling you that it won't be risky. We won't be anywhere near the Municipal Building. The demonstration is three blocks away. We'll meet people on the way to the demonstration and on the way back. Don't worry, we'll be safe."

"No one in Hesterville will be safe."

Chapter Twelve

As the Fourth of July approached, I became very agitated. I couldn't sleep. I couldn't eat. I couldn't concentrate on my work for my clients, let alone the new book I was writing. I was cranky and couldn't have a normal conversation with June. Fortunately, she was understanding and stayed out of my way for the most part. We didn't discuss the situation, but we both knew what was in each other's heart.

"I'm going to Hesterville on the Fourth of July," I said to her one day.

"Adrian! You're not serious!"

"I am, June."

"But why?"

"To see my clients. There's paperwork to sign and a fee to collect."

"You're going for the money? Tell them to come to Manhattan on a business day!"

"Come on, June. You know why I'm going."

She didn't reply. Tears formed in her eyes.

"I have to keep an eye on David."

"Why, Adrian? What can you do?"

"I'll eat my heart out if I stay here, in the dark about what's happening there. Maybe I'll give him a hand."

"You're going to put *tefillin* on people?"

"I'm not going for that. I just want to be near David. He's

excited that, as he believes, he's doing something meaningful. I want to share the moment with him. And I want to keep him safe."

"He'll be just as safe without you there. He'll be far from the demonstration. If you think it's not safe, why are you risking your own life? What about me? I don't want to be a widow again."

"You won't be a widow. You said yourself that it was safe."

"But you think it's not safe. Don't you have a responsibility to me? I don't want to lose you. You're my whole life!"

She was right. I was putting her at risk.

I sighed. "June, my dear wonderful beloved wife, I beg your permission to go. I can't begin to tell you how important this is to me."

"I know how important it is to you," she said quietly.

She slumped in her chair and buried her face in her hands. She sat that way for a long time, not moving, not making a sound. Finally, she raised her head. I saw resolution in her eyes. She would accept no argument. But I was not ready for what she said.

"I'm going with you, Adrian."

I was taken aback. "I can't let you do this. I know you love David, but you have no need to go. Why put yourself at risk?"

"Don't waste your time and effort, Adrian. I'm going to stand beside you on the deck of the *Titanic*, and if the ship goes down, we go down together."

Chapter Thirteen

The Fourth of July was a beautiful day. Wispy white clouds rode high in the bright blue sky. It was very hot, but there was a gentle breeze as we left our brownstone. I decided to drive myself. I wanted more control of my time; a driver would just be in the way. Waze would get us to Hesterville just fine.

I called Ackerman from the highway.

"Mr. Ackerman, good morning. It's Adrian Taylor. I'm with my wife. We have you on speaker."

"Mr. Taylor! And Mrs. Taylor! I've never met you, but I have to tell you that your husband is a prince."

She laughed with pleasure. "You're so kind, Mr. Ackerman. He's indeed a prince. I know it better than anyone else!"

"You sound like a great lady," said Ackerman. "A lady fit for a prince!"

"Okay, enough of this," I said. "How are you, Mr. Ackerman? How's the family?"

"I'm fine. The family's fine. I'm on my way home. Today, I stay indoors, just to be safe. How are you enjoying your holiday?"

"That's what I'm calling about. We're on our way to Hesterville. Can we park our car in your gas station?"

"What are you saying, Mr. Taylor? You're coming here? Today?"

"Yes, we're on our way. I'm calling you from the car. We should be there in a little over an hour according to Waze."

"Of course you can park your car in my gas station. If I knew you'd turn around and go back, I'd say no. But why are you coming here? You don't live here. If you want to talk with us, we'll come to you tomorrow."

"It's a long story. Perhaps I'll tell it to you at a different time."

"You really shouldn't come here. Nothing can be that important. You don't know what's going on here, Mr. Taylor. Pickup trucks full of rough characters and motorcycle riders have been pouring into town since the crack of dawn. There must be hundreds already. Maybe thousands. They're having tailgate parties in the municipal parking lot, and they have a stage and loudspeakers set up near the building."

"Is there a police presence?"

"Absolutely. Just about every police officer in Hesterville is out there, and I saw many police cars from neighboring towns. I even saw squad cars from Scranton and Wilkes-Barre. The police are heavily armed and wearing riot gear. They must be sweating bullets. Oops, I didn't mean to mention bullets."

"What else?"

"They've put up barricades in a one-block perimeter around the Municipal Building to contain the crowd."

"Can I interrupt, Mr. Ackerman?" said June. "Did you see any medical people?"

"Lots of EMTs. There are some ambulances parked a block away."

"Good," she said.

"But we probably won't be needing those. The police will have things well under control."

"But you're going home," I said.

"Yeah. I don't mind watching on television in the comfort of my own home. I'm sure it'll be covered live."

"Are there counter-demonstrators?"

"Yes. Loads of them. They're gathered behind

the barricades."

"Did you pass by the Chabad House on Columbus and Jamestown?"

"I know where the Chabad House is. Everybody knows. Yeah, I passed by a few minutes ago."

"And?"

"There's a big white van parked on the Jamestown side, right near the corner. There are tables set up near the van. It says Mitzvah Tank on the side. There are a few Lubavitchers, maybe six or seven, young men stacking leaflets Why do you ask?"

"I heard that Chabad would have a presence today in Hesterville. Are they out of harm's way?"

"Oh, sure. They're far away. I guess they want to reach out to the Jewish kids who come to demonstrate against the roughnecks. Give them Shabbat candles and things like that. Those Lubavitchers are good people. I like them."

Chapter Fourteen

We parked the car in Ackerman's gas station on Columbus Avenue ten blocks south of the Municipal Building. The police had blocked the north end of the avenue to the protesters. The demonstrators would be arriving that way, and the police wanted to avoid direct confrontations.

June and I joined the throngs of people of all ages, all genders and all colors walking toward the barricades that cordoned off the demonstration area. Many of them carried placards. "Down with Bigotry and Racism." "Humans Are Not Animals." "Love Makes the World Go Round, Hatred Makes It Go Down." "All People Are Made in God's Image." "Democracy Embraces All People." And many more.

An undercurrent of gravity ran through the walkers. Their faces and body language displayed a variety of emotions. Anger, idealism, disgust, frustration, agitation, anguish, alarm, desperation. But regardless of what every individual was feeling, they were all united in a sense of the gravity of the situation. It was an important day. A critical day. A monster had risen from the slimy depths of society and was gathering strength. It had to be stopped before it tore apart their beloved United States of America. June and I shared their urgency and many of the other emotions as well.

The sides of the avenue on both sides of the walkers were

packed with hundreds of onlookers. We passed the Shiloh Gospel Church just when a stream of black people in their Sunday best were emerging from Sunday services. Parents hustled their children away, but many others remained to watch the spectacle.

As we approached Jamestown Road, I could see the Mitzvah Tank in the distance across the avenue to our left. It was parked right off the avenue in front of a nondescript square box of a building, which I recognized as the Chabad House. A few bearded young men in white shirts and colorful yarmulkes stood beside three folding tables covered with stacks of leaflets and assorted religious articles. Some of the passersby stopped to view the display. One Lubavitcher was offering Shabbat candles to young women who appeared Jewish. Another was helping a young man in shorts and sandals put on *tefillin*.

June pulled a small but powerful pair of binoculars from her ample handbag and trained them on the Mitzvah Tank. "Adrian! Look! That's David doing the *tefillin* thing!"

I took the binoculars and looked. It was indeed David. He looked happy and excited as he wrapped the black leather straps around the young man's left arm. Four other young man were waiting their turn. Most of them had probably never put on *tefillin* in their lives. Perhaps just on the day of their bar-mitzvah. Their Judaism did not play an important role in their lives, certainly not to the extent of strapping on *tefillin* every day. But on that day, it seemed eminently appropriate. I am Jewish, they were declaring, and I'm proud of it.

I studied David's face while he was giving random Jewish people a distinctly Jewish experience. I could read that face so well, and it was clear that he felt he was doing something terribly important, something extremely meaningful, that he was playing a small role in something historical. He was oblivious to the hatred and malice that hung over Hesterville like a noxious cloud. He looked inspired. He was fighting evil with good. He was on the side of the angels.

June and I stepped into the doorway of a hardware store to make a plan. We didn't want David to see us. We needed to find a vantage point from which we could observe the demonstration in the municipal parking lot and also watch David unobserved. I looked up and saw some people gathered on the roof of a four-story apartment building The roof was our best bet.

The stairs to the roof were crowded with others who had the same idea, but we pushed our way through and found a spot at the edge of the roof. I let June look around first, and then I took the binoculars.

First, I looked at the Mitzvah Tank. Activity was strong, and David was intensely involved. Every once in a while, he turned in my direction, and I could see the excitement on his face. I envied him. When had I ever felt such a surge of excitement? Not when I was in Congress. That was a disaster. Not even when I held the first copies of my newly published books. Of course, I was profoundly pleased, but in my mind, it was on to the next thing. The moment itself was disappointingly anticlimactic. As for the times of the writing, they were deeply exciting and fulfilling. But I had never experienced a single point in time, a single moment, when my head glowed and I breathed joy. David was experiencing just such a moment, and although I had begged him not to come, I was happy for him.

I turned the binoculars to the north. The low buildings between us and the municipal building did not obstruct the sight lines. I had never seen such a spectacle. I had been to places with huge crowds. I was in Berlin when Barrack Obama drew two hundred thousand cheering people when he was running for President. I had been to the Super Bowl more than once. I was in many places. But this was different.

The municipal parking lot was completely filled with demonstrators wearing tee-shirts or jackets emblazoned with the slogans of their respective groups and baseball caps with the emblem of the American Identity Party. Numerous more demonstrators jammed the northern part of the avenue as far as I could see. I saw many men and women of all ages but no children. They were all white. A long row of pickup trucks was parked on the avenue in front of the municipal parking lot.

The barricades were set up below us about a block from the demonstration area. Hundreds and hundreds of walkers had reached the barricades. The southern part of the avenue was clogged with them. They stood shoulder to shoulder with an air of expectancy, although no one knew what to expect.

The police were present in force. Governor Cimarron had considered calling out the national guard, but he decided that would be too incendiary. Instead, he requested that other townships send reinforcements, and I could see many police cars in a variety of makes and colors. The Hesterville police chief was in overall command, but coordination would be difficult. The police presence was heaviest at the barricades around the perimeter of the demonstration area, but many police also circulated through the crowds.

There were ambulances parked both on the south and the north parts of Columbus Avenue, and television trucks at the barricades. The media were not allowed into the demonstration area. Nonetheless, some enterprising newspeople had managed to get through with cameramen, and they were interviewing demonstrators for the live audience. A news helicopter hovered overhead.

As I watched, Farragut walked onto the stage. He nodded to the AIP dignitaries and waved to the raucous multitude. Then he stepped to the podium and raised his hand for silence. A sound technician adjusted the microphone for him and tested it.

"Welcome! Welcome!" Farragut shouted. The loudspeakers screeched, and he lowered his voice without lowering the intensity. "What a beautiful sight! I look around at the precious faces of my brothers and sisters in the American Identity Party, and tears come to my eyes. We've been sleeping long enough, my friends, and right here, in front of my eyes, I see the awakening of our people. We will not be silent while our beloved America is taken from us by others. We fought for this land. We spilled our blood for this land. This is our America! No one else is welcome in our America. If they want to be here, it can be only on our terms. Only we are the owners of this wonderful land. Only we will decide who comes and who leaves."

He paused and looked around. Then he raised two fists into the air.

"Repeat after me. Our America for our Americans!"

The crowd erupted in a roar. "Our America for our Americans!"

"Again!" shouted Farragut.

The roar was even louder. "Our America for our Americans!"

"Again!"

"Our America for our Americans!"

He raised his hands for silence.

"What should we do about the illegal immigrants?"

"Send them back!"

"Where should we send them?"

"Where they came from!"

"What should we do about the fake Americans?"

"Send them back!"

"What should we do about the Hispanics?"

"Send them back!"

"Where should we send them?"

"Mexico!"

"What should we do about the blacks?"

"Send them back!"

"Where should we send them?"

"Africa!"

"What should we do about the Jews?"

"Send them back!"

"Where should we send them?"

"Poland!"

"What should we do about the Asians?"

"Send them back!"

"Where should we send them?"

"Asia!"

"That's right, my friends. Send them all back. We don't want them here. Unless they serve our interests." He raised his fists. "And who makes the rules? Who lays down the law?"

"We do!"

"That's exactly right, my noble brothers and sisters. This is our land. No one will replace us. Do you agree?"

The crowd exploded with a primal roar, sudden and powerful as a thunderclap, and then the chants began.

"The spics will not replace us! The niggers will not replace us! The Jews will not replace us! The gooks will not replace us! The spics will not replace us! The niggers will not replace us! The Jews will not replace us! The gooks will not replace us! The spics will not replace us! The niggers will not replace us! The Jews will not replace us! The gooks will not replace us!"

Farragut lifted his hands, and the chants subsided.

"Let's have a round of applause for our good friends in the media. They are witnessing this historic gathering, and I'm sure they'll report to their viewers with fairness. Come on, a round of applause for the media."

There was a ripple of unenthusiastic applause, but Farragut was pleased. The media was not the enemy of his people. Without the media, they would sink into obscurity.

"And now … the time has come. We have to take this event to the next level. We will march. Let's light our tiki torches!"

A sea of tiki torches sprang to flaming life all over the demonstration area. There were at least a thousand. Maybe two thousand. I didn't count.

"Get ready! And remember, we are not savages. The march

must be peaceful. No violence!"

The instructions were met with loud snickers, and the crowd surged toward the avenue. The beds of the pickup trucks quickly filled with demonstrators. The others lined up on the sides or behind them. Most had tiki torches. Some waved placards aloft.

Farragut thrust his fists into the air.

"Gentlemen! Start your engines!"

Chapter Fifteen

The pickup trucks drove straight at the barricades below us. The police trained their weapons on the approaching vehicles, but they only fired into the air. The trucks gathered speed. At the last moment, the police offices and crowd gathered behind the barricades scattered, and the first pickup truck smashed though the barricade. The other trucks followed close behind.

The pickup trucks slowed a little to allow the swarming marchers to catch up, then they headed south on Columbus Avenue. The marchers waved their tiki torches and shouted, "The spics will not replace us! The niggers will not replace us! The Jews will not replace us! The gooks will not replace us!"

The counter-demonstrators hung back from the procession and shouted curses, epithets and slogans from the safety of the sidewalks. David and the Mitzvah Tank were parked on Jamestown Road. They were out of the path of the marchers. I prayed they would be safe.

June pulled at my arm frantically. "Adrian, look! They're slowing near the Mitzvah Tank!"

The lead pickup had indeed slowed almost to a crawl. Through my binoculars, I saw a burly man with long blond hair and a tattoo on his neck lift a black tube from the bed of the truck and point it at the Mitzvah Tank. In a feverish haze, I looked for David. He was handing candles to a young woman in front of the Mitzvah Tank.

It took me a moment to identify the tube, but there was nothing I could have done right then and there. All I could do was watch in horror as the man in the truck pulled the trigger of the grenade launcher. There was a wispy tail of white smoke as the grenade flashed through the air and struck the Mitzvah Tank The white van exploded in a ball of flame. David and the young woman were flung through the air like a pair of rag dolls.

Immobilized by shock, I saw the pickup truck speed up a little and slow down near the Shiloh Gospel Church. The man fired again, and the front of the church crumpled. As I was told later, he also fired a grenade into Cortez's pharmacy a few blocks away.

"David!" June's scream penetrated my fog. "David!"

The enormity of what I had just seen suddenly hit me like a blow to the sternum. My scream was even louder, but it did not escape into the air. It ripped through my heart and tore it to shreds.

We flew down the stairs and ran to David, but the police had cordoned off the area and wouldn't let us through. I tried to push my ways through, but they grabbed my arms and pulled me back.

"You can't go there, sir," a sergeant said to me. "It's a crime scene."

"You have to let me through," I shouted. "That's my grandson."

"I'm awfully sorry," he insisted. "We have medics on the way."

I was beside myself with fury. "Let me through! I'm Congressman Adrian Taylor! If you don't let me through, I'll have your badge!"

The sergeant looked at me with indecision in his eyes.

June stepped forward. "Officer, let us through."

"Who are you, ma'am?"

"I'm June Taylor, the Congressman's wife. I'm a doctor. Let us through to see if we can help our grandson."

The sergeant stepped aside and let us in.

David's crumpled body lay immobile on its side. He was unconscious. His face was ashen and covered with blood, as if all the blood from within had been squeezed out and splattered over his face.

"Is he breathing?" I whispered.

"Very faintly," said June. "I can hardly find a pulse. Here, help me with this abdominal wound, he's bleeding heavily." She ripped off her jacket and handed it to me. "Take this and try to staunch his bleeding."

She stood up.

"Where are you going?" I asked in a panic.

"I have to see to the young woman. I'm right here if you need me."

I placed the balled-up jacket over David's wound and pressed with all my might.

"David, my dear sweet David," I pleaded. "Please open your eyes. If just for a second. David, I love you. David, you can't leave me. David. David. David."

There was no reaction. I wept and kept pressing the jacket on the wound. I would not let the life seep out of him. I staunched my tears for a moment.

"What's with the young woman?" I managed to ask June.

"I think she's gone. I'm still trying to find some vital signs. There's not much blood. She must have hit her head when she was thrown."

The ambulance pulled up, and the first responders jumped out. They lifted David gently, laid him on a gurney and hooked him up to an IV. Suddenly, David went into a convulsion and opened his eyes. Then his eyes began to roll into his head.

June grabbed his hand. "Stay with us, David. Stay with us!"

She squeezed his hand, and I thought I saw an almost imperceptible squeeze in return. His convulsion passed, and he closed his eyes.

"Where are you taking him?" she asked the medics. "I'm a doctor, and I'm also his grandmother."

"Hesterville General is on the other side of town. He'll be in good hands. It's an excellent hospital, and we have to get him there right away. There's no time to waste."

Chapter Sixteen

June went along with David in the ambulance, while I ran to get the car from Ackerman's gas station. There was only room for one in the ambulance, and she was the doctor. It was more important for her to oversee David's care, while I would only get in the way.

When I arrived at the hospital, June told me that David had been taken into surgery and that she had spoken to Margaret. We sat on chairs outside the operating room, not knowing what to say to each other. There were no questions to ask. We both knew the answers. After a while, June patted my knee and gave me a wan smile.

"The doctor seemed competent," she said. "Let's hope David pulls through. He's young and strong."

"Maybe God will save him. He certainly deserves it. He was doing God's work."

She shrugged. "Who knows what God will do? I hope you're right."

"Should I pray?"

"Sure. I'll pray with you."

"I don't know what to say. I don't remember the last time I prayed."

"Just say whatever's on your mind. You're a terrific lawyer. Plead your case. Give it everything you've got. I'll do the same."

We prayed for fifteen minutes, and then we got tired. If

God heard my argument, He'd get it right away and would rule one way or the other. What was the point of praying and praying? Did I think I could wear Him down?

A nurse came out of the operating room.

"Doctor Taylor, Congressman," she said. "Maybe you should go down to the cafeteria for a coffee and a bite to eat. It's going to take a while. Hours and hours. We'll call you if there's any change. We have both your numbers."

"How is it going?" asked June. "What is the doctor doing?"

"I can't get into it in great detail," the nurse replied. "Your grandson has lost a lot of blood, and there's damage to his internal organs. The doctors are doing everything in their power for him. Let's hope for the best."

"I can't leave," I said.

"I understand," she said. "There's a small waiting room down the hall. The chairs are more comfortable. And there's a television. If there's anything, I'll run there and call you. You'll be just seconds away."

"All right," I said. "We'll do that."

"I'll go down and get us some snacks," said June. "Margaret should be here any minute, so you won't be alone if it takes me a little while."

"I dread the moment she arrives."

I turned on the television and tuned to CNN. They were reporting about nothing except for the demonstration. Interviews and interviews with police officers, politicians, walkers, marchers, townspeople. Talking heads pontificated and analyzed from every angle and perspective. What was there to talk about? There was no mystery to what had occurred. The only mystery was the identity of the man who fired the rocket-propelled grenade.

"For those of you just joining us," the commentator was saying, "there was a violent attack in Hesterville by members of the white supremacist American Identity Party. In the aftermath of the rally, rocket-propelled grenades were fired by an unidentified assailant at three targets – a Chabad House, the Shiloh Gospel Church, the majority of whose members are African American, and a Hispanic-owned pharmacy.

"A young man and a young woman were critically injured at the Chabad House. Several other young men were also wounded, but not as seriously. Three people died in the attack on the church, and eight more were injured. The building was destroyed. No one was injured at the pharmacy, because it was closed at the time, but it is in shambles. Let's go to the video."

The video was clearly spliced together from different cameras. It was gruesome. It began with footage of the vast crowd in the demonstration area, including many closeups of red-faced, fist-shaking, screaming demonstrators, and excerpts of Farragut's harangue. There was a clip of the pickup trucks smashing through the barricade. There was a clip of June and me kneeling over David with the young woman lying inert a few feet away. Her name, as I learned later, was Kimberley Ann Adams. She was eighteen years old. There was a clip of the carnage at the black church. There was also a clip of the shattered pharmacy, it's storefront no more than a black gaping maw. The commentator was mostly silent while the video clips were playing. They spoke for themselves.

"The FBI has deemed these hate crimes and is investigating," he continued after the raw images came to an end. "Senator Farragut, chairman of the American Identity Party, expressed shock at what happened. He sent his condolences to the victims and their families and says he will keep them in his thoughts and prayers. The senator claims he is innocent of inciting to riot, because he begged the crowd to march peacefully and eschew violence. If no criminal charges are brought, there are bound to be civil suits. The consequences of this horrific tragedy promise to reverberate through American society for a long, long time. And now to our Washington correspondent."

A middle-aged woman appeared on the screen. She was

standing on the street with the White House behind her.

"All of Washington is in shock," she said. "The President was outraged at what he described as one of the worst acts of domestic terrorism in American history. He promised to hunt down the criminals and bring them to justice. Leaders of both parties have expressed their sorrow and anger. They condemned the act in the strongest terms and promised to work together to destroy this cancer on the American body politic."

I shut off the television. I couldn't bear to hear another word about strong condemnations and thoughts and prayers. They meant nothing. They were just excuses for doing nothing. If any of these people would do something, we wouldn't need their thoughts and prayers or their strong condemnations.

Was I responsible for what had happened to David? Was I so opposed to his going to Hesterville because I had a premonition of doom? I had no premonitions. In fact, I really thought he would be safe. I was just being extra cautious. Why go there when you don't have to? Why take a chance of visiting Paris when you can vacation in other places? But should I have put my foot down? I had no authority over him, legal or moral, and he would not have listened to me. I dropped my head into my hands and sobbed until I could barely catch my breath.

I heard someone come in and looked up. It was Margaret.

Chapter Seventeen

The dreaded moment had come. Margaret sat down without a word. She was seething. Gerald came in a minute later and sat down beside her. He nodded to me, then he studied his shoes. I wondered who would be the first to break the deadly silence. Of one thing I was sure. It wouldn't be me. I didn't think it would be Gerald either.

"It's all your fault," said Margaret. "My baby is in there fighting for his life. My only child! And it's all your fault."

"Oh, really? How is it my fault? I tried to stop him. June tried to stop him. But he wouldn't listen."

"You mean he told you he was coming?"

"He did."

"When?"

"At Pop's birthday party."

"You knew all along, and you didn't tell me! Didn't you think I should know? I'm his mother, for crying out loud! What kind of a father are you? What kind of a grandfather?"

"Do you think he would have listened to you if you'd told him not to go? Don't forget that you're the one who threw him out of the house when he didn't leave Chabad. Did he listen to you then?"

"You should have told me! I blame you!"

"Really? Really?" I was furious with her for blaming me even though I knew I was not to blame. Perhaps I should have restrained myself. Perhaps I should have given her some slack considering that she was his mother after all. But her unfair and unreasonable accusation hurt me so deeply that I just wanted to retaliate. "Maybe you're the one that's to blame, Margaret. Did that ever occur to you? If you had let him live at home and keep kosher in his room, he wouldn't have gotten so involved with Crown Heights. He would have been Chabad from a distance. He would never have volunteered to go to Hesterville."

She stared at me with horror. "So now it's my fault?" she snarled. "You just can't accept responsibility, can you? You never could." I didn't know what she meant by that last remark, but she didn't give me time to think about it. "Let's forget about telling him not to go. I'll admit that, considering where he was, he would not have listened to you and not to me either. But why was he there in the first place? Why was he in Hesterville?"

"What do you mean? Did you think I told him to go? He volunteered!"

"I know why they sent him. I heard it on the radio on the way here. They would have sent only Lubavitchers experienced in outreach, and he did not exactly qualify for that. But they accepted him anyway, because he convinced them he was familiar with Hesterville. Why was he familiar? Because his grandfather, the famous Adrian Taylor, took him there to the meeting with the township committee. I heard it on the radio."

"That's ridiculous," I fumed. "I took him with me, because I wanted him to get some experience with lawsuits. I was hoping he'd go back to college even if he stayed with Chabad. I could not have known that he'd volunteer to man a Mitzvah Tank near a riot."

"We all saw what happened at Tulane. We all heard about the American Identity Party. Did you think they'd stand by while people waved Israeli and Mexican flags on the Fourth of July? You must've known that you were opening a can of worms!"

"So you're saying that I shouldn't have taken the case when my clients were being denied their right to free speech?"

"You could do whatever you damn well wanted to do, but you didn't have to drag David into it."

This was getting crazier and crazier. I realized I was dealing with an irrational, hysterical mother. She had to blame someone, because she couldn't bear to face up to her own culpability. Nonetheless, I couldn't let her accusations pass. I was about to respond that she had driven David into the arms of Chabad by her domineering mothering, but just then, June came back. Rabbi Gutmacher was with her. Both were holding bags.

"This is Rabbi Gutmacher," said June. "I met the rabbi downstairs. He said that David is his student."

"He is," I said. "Thank you for coming, Rabbi Gutmacher."

"I came as soon as I heard," said the rabbi. "I brought sandwiches and fruit. It won't do David any good if we faint from hunger."

"And I brought snacks and drinks," said June.

"Great!" said Margaret. "Let's have a picnic while my son is dying!"

"Margaret, dear," said Gerald, "Maybe you should have something to eat. You'll feel better." It was the first thing he had said since he came.

Margaret was about to say something, but then she changed her mind. She took a sandwich from the rabbi's bag and a bottle of water from June's. All of us followed suit, and we ate in silence. I was grateful for the few minutes of peace. I was also grateful for the interruption before I hurled my latest accusation at Margaret. It would have been a mistake; there was nothing to be gained.

Night was falling, and still we heard nothing from the operating room. I wondered if that was a good sign, but I said nothing. Rabbi Gutmacher was reciting Psalms. Gerald was on his cell phone for want of anything better to do. I couldn't tell if he was reading messages, consuming news or playing games, but I could see that his eyes were glazed and that his mind was somewhere else. June was reading a magazine. Margaret and I were watching the news without speaking to or looking at each other.

After about five hours of waiting, the nurse appeared again. "I know you're all anxious," she said, "so I came to tell you that David is still in surgery. The doctors have managed to stabilize him, but there are some complications. Say some prayers. I'll be back as soon as I have anything more to report."

"What does that mean?" Gerald asked June in a shaky voice. "You're a doctor. Please explain that to me. Be honest. Please."

"I'm a dermatologist, Gerald," she replied. "I haven't dealt with traumatic injury since my residency days. But I'd guess that they hooked him up to a heart-lung machine and stopped the internal bleeding. They're trying to repair the damage to his organs, and maybe it's not going as well as they would like."

"What are you saying, June?" breathed Margaret. "Tell me the truth!"

"I'm saying that we should hope for the best but be prepared for the worst. I'm so sorry."

"You should be. You're also responsible for this."

"Adrian and I were by David's side less than a minute after the attack. We may have saved his life."

"I'll thank you if he lives," said Margaret and burst into tears.

Another hour of tense silence passed by. We all kept looking at the door, but the nurse did not return. I told myself that it was a good sign.

Rabbi Gutmacher cleared his throat.

"May I bring up an unpleasant subject?" he said. No one objected so he plunged ahead. "Dr. Taylor is right. We should hope for the best but prepare for the worst. If the worst happens, Heaven forbid, the family should already know what has to be done. I'll get straight to the point. If David passes away without recovering consciousness, Heaven forbid, I think we should honor his wishes even if he doesn't get a chance to express them himself. As the parents, Mr. and Mrs. Goldfield, do you agree?"

Gerald nodded. "Of course, we should do whatever he would have wanted to do. I think that's only right."

"And you, Mrs. Goldfield?"

Margaret's hair was disheveled, her makeup was smeared, and her cheeks were stained with her tears. Comprehension dawned in her reddened eyes. She threw back her shoulders in defiance and glared at him.

"Oh no, no," she said and wagged her finger at the rabbi. "No, no, no. A hundred times no. Don't even think about it. You are not involved in this. I'm his mother, and I've made my decision. He'll be cremated, and his ashes will be buried in the family plot. You took him from me in life, and now you want to take him from me in death? No!"

"Think about you son, Mrs. Goldfield," said the rabbi. "If he were to regain consciousness for a short while and realize that his time was limited to minutes or hours, what would he say? Would he want to have his funeral according to Jewish tradition? Or would he want to be cremated? What's more, do you think he'd ask to be buried in Montefiore Cemetery near the mausoleum in which the last two Lubavitcher Rebbes were laid to rest?"

The rabbi was right. David would want a traditional Jewish burial and internment. Even though he'd been in Chabad for less than a year, he'd given his life for Chabad ideals, and Chabad had given him inspiration and fulfillment until his last breath. He'd want a Chabad funeral, and he'd want to be connected forever by being buried in the hallowed ground near the Lubavitcher Rebbes. But I was sure Margaret wouldn't hear of it.

"I appreciate your concern, rabbi," she said. "Perhaps you

should have shown your concern by advising him not to go to Hesterville."

"He didn't ask me. And if he did, I don't know what I would've told him. I'm sorry you blame me, Mrs. Goldfield, but now is not the time for blame. It's the time for decisions."

"And I've made my decision. He'll be cremated, and his ashes …" She burst into tears. "My God, his ashes! I can't believe what we're saying! But if my baby doesn't survive, his ashes will be buried in the family plot in New Jersey. Do you agree, Gerald?"

Gerald clearly did not agree, but he could not contend with his wife in her fury. His shoulders slumped, and he shrugged. That was the most spousal defiance in his capability.

"Then that's settled," said Margaret.

"I ask you to reconsider, Mrs. Goldfield," said the rabbi. "It is a great mitzvah to honor the wishes of the … his wishes. What do you honestly think David would have wanted?"

"You want him to defy me in death? Is that what you want? It's not enough that you lured him away from me during his lifetime. Do you want to keep him apart from me forever?"

"This is not about you, Mrs. Goldfield. It's about David. It's about honoring his wishes. I'm pleading with you. For the sake of David's eternal soul, let him have what he would have wanted."

"I'm his mother! I'll decide what he would have wanted. I don't want to hear anymore."

The rabbi sat down in glum defeat. He buried his eyes in his book and continued to recite Psalms. Margaret was triumphant, but she knew perfectly well that it was not important to David to be buried next to Harry and Ruth Schneiderman, his great-great-grandparents. There was no doubt about what he would have wanted. And yet, she insisted on standing in his way. Why was she doing it? Was it to gain a victory over David that she couldn't gain during his lifetime? I had to stop her. I had to do it for David. I would never again be able to do anything for David, but I could stand up for him now.

"Margaret, let's talk a little more," I said.

"Aha, you're on the rabbi's side. Of course. I should have known. I bet you were happy when David moved out of the house and went to live in Crown Heights, weren't you? The sweet taste of revenge. Maybe you even put him up to it. And now, you want him buried in Crown Heights, and your revenge will be complete. Separation forever."

"Margaret, you're hysterical. Take a deep breath and let it out slowly, and let's have a calm conversation. Is that okay?"

"What if I don't want to have any more conversations?"

"I'm his grandfather, and I loved him with all my heart. I have some say in the matter. Put your anger and fury aside. Think about your love for your wonderful son. Let's talk."

"I don't want to talk."

"Then I'm going to talk to Gerald."

"Gerald and I are one. He's not going to side with you against me."

"Then we'll leave Gerald out of this. You talk to me."

"I don't want to talk anymore. I'm exhausted. You're a bunch of ghouls talking about burying a boy who's still alive. In any case, I'm his mother, and I've made my decision. It won't change."

"Let me point out, Margaret, that David is not a minor over whom you have control. He is an adult. Your position as his mother and closest kin is to give an honest evaluation of what his wishes would have been. Your decision is to suit yourself, not to honor David's wishes."

"You're accusing me of dishonesty."

"I'm not accusing you of anything. I'm just saying that you're being overly emotional. It's understandable, of course. But think with your head and with the love in your heart. You must let David have his wishes. He's at your mercy right now. Don't take advantage of it."

"I'm doing the right thing. He never should have gone to

Chabad. I'm going to bring him home where he belongs."

I sighed. I had tried my best. Now, I would have to take a different approach. "I won't let you do it, Margaret. It would be unconscionable. I'm sorry, Margaret, but I'm going to have to fight you on this. For David, whom we love."

"And how are you going to stop me? I'm his mother! I have legal standing, not you."

"I'm going to get an injunction. I have enough connections, and I can get it within hours. Then we'll have a hearing before a judge. We'll let the judge decide what David would have wanted. I'll bring witnesses to the life he'd chosen for himself. I'll tell the judge that you threw him out of the house. June and I'll testify to his state of mind during his last hours. I'll tell him that David gave his life for a mission in which he believed strongly. What do you think he'll say? What do you think the press will say?"

She blanched. "You wouldn't dare! You would humiliate me like that?"

"I would. You know I would. This is the last thing I can do for David, and I will do it to the best of my ability."

"And Margaret be damned!" she yelled.

"It doesn't have to be that way, Margaret. It doesn't have to be a war. Be completely honest and unemotional for a moment. What is the objective truth? What would an objective judge say?"

"You're an evil man, Dad. The great Adrian Taylor is nothing more than a snake in the grass!"

I did not respond, and she fell silent for a long minute.

"All right," she whispered. "For David."

We sat in silence, all eyes fixed on the door. I took no pleasure in my victory over Margaret. At least, I convinced myself I didn't. I knew she'd never forgive me. I was paying a high price, but I couldn't let David be buried anywhere other than where he would have wanted. I owed it to him.

It was close to midnight when the door finally opened. This

time it was the doctor. One look at his exhausted face told the entire story. Margaret shrieked and covered her face with her hands. Her body shook with heartrending sobs. Gerald put his arm around her shoulders and whispered to her.

As for me, what can I say? I had never experienced such sorrow in my entire life. I didn't cry, but I felt as if my chest was clenched in an iron first. I couldn't breathe. I felt as if my heart would stop beating. June led me to a chair and gave a bottle of water.

"I'm so sorry for your loss, Mr. and Mrs. Goldfield, Congressman, Dr. Taylor," the doctor said. "We did everything humanly possible, but the shrapnel had caused too much damage. We lost him. I'm so sorry."

The doctor slipped out of the room, and Rabbi Gutmacher took out his cell phone.

"I'm going to call the burial society. They'll be here in an hour."

Chapter Eighteen

Following venerable Jewish tradition, the funeral was set to take place the very next day; delayed burial of the body was considered painful to the soul of the deceased. Rabbi Gutmacher took charge of all the arrangements. He told us to be in front of the World Headquarters of Chabad-Lubavitch at 770 Eastern Parkway in Crown Heights at noon. He asked us to be on time. The press had reported extensively on David's death and on the time and place of the funeral. There was sure to be a large crowd.

Rabbi Gutmacher also took care of the arrangements for the Shivah, the traditional seven-day mourning period observed only by parents, children and siblings. Margaret and Gerald chose to have only one day of Shivah for a few hours in the evening. Rabbi Gutmacher asked if I would act as a surrogate for the rest of the Shivah period. I consented.

I also agreed to observe the Shivah in Crown Heights instead of my own home. Friends of David would be coming in all day, and I wanted to hear their stories and impressions. It would keep him alive for a little while longer. It would be a consolation. Rabbi Gutmacher arranged a house for us on Union Street, around the corner from 770. At my request, he set us up with a television so that we could be on top of the news during lulls in the visiting period and at night after everyone left.

We finally got to sleep just before dawn. Physically and emotionally exhausted, I slept the sleep of the dead and woke up disoriented a few hours later. June was fast asleep.

Was it all a horrible dream? Would David answer if I called him on his cell phone? I reached for my phone, but then I was struck by reality and put it down. It was not a dream. The ache in my heart was too real. The memories flooded my mind and threatened to drown me in unspeakable sorrow. In twenty-four hours, my life had been completely shattered. It was too much to bear. I wanted to bury myself under my covers and not come out for the rest of the day, but there was a funeral to attend, the funeral of the beloved grandson whom I'd never see again.

Pedro, my driver, came for us at ten-thirty just in case there would be traffic in Brooklyn because of the funeral.

"I'm sorry for your loss," he told us when we got into the car. "*No hay nada a decir.*" He was right. There was nothing to say. Only that there was nothing to say.

"Please turn on the radio," I said. "I want to hear the news."

Numerous federal and state government officials from the President down, and indeed from all over the world, were expressing condemnation, outrage and the deepest sympathy for the victims and their families whom they promised to keep in their thoughts and prayers. The Senate and the House both called for investigations. A few Congressmen demanded the American Identity Party be declared a terrorist organization for advocating the violent overthrow of the government. One of them called for reconstituting the House Un-American Activities Committee of the Fifties to root out them and their sympathizers just as the Communists had been uprooted.

Bishops, cardinals and leading evangelists were vociferous in their censure of the American Identity Party and the demonstrators. One fire-breathing pastor called them heathens and pagans and swore that they would be consigned to the nethermost regions of Hell for all eternity. I wondered how much this threat would affect the demonstrators, but perhaps it might influence their mothers. Many Muslim imams added their voices in denunciation, as did the Anti-Defamation League. Even the Pope weighed in with an emotional statement from St. Peters Square.

The Department of Justice was considering charging Frederick Farragut and Sanford Johns with incitement to riot, and the FBI was in hot pursuit of the lead pickup truck and its occupants. They were studying surveillance feeds from many businesses along Columbus Avenue, and they promised to apprehend the culprits very soon.

Voices on the right, on the other hand, called for calm and patience. Instead of going after the American Identity Party, they claimed, we should address the root causes of the movement, which are economic deprivation and unchecked immigration. If people felt secure in their jobs and their livelihoods, they would not be drawn to such violent movements. We should talk to them and listen to their grievances. Furthermore, they suggested, perhaps the shooters were suffering from mental illness caused by their economic stresses. I wondered if they had listened to Frederick Farragut's tirades and the Natural Humanist ideology of Sanford Johns. Weren't their racial and xenophobic grievances clear enough?

There was also a report from Crown Heights. The streets were jammed with vehicles headed for the funeral. Thousands of people were pouring out of the subway station at the corner of Kingston Avenue and Eastern Parkway, a stone's throw from the Chabad headquarters at 770. There was no evidence of counter-demonstrators or any attempt to disrupt the funeral, but police and security personnel were everywhere, including the rooftops.

It was good that we had left Manhattan early, but it was still possible that we would be delayed by the traffic for hours. I made a few calls, and a police escort met us on Flatbush Avenue and guided us to our destination. We arrived with a few minutes to spare.

Rabbi Gutmacher met us in front of the building and led us to a row of chairs set up for the family on the large brick terrace of the building next to 770. Margaret and Gerald were already there. Margaret was dressed in black with a black pillbox hat and a black veil over her face. My siblings were there as well, but my father's assistant had called in that they were delayed in traffic. They had left their car on a side street and were taking the subway. The start of the funeral was postponed for fifteen minutes until they arrived.

The members of the Chabad burial society brought out the plain pine coffin covered with a Velvel cloth and placed it on the landing at the top of the stairs. Before taking the microphone, Rabbi Gutmacher whispered in my ear that he would like me to say a few words afterward. It had occurred to me that I might be asked, but my thoughts were not formulated yet.

"In the custom of Chabad, eulogies are not delivered at funerals," Rabbi Gutmacher began, "Therefore, what I am about to say is not a eulogy. Considering the gravity of the situation and the size of the assemblage, we felt it appropriate that some thoughts be expressed. This is a very sad day for the Jewish people and indeed for all people of good will. We have seen the ugly face of evil, and we are horrified. How can this be happening in our beloved America? A young man and a young woman are cut down as he handed her candles to illuminate the holy Sabbath and bring her closer to God. African Americans emerging from their church after Sunday services are killed and maimed. Our hearts are broken. We cry out to the Almighty in anguish and plead with Him to strike down His enemies. O God in Heaven, the fate of this blessed land is in Your hands. Do not abandon us!"

He paused to survey the multitudinous crowd.

"I look up and down Eastern Parkway," his voice echoed over loudspeakers placed near and far. "I see no cars, only thousands and thousands of sad people. Men, women, children. I see Jews, African Americans, Hispanics. I see so many, many good white people. I see Christians. I see Muslims. All of us, despite any differences we might have, must join hands in the spirit of America at its finest. We are all the children of God, formed in His image. We must look at each other with friendship, love and compassion. We must strengthen the bonds of liberty and tolerance. That is how we will defeat the evil with the help of the Almighty. This how we will ensure that this young man has not died in vain."

His voice choked with emotion, and he paused to compose himself.

"David Goldfield was my student. I loved him, and I miss him terribly. We all do. He was such a wonderful young man, full of life, charismatic, smart, idealistic, friendly, kind, thoughtful, such a special young man. But what was most special about him was his need to have a meaningful life, to do something important with his life. David, I know you hear me still ..."

He sobbed and wiped his face with a handkerchief.

"David, my beloved David, my golden David, you may have lived a very short life, but it was a supremely meaningful one. You came to us seeking inspiration. You wanted to get close to God. You will be honored in Heaven as the holy martyr you are. Any Jew killed because he is Jewish is considered holier than all the angels in Heaven and is brought very close to God for all eternity. But you, David, are the holiest of martyrs, because at the moment of your death you were bringing people closer to the Almighty. You are the holiest of the holy.

"You will be laid to rest near the Rebbe. You will go down in history as a legend, an exemplar for people all over the world. People will pray at your grave. David, my dear, dear David, you have been taken from us, but you will never be forgotten."

He concluded with a short Hebrew prayer that I did not understand, and then he beckoned to me.

I got up and stood near the plain pine coffin. It somehow seemed more appropriate than an elaborate carved casket with satin padding. There was no luxury in death; all the departed were equal in death's grim reality. My dead grandson lay in this pine box. He would soon be buried in the ground. I had no desire to lift the cover and look at him. I didn't want that image in my mind along with the other memories.

I looked out at the enormous crowd that filled Eastern Parkway and spilled into the cross streets as far as I could see.

"I want to say just a few words," I began. "The rabbi has already said all that needs to be said. I want to make just one point. David was my grandson, my only grandchild, and we were exceedingly close. He was an idealistic young man. He did not seek his pleasure in material things but in spiritual fulfillment. He was a happy young man. His face shone with happiness, and at moments of special happiness, his face shone like the sun.

"When he was ten years old, I took him to Phoenix to see the Super Bowl between the New York Giants and the New England Patriots. He was a rabid Giants fan, and he was so excited, he could hardly sit still. Well, you all know what happened there. David Tyree caught a pass from Eli Manning against his helmet, and then Plaxico Burris caught a pass in the end zone for a stunning comeback victory. The happiness on David's face was beyond description. It was the happiest I had ever seen him. Until yesterday.

"My wife and I were there in Hesterville. We watched him with binoculars from a roof across the street. I saw his face as he manned that Mitzvah Tank. He was happy! He was oblivious to the tension and the roaring hatred all around him. He was serving his people and God. He was happy.

"I saw his face the moment before the grenade struck as he was handing Shabbat candles to a young woman, two precious Jewish souls on a little island of holiness. I saw the look of transcendent happiness on his face, and I envied him. I did not recall any time in my life when I'd felt such an intense burst of happiness, and I envied David, who'd managed to achieve a peak in his young life that most people never even approach. I envied him, and I loved him, and I was happy for him. And then he was gone.

"But as the rabbi said, he is not gone. The legend of his martyrdom will go down in the annals of Jewish history and American history. The effects of his sacrifice will be with us forever. We will never forget him. And we will do our best to make sure that he did not die in vain."

The rabbi said the Mourner's Kaddish and announced that the burial would be in Montefiore Cemetery in Queens if anyone wanted to attend.

The procession began. Black-hatted Lubavitchers pushed forward for the honor of carrying the coffin. There was hardly an inch of coffin that did not have a hand attached to it. A sea of silent humanity followed the coffin down Eastern Parkway all the way to Lincoln Terrace Park on Rochester Avenue, where a hearse for the deceased and cars for the family were waiting.

Chapter Nineteen

The house on Union Street came fully stocked with food and drinks. I asked Rabbi Gutmacher to make sure no people came to pay their respects until the following afternoon. June and I had a light lunch and went to sleep. I woke up after dark. June was still asleep. I roamed the house for an hour or two, unable to get away from my thoughts. There was a pile of newspapers on the coffee table in the living room, but I could not bear to look at them. It was surreal.

After a while, I stumbled back to bed and slept until morning. When I awoke, I found June fully dressed and ready to go to her office. She didn't want to cancel her patient appointments. She prepared a nice breakfast and promised to return in the evening. Pedro would drive her back and forth.

In the afternoon, Rabbi Gutmacher informed me via email that he had posted instructions in the synagogues that the doors would not be open to the public until Tuesday. He asked, however, if he could come with a few important members of the Lubavitch community later that afternoon, and I said yes. I really didn't want to be alone. I was rested and bored. And I wanted to talk about David.

Rabbi Gutmacher arrived with two older men with white beards. I sat in a low chair that had been set up for me, and the men sat in a semicircle around me. No one said a word. They just sat there silently. I didn't understand it. Did they come just to look at me?

"Why doesn't anyone say anything?" I asked after a while.

"According to Jewish tradition," said Rabbi Gutmacher, "the mourner speaks first. A visitor could offer a well-intentioned word of consolation and unwittingly cause the mourner pain. It is safer just to respond."

"You mean something like God takes the good ones?"

"Exactly."

"I understand. Why don't you tell me about David as you knew him? This was his life at its end, and I want to know as much about it as I can. David will live forever in my memory. This part cannot be missing."

The conversation began with David's time in Crown Heights, but it soon veered to the worsening political situation in the United States. My visitors were intelligent and informed. The discussion went deep into the psychological causes of antisemitism and racial bigotry.

One of the men asked what percentage of American whites were supremacists, either overtly or by unspoken agreement. I speculated that it might be as much as ten percent. He suggested that closer to ninety percent were supremacist sympathizers at least to some degree. I hadn't seen it from personal experience, but perhaps racial epithets and supremacist sympathies would not be voiced in front of a Jew by middle-class and upper-class people. How could I know what they were saying behind closed doors?

The next two days were exhausting. June had cleared her appointments to stay and take care of me. The house was crowded from morning until late at night. My only respite was the few times that June tore me away to eat something and take a breather.

I didn't really want a breather. I would never get another opportunity like this. Like a parched traveler in the desert, I drank in wonderful reminiscences of David by friends, neighbors and rabbis. The young men who were with David in Nepal for Passover told numerous stories about the inspiring experience. A cell phone on the table captured every word spoken during the whole time; unfortunately, it reminded me of the meeting with the township committee in Hesterville and made me sad.

Wednesday evening, Pedro drove June and me to Margaret's house in the Park Slope section of Brooklyn. My entire surviving family was there. Margaret and Gerald sat on a sofa in the den and greeted friends, neighbors and colleagues who came to pay their respects. Margaret looked drawn and sleep-deprived. Her eyes were red and puffy. But she mustered the strength to be gracious to her visitors. Gerald looked dazed and disoriented, offering only muttered monosyllabic responses to remarks addressed to him. I assumed he was sedated. Margaret was not.

After the door closed behind the last visitor, the family remained together in the den. No one spoke for a while.

Margaret broke the silence. "How is it going in Crown Heights, Dad?" she said. There was a resentful edge in her voice, as if I was usurping her prerogative to be the principal mourner.

"It's been exhausting," I said, "but rewarding. The house was crowded all day with people telling stories about David. There was a lot about Nepal. I have everything recorded."

Her eyes opened wide. "Can you send me the audio?"

"Of course."

She bit her lower lip. "You know, Dad, I still blame you. You got him involved with Hesterville, and look where it led. I've lost my baby, my only child, my reason for living." She fought back her tears. "But I admit, after the fact, that holding the funeral in Crown Heights was the right thing. I've never seen such a funeral. It was a historic event. A real martyr's funeral. It gave my David honor. Maybe his life was not completely wasted, but it was unfairly cut short. We shouldn't be sitting here mourning him. It's not right. It's not –" Her voice broke, and she buried her face in her hands.

My father cleared his throat. "Margaret, sweetheart, maybe we should talk about other things."

She looked up, her face wet with tears. "Other things? What other things? Should we talk about the weather? The elections?" She stopped herself. "I'm sorry, Grandpa. You don't deserve this. You didn't do anything. What other things? What do you mean?"

"Well, what are we going to do? Are we just going to lick our wounds? Or are we going to strike back?"

"Strike back? How can we strike back?"

"We can sue them for a billion dollars. Let the FBI go after the shooters and the inciters. We can bring a civil lawsuit for wrongful death and violation of civil rights. It will strike a blow against the haters, and it will be a catharsis for the family."

Margaret looked to me. "Can we do this?"

I nodded. "Yes, we can."

"Whom will we sue?"

"Everyone," I said. "The American Identity Party, Frederick Farragut, Sanford Jones, the particular group the shooters belonged to and its leaders and anyone else that comes to mind."

"You see, Margaret?" said my father. "We can hit them where it hurts."

I actually thought it was a good idea. We would have to get a different attorney to bring the suit for us since I would be one of the plaintiffs, but my legal expertise and experience would be put to good use.

"Let's do it," said Margaret.

Chapter Twenty

Thursday was a long day. There were many more visitors, including some of my friends and colleagues, members of the media and government officials. The Governor of New York and the Vice President also came by for a short while. Their visits were televised.

We closed the doors at seven o'clock. We'd had enough. It was time to go home. I told Rabbi Gutmacher that we'd be leaving in the morning. He very graciously did not press me to stay for the entire seven-day Shivah period. He just asked if he could come back after dinner to speak with me privately, and of course, I said yes.

He arrived at nine o'clock. June had already retired, and we were completely alone. He took a sip of the coffee and wiped his lips. He looked serious, and I wondered what was on his mind. Was there a new issue?

The rabbi took off his hat and jacket and took a deep breath.

"Mr. Taylor, all of us in Crown Heights and in Chabad Houses all over the world are grateful to you for agreeing to observe the Shivah among us. This tragedy did not strike just your family. It struck all of us in the greater Chabad family and Jewish people everywhere."

"And Christians and Muslim as well."

"Absolutely. And secular people of good will. What you've done kept David's story in the news for a week, when it could easily have been forgotten when the next atrocity occurred. I don't know if you heard about it, but there was a shooting in Alabama two days ago."

"I did not. Was it related to the American Identity Party?"

"Probably not. Some maniac with an assault weapon shot up a supermarket. Killed a few people before the security guard shot him. Something like that happens all the time. And if it's not violence, then it's something else. A plane crash. An abuse scandal. Tweets from the President. A messy breakup in Hollywood. There's always something to distract the public's attention. But David's story is still on top of the news. And it's all because of you."

"Well, I see what you're saying," I said. "But what happens now? How do we hold the public's attention? How do we prevent the outrage from subsiding? How do we keep David's memory alive?"

"That's what I want to discuss with you."

Here it comes, I thought. He was about to ask me to donate a synagogue or a school building in David's memory. They'd put his name on the building, and his memory would be preserved. I did not want to do that. It would cheapen the tragedy, as if posting his name on a building would be a kind of happy ending. I understood that Chabad needed money, but this was not the time to bring it up. Yet what could I say? He had been David's teacher, and he had orchestrated the entire week. How could I turn him down without at least a nice contribution? It would be ungrateful.

I braced myself. "I'm listening."

"The story will inevitably fall out of the news," he said. "The hearing in Congress and the FBI investigations will drag on. Every once in a while, they'll pop into the news for a day or two, and then they'll fade out again. What do we want to accomplish by keeping the story in the news?"

"We want action. We want to bring down these monsters. We want to save the republic."

"I agree. We can't wait for the ponderous government to take action. We must do it ourselves, and we must do it now. We must strike a mortal blow at them. We must cripple their movement."

Clearly, he was not angling for a contribution to Chabad in David's memory. At least, it didn't seem like it.

"Do you have any ideas?" I asked.

"Perhaps. One idea is to bring a civil suit against them."

"Our family has already discussed it in Margaret's house on Wednesday, and we decided to do it."

"Excellent. You must sue for as much as you can get, but even if you're rewarded billions, it will not be a mortal blow."

"Why not?"

"Well, first of all, the lawsuit is bound to drag on for years. They'll resort to all kinds of ploys to delay the trial until the public outrage dies down. Even if you win and are rewarded megabucks, there'll be appeal after appeal after appeal. After all the appeals are exhausted, even if they actually have to reach into their pockets and pay, what will you have accomplished? That they'll have to scramble to pay the judgment? That is not an existential threat. It's just a major nuisance. There are enough sympathizers and fellow-travelers to keep them afloat."

"Are you saying we shouldn't sue?"

"No, by all means, sue for everything they're worth. But you must understand the limitations of a civil lawsuit for damages."

"I understand. Nonetheless, it's the best option I have, other than getting a gun and shooting the whole lot of them."

"Maybe not," said the rabbi. "Maybe not."

"What do you mean?"

"I think you may be able to really damage them."

"How so?"

He pulled a newspaper clipping from his pocket and handed it to me. "This is from the New York *Times* in the metropolitan section. Read it, then we'll talk."

I put on my reading glasses and began to read. It was a small article about Lavender Williams, an African American schoolteacher in the Bedford-Stuyvesant section of Brooklyn, who had been fired from her job after using the Bible as a historical resource in her sixth-grade history class. She was apparently a well-educated woman. She filed a complaint with the Board of Education. They turned down her petition, because it violated the separation of church and state. That was basically it.

I took off my glasses. "I don't understand. What does the firing of a religious fanatic have to do with us?"

"Why do you think she's a religious fanatic?"

"Because the Bible is not history."

"Do you believe the Bible is true or do you think it's a myth, as Sanford Johns claims?"

"It's not only Sanford Johns," I said. "That's the universally accepted opinion in academia. I know that Chabad thinks it's true. Every word of it. And it seems that Lavender Williams is a good Christian and agrees. But that's a matter of faith. It doesn't belong in the classroom. That's teaching religion in a public school. It's unconstitutional. It violates the establishment clause."

"I don't think she was teaching religion. She was teaching historical information that's derived from the Bible."

"Look, even if the Bible is true. Even if God split the Red Sea for the Israelites and drowned their Egyptian pursuers, the Bible is not a valid historical record."

"Are the ancient steles in Egypt and Mesopotamia historical records?"

"Steles are large slabs of stone with engraved inscriptions. We can date them with reasonable accuracy to the times they describe. So we accept their information as history. If we didn't know when the steles were erected, we could consider them fiction."

"But now you consider them historical?"

"Yes."

"Is everything they report historical?"

"Not necessarily," I said. "There's usually a strong supernatural element. Victories are achieved because the gods came down and hurled lightning bolts at the enemy. Things like that. But the underlying story is fairly reliable. They didn't erect steles with fictional tales for the people of their times. You don't boast about a victory over your enemy if the enemy is occupying your cities."

"I agree. But why can't you give the same respect to the Bible? Why can't you accept the Biblical stories as reliable even if you discount the supernatural elements? In fact, that is what the teacher was clearly doing, using the Bible as a resource for the underlying history and omitting the supernatural element. I don't think she told them that God spoke to Moses."

"My dear rabbi, if the Bible was inscribed on a stele that we can date back to the general vicinity of the period it describes, I would agree with you. But we have no biblical stele, just the printed Bible. The oldest copy of the Bible extant is no more than a few hundred years old. Who knows when it was originally written?"

"You know, there are conflicting theories about the reliability of the Old Testament. Some scholars believe it's very ancient, based on the language and the culture it describes. I recommend *On the Reliability of the Old Testament* by Kenneth Kitchen. Dr. Kitchen, who passed away recently, was Professor of Orientology at the University of Liverpool. He was expert in the ancient languages of the Middle East. He could read hieroglyphics, hieratic, demotic and cuneiform as easily as you read English. He was recognized as one of the greatest scholars of any kind in his time. I suggest you start your research with his book. Then we'll take it from there."

I gave him a long look. "All right, where are we heading?"

"I think this teacher should sue, and I think you should

bring the lawsuit. If you take the case, Mr. Taylor, and if you establish to a reasonable degree that the Bible dates back to deep antiquity, you will have undermined the ideological foundation of the neopagans. Then we can work together with our Christian and Muslim friends to convince the neo-pagan rank and file that the American Identity Party is the road to Hell."

Chapter Twenty-one

We didn't speak again about Lavender Williams for two weeks. The undertaking he proposed would require enormous expense and effort, and the chances of countering a century of academic biblical thinking were slim at best. Rabbi Gutmacher asked me not to respond right away, just to think about it for a while. If he didn't hear from me again, he would know what I had decided.

His idea was a long shot at best, and he knew it. It involved serious risk for me. College-educated people would wonder why I would become a Bible thumper late in life. What had happened to the liberal Congressman from Manhattan, the respected historian, the progressive professor of law? Did I no longer believe in the establishment clause? As for my friends and colleagues, they'd think I'd simply gone off the rails because of David's death, that I was undertaking this quixotic venture for my Chabad grandson who'd been murdered. And who knows, maybe there would be a certain amount of truth in that.

I could defend my reputation by saying that everyone is entitled to legal representation in court, even confessed murderers. Why shouldn't I represent a schoolteacher in Bedford-Stuyvesant who asked for my help? But there was a problem with that. It was a lie.

This mission impossible, if I chose to accept it, would not

have been initiated by Mrs. Williams. It would be initiated by me. Of course, I could have Rabbi Gutmacher suggest to her that she call me, and then technically, she would be asking for my help. Nonetheless, it would be a lie, something of which I don't approve.

I pride myself on never lying. I don't find it necessary. If I don't want to admit to something, I say nothing at all. Lawyers know how to avoid answering questions without being pinned down. It's one of the first requirements of being a lawyer; don't lie, but don't tell the truth. I was not going to lie about who initiated the representation. Besides, Mrs. Williams was bound to find out that the suggestion had come from me; if we entered on a lawyer-client relationship, it would be difficult to hide it from her. Should I ask her to lie as well?

No, the everyone-is-entitled-to-representation argument would not fly. The public would know that I'd gone after this case, and my academic reputation would be on the line. Defeat would be humiliating. People would either scorn my newfound religious fanaticism or pity me for becoming unsettled by personal tragedy. Did I want to undertake an endeavor with such low prospects for success and vindication and such a high risk of defeat and humiliation? Would a win in this case enhance David's memory by association? Would a defeat tarnish it?

For a full week, I didn't give the question too much thought. I was so depressed I could barely drag myself from bed. I didn't go to the office at all. I knew that all the staff would console me with soulful eyes, hugs and pats on the back, and it would make me even more depressed. I just wanted to wallow in my sorrow.

I am usually not a wallower. I try to take my hits like a man and move on. I don't let my emotions take me over. But now, I gave in to my sorrow and pain. I just accepted my suffering helplessly, without resistance. I actually luxuriated in the agony. Perhaps I was afraid that if I stopped suffering David would fade away. But how long could I continue in this state? Wasn't it inevitable that David would eventually fade into distant memory? Wasn't that the way of the world?

Then it struck me. Lavender Williams! If I took the case, David would be with me for as long as it lasted. It might be months or even years, and when the inevitable time for separation arrived, I would be more ready to say good-bye. I pulled myself together and left my depression behind.

I did not decide then and there to take the case. I decided to explore it.

When I returned to the office Monday morning, I asked Nancy Hannah Mikhail, one of the young associates, to get me as many sources as she could find presenting all views on biblical criticism and archaeology, including Dr. Kitchen's book. I knew that most of the books would reflect the academic orthodoxy, but I was sure there would also be a number of books for the other side. Then I called for Paul Blake, the office investigator.

Paul Blake was a large man with massive arms and a deceptively innocent look. As an army major stationed in Afghanistan, he had served as an investigator for the military police. After the army, he came to us. He was like a tenacious bulldog with a sharp brain. He never accepted failure, even if it meant crossing some lines.

"I have a job for you, Paul," I said. "I want you to investigate a schoolteacher in Bedford-Stuyvesant."

"Really? Is this for a divorce case? Child molestation? Drugs?"

"Nothing of the sort. It's for a civil suit. The schoolteacher is the prospective client. I need to know all about her. Everything."

I handed him a printout of the article, and he read it quickly.

"Should I give this top priority and drop everything else I'm doing?"

I thought for a moment and shook my head. "I'll be patient.

It's not especially urgent, but please do it as soon as you can."

"All right, boss. I'm ready. Shoot."

"This is what I know. Her name is Lavender Williams. She teaches sixth-grade in Bed-Stuy. Cushman Middle School, corner of Reid Avenue and Willoughby Street. She was fired for using the Bible in history class. She is African American. I know only what it says in that article. That's it."

Blake stood up. "It's a start. I'll see what I can find on Google, and then I'll get to work. Give me a couple of days."

Nancy Hannah reported that she had found plenty of sources on the subject, including books that were not yet available online. There were too many to carry away, and she was having them delivered. They would arrive later today. She had placed additional books on order. They would be delivered tomorrow.

The books came late in the afternoon in two large cartons deposited on the floor in my office. I opened one of the cartons. It must have contained a dozen or more books. Dr. Kitchen's book was among them. I love the look and the smell of new books. They're intoxicating. Well-worn books have their own charm. I looked through the collection, picked out four volumes and brought them to my desk. I left Dr. Kitchen's book in the box.

It was past six o'clock, and the office was emptying quickly. I called June and told her I'd be late. Then I began to read.

I spent an hour or so scrolling through the online articles, and then I turned to the books. I looked at the bios of the authors, the tables of contents, read a few paragraphs here and there, and I got a sense of the authors' personalities and points of view. Only one of the four I chose at random supported the Bible to some extent, but I couldn't buy into it if I didn't read the other books as well. I'd start with these four books. There were still two cartons of unread books on the floor, and there'd be more coming tomorrow. I had to go through all of them, maybe not read every word but scan them carefully.

I decided to take one of the books home with me. My first inclination was to take the one that supported the Bible, the point of view I'd be defending, but then I thought it'd be best if I read the books of the detractors first. I'd evaluate them better if I faced the full brunt of their arguments without any defenses.

Over the course of the week, I thoroughly read all the books referenced in other books. These seemed to be the most important. I went through the others as well, but not as thoroughly.

I was surprised to discover that the issue of biblical criticism was far from resolved even in academia. Most critics followed, in one form or another, in the footsteps of Julius Wellhausen, a German professor of theology around the turn of the twentieth century. His most influential book was *Prolegomena zur Geschichte Israels*, an introduction to the history of Israel. Despite its many flaws, it was accepted in academia as the most rational and authoritative reading of the Bible. The case, if I chose to accept it, would revolve around this book and its academic descendants.

On Friday morning, Blake submitted a written report on Lavender Williams. She was forty-five years old, married to Major Marvin Williams, fifty-five years old, a career officer stationed in Afghanistan. He was home on leave for the next two months. Twin daughters, Mahalia and Shawana, ten years old. The Williams family lived in a single-family home at 634 Berkeley Place in Bedford Stuyvesant. They owned the house and carried a small mortgage. Mrs. Williams had a master's degree in education from Brooklyn College and another in history from Columbia University.

Blake had placed her under surveillance the entire week. He'd also spoken to colleagues and neighbors without discovering anything suspicious. His research had uncovered a wealth of financial, educational, familial and other information, which he included in the report. The information was being analyzed and verified by one of Blake's associates. Blake had found no skeletons in her closet, but he would continue digging.

All in all, at first glance, she checked out well. It was time to call Rabbi Gutmacher. I had not yet come to a decision, but further discussions were in order.

Chapter Twenty-two

Pedro drove me to Brooklyn on Sunday. My closest colleagues knew about my new reading regimen and my interest in Lavender Williams, but they thought it was just a passing phase. I didn't want to bring Rabbi Gutmacher to the office before I made my decision. Instead, we had agreed to meet in Crown Heights.

Before meeting with Rabbi Gutmacher, I wanted to see the school where Lavender Williams had taught and the place where she lived. My knowledge of Brooklyn, except for Park Slope, was limited. I asked Pedro if Bed-Stuy was on the way to Crown Heights, and he said it was if he took a different route.

We took the Williamsburg Bridge into Brooklyn. It was unfamiliar to me; I didn't remember the last time I'd been on the bridge. It was a stately old bridge, a venerable gateway into a different world.

We came off the bridge and proceeded on Broadway under the elevated tracks. There was a luster to the darkened avenue as the sunlight filtered through the tracks, sweeping across the hood of the car in long slender stripes. The first few blocks featured stores that catered to Chassidic people, but then the street became Hispanic. Small clusters of men and an occasional woman stood on the sidewalks, smoking, laughing, taking clandestine sips from bottles in paper bags. The car turned into Tompkins Avenue, and we arrived at Berkeley

Place a few minutes later.

Berkeley Place was a quiet tree-lined street of tidy row houses, an island of gentility in the mostly disadvantaged Bed-Stuy section of Brooklyn. Lavender Williams lived in a freshly painted walk-up duplex. The stone steps gleamed, and the shrubbery in the pocket garden was carefully trimmed. Most of the cars parked along the street were late model, probably leased, as well as a small number of luxury vehicles and older cars. No jalopies. The people walking on the street were African American middle class. I didn't see any white people.

I saw as much as I could see in a pass-by inspection, and we headed for the Cushman Middle School on Reid Avenue and Willoughby Street. It was an aging brick fortress free of litter and graffiti. Young black men were playing basketball in the yard.

We followed the Utica Avenue bus down Reid Avenue into Crown Heights. Rabbi Gutmacher was waiting for me in a kosher restaurant on the corner of Nostrand Avenue and Crown Street called Alenbi. I gave Pedro a few dollars to take care of himself while I met with the rabbi. I did not know how long the meeting would take.

The restaurant served something called Modern Israeli cuisine. The place had a Middle Eastern décor, and Middle Eastern music played softly in the background. Rabbi Gutmacher recommended dishes called drunk liver, yassu soflakisitis and chicken mushakan. They were strange and exotic and altogether excellent.

We ordered coffee and the conversation turned to the business at hand.

"So tell me, Mr. Taylor," said the rabbi, "have you reached a decision?"

"Almost, but not quite."

"How does your wife feel about it?" he asked.

"She assured me that, since she won't be personally affected either way, she supports any decision I make."

"Did she give you any advice?"

I shook my head. "I asked for her advice, but she declined. She said the decision should be mine alone. She trusts my judgment."

"Smart lady. So, what's your judgment?"

"I'm conflicted. The safest choice is to decline."

"But the safest choice is not the route to greatness, is it, Mr. Taylor?"

I nodded. "No, it's not. I know that to take this case and win it would be a great thing. It would be historic. But the chances of a victory are remote. Is it worth the risk? It could backfire."

"That doesn't sound like an almost."

"But it is. Your idea is bold and ingenious. And high risk. I'm inclined to do it. Almost inclined to do it. But! I have to overcome my reservations. I'm not quite ready to pull the trigger."

"And how do we accomplish that? Do you have any ideas?"

"I do," I said. "I think you should make an approach to Mrs. Williams. See if she's interested in this battle. If she is, arrange a meeting of the three of us. Also her husband if he's available. No commitments on anyone's part. If I think she'd be a really good client, and that her husband would not be a liability, I'd probably make my decision right then and there."

"What do you mean by a very good client? Does she have to gain the sympathy of the jury?"

"Actually, she does. Juries are influenced by their perception of the client. Do they want to reward them? Or do they want to punish them? So, if she turns out to be an overbearing, angry, untelegenic woman, I think I'll take a pass. But there's something else …"

The rabbi just sat there with quiet patience. He did not prompt me.

"You have to see this trial in the context of what's happening with the American Identity Party these days," I said. "There will inevitably be white people on the jury who secretly, perhaps subconsciously, sympathize with some of the positions of the AIP, at least to some degree. If they see Mrs. Williams as a threat …" I shrugged. "Well, you understand."

"I do. So let's move this forward. We'll meet her, and you'll decide." He gave me a curious look and cocked his head. "Do you have any other reservations, Mr. Taylor?"

I smiled. He was quite perceptive.

"Not really a reservation," I said. "Just a concern. We're going to sue for, let's say, fifty million dollars. But it's not about the money, of course. It's about striking a blow at the American Identity Party and the Church of Natural Humanism. But fifty million dollars is a lot of money. It's quite possible that we may be offered a settlement during the trial."

Rabbi Gutmacher shook his head. "No, we can't accept a settlement. It will defeat the whole purpose of the trial."

"But what if Mrs. Williams wants to settle?"

He stroked his beard. "I see the problem. Can we have her sign an agreement not to settle?"

It was my turn to shake my head. "It's not legal."

"Maybe she can give us a verbal commitment not to accept a settlement if it's offered. Maybe she'll buy into what we're trying to accomplish. We'll ask her to give us her solemn word."

I couldn't help but smile. "In the immortal words of Yogi Berra, verbal agreements aren't worth the paper they're written on. Solemn words are wonderful, but if there's an offer of three or four million on the table, how reliable are they? I wouldn't fault her for changing her mind."

His shoulders sagged, and he gave me a doubtful look. "So what do we do? Should we take a chance on her?"

"No, it's too risky. But there is a way. She can sell her prospects in the lawsuit. Let us say, for argument's sake, that I pay her two million dollars for whatever she wins in the lawsuit. The money is put into escrow. She gets the two million regardless of whether we win or lose as long as she goes through with the lawsuit until the end. She would not be in a position to settle, because the reward would not be hers. Any settlement would have to go through me, and I would reject it."

"Do you have two million dollars to offer her?"

"I do."

"And are you willing to risk it?"

"I am."

His eyes lit up. "So it's solved! We can go ahead."

"Except for one detail. As her lawyer, I cannot make such an agreement with my client. Someone else would have to offer her the two million."

"Do you know anyone who would do it?"

"I do, but I would have to ask him."

"Who is it?"

"It's you. More precisely, your yeshivah."

"My yeshivah? We don't have two million dollars! We don't have even a small fraction of it."

He was getting frustrated. I don't know why I couldn't have told him my plan straight out without all the drama. It's just a bad habit of mine. June does not tolerate it.

"Relax, rabbi," I said. "I'll donate two million dollars to your yeshivah, anonymously, on the condition that you use it to buy the rights from Mrs. Williams. I hope we win and that my donation will translate into many millions for you. Is that acceptable?"

He grabbed my hand. "It's a deal," he said. "Now let me go find Mrs. Williams. I'll call you if she wants to meet. Do you want dessert?"

I heard from Rabbi Gutmacher two days later. Lavender Williams and her husband were willing to meet with us on Sunday.

Chapter Twenty-three

Friday was devastating. A dozen coordinated acts of domestic terrorist acts shook the country to it very foundations. Black businesses, Hispanic churches, synagogues and mosques were attacked with grenades and automatic weapons. In Grand Central Station in Manhattan, five masked attackers with assault rifles cut down the security guards first and then sprayed the commuter crowds with a relentless hail of bullets. Casualties were high. Eighty-three people were murdered and over two hundred injured. The attackers escaped.

June and I sat up late Friday night watching the reports from Atlanta, Tulsa, Spokane, Baltimore and New York City. The horrific scenes were almost identical. Yellow crime scene tape. Police cars and ambulances. Body bags and stretchers. Weeping people. A sea of pain and horror.

Saturday morning, Frederick Farragut of the American Identity Party issued a statement that the party was not responsible for the carnage. He condemned the attacks and offered his deepest sympathies to the victims and their families; as always, his thoughts and prayers were with them. Methought he didst protest too much. I could almost hear the taunts between the lines. He also took the opportunity of his statement, which was bound to get wide circulation in the media, to announce an American Identity Party rally in Central Park at the end of the summer and invite sympathizers from near and far to attend.

I was sick to my stomach all day. Was I witnessing the disintegration of my beloved America? How could all this end well if angry mobs were better armed than the police? Is this what the founding fathers had in mind when they wrote the Second Amendment into the Constitution? Did they foresee that it would lead to chaos and mayhem?

I could understand that people need handguns to protect their homes and families. Even shotguns. I could understand that people need hunting rifles to provide food for their families or sport for themselves. But does the Constitution state that there should be no limits? Should people be allowed to own military grade weapons? Should they be allowed to own grenade launchers? Tanks? Fighter jets? There had to be a limit. And why couldn't gun ownership be regulated? Why couldn't every gun's provenance and ballistic signature be registered and stored in a national data base like fingerprints are? Something had to be done to stop depressed teenagers from shooting up schools and domestic terrorists from killing innocents like my poor grandson. What would it take to bring about a change?

Rabbi Gutmacher called me Saturday night. Mrs. Williams was expecting us in her home at noon. I told him I'd pick him up and we would arrive together. We'd compare notes in the car.

Sunday was overcast with occasional drizzle. Pedro drove me to Crown Heights via the Brooklyn Battery Tunnel and the Gewanes Expressway. It was not as interesting as the Williamsburg route, but it got us there more quickly. Rabbi Gutmacher was waiting in front of 770. He was holding an unopened umbrella. I guess a little drizzle doesn't scare a Lubavitcher.

Marvin Williams greeted us at the door and led us to a long room divided by furniture into sitting and dining areas.

The sitting area featured a comfortable leather sofa and two upholstered armchairs arranged around a low coffee table. An upright piano stood against the wall. The dining area featured a mahogany table and eight chairs under a modest crystal chandelier. There was also a china closet and a sideboard covered with family photographs. There was a plate of pastries on the coffee table.

Lavender Williams greeted us with a gracious smile. She invited us to sit in the armchairs, while she and her husband sat on the sofa. They were a striking couple, tall, dignified, dark-skinned with chiseled features. They reminded me of Michael Jordan and Michelle Obama.

"I'm so pleased to meet you, Congressman," said Lavender. "I have to tell you that I was disappointed when you retired from the House. I had high hopes for you."

"Well, I'm sorry to have disappointed you, Mrs. Williams. I guess I wasn't cut out to be a politician."

She flashed me a brilliant smile. "You didn't disappoint me, Congressman. Not at all. I respected your decision. A man of your talents shouldn't waste his time in Congress. It really was unrealistic to expect a Congress of altruistic, high-minded civil servants."

"You have a lovely home, Mrs. Williams," I said.

"Thank you so much. You can call me Lavender."

"That's very kind of you, but I prefer to keep my attorney-client relationships on a formal basis. I've found that it works better that way. But I would ask you to call me Mr. Taylor instead of Congressman. It brings back bad memories."

She chuckled. "I hear you loud and clear," she said. "So shall we get down to business? Do you think we have a case?"

I liked that she moved the conversation along without being aggressive. I also liked that Marvin was not inserting himself into the conversation. He knew his turn would come, since we had asked him to be at the meeting.

"We may," I said. "But it's a long shot at best."

"But if you're ready to do it, you must think there's a chance."

"Did Rabbi Gutmacher explain my motivation to you?"

'Actually, he did. Marvin and I are really sorry for your loss. He said you wanted to strike a blow against the AIP. I'm on board with that."

"I'm pleased to hear it." I looked at Marvin. "And you, Major Williams? Are you also on board?"

"Yes, sir!" he said. I thought for a moment that he would stand up and salute. "I fully support my wife's decision, sir."

"As I said, the case would be a real long shot. I'm motivated to do it despite the long odds. It's the only meaningful thing I can do for my grandson. If we fail, at least I'll know that I tried. Are you ready to get into this on that basis? It will be a long, difficult and grueling process, and the chances for success are exceedingly slim."

"I am," said Lavender.

"Why?" I asked. "Is it because you want your job back?"

"That would be nice, but it's a matter of principle."

"Are you really convinced that the Bible is historical?"

"I am."

"Are you a Christian?"

"Yes."

"Does your faith have anything to do with it?"

"Maybe a little. It gives me a bias, but those who deny the truth of the Bible also have a bias. Wellhausen was a known anti-Semite."

"And you disagree with him?"

"I accept the wisdom of the ages. The Bible was always accepted as the truth, at least in the core story if not in every detail. I accept it as the truth."

"Were you told to desist?"

"I was."

"But you continued to use the Bible in history class?"

"Yes."

"Wouldn't it have been easier to just let it go?"

Lavender exchanged a look with her husband before responding. "Look, Mr. Taylor, religion is the bedrock of the black community, especially in neighborhoods like this one. Most of our leaders are pastors. Our young people need Jesus. If you undermine the Old Testament, you discredit Jesus, because Jesus certainly believed in the Old Testament."

"I understand," I said, and I did. "But your position will not win the case for us. Anyway, let me ask you this. How's your financial situation? Have you taken another job?"

"It's still summer vacation. I'll find something. In the meantime, I'm doing some tutoring. Between that and my husband's army salary, we'll manage." She grinned and shrugged. "If we win, I'll be able to retire and send my kids to college without student loans. We're counting on you to do your magic, Mr. Taylor."

"I'll do my best, but I have a serious concern. There's a scenario in which our interests will not coincide. We're going to sue the principal of the Cushman School, the Board of Education, the City of New York and whoever else we can add to the list. It's possible that at some point the defendants will offer a settlement."

"All right," she said, drawing out the words into a question without a question mark.

"Let's say we sue for fifty million, and let's say they offer a settlement of three million just to save themselves the cost, the bother and the risk of a lengthy lawsuit. What would you say? Would you accept the settlement?"

She looked at her husband, and he looked at her.

"Let me address the question to you first, Major Williams," I said.

He pursed his lips before he answered. "I suppose I'd be inclined to accept. You know, a bird in hand and all that. Three million dollars is a lot of money. Of course, one million goes to you, but two million is also a lot of money. It would be completely up to my wife, but if she wanted to ask for my advice,

I'd say yes."

"Thank you for an honest answer, Major Williams. And now you, Mrs. Williams. What would you do?"

"I know what you want me to say. You don't want a settlement, because that would defeat your purpose. I get it. I don't want a settlement either. But to be perfectly honest, if there was an offer of three million dollars on the table, would I turn it down? I can't say for sure."

I nodded. "You've both been honest with me, and I appreciate it. But I can't risk going down this road and ending with a settlement."

Lavender's face fell. "So you're turning down the case. It was too good to be true, but I understand. What if I gave you my word that I wouldn't accept a settlement? What if I gave it to you in writing?"

I shook my head. "It wouldn't work. If you chose to settle, I couldn't stop you. There's only one way I can prevent you from settling."

She moved to the edge of her seat. "And how's that?"

"By making sure the award does not go to you but to someone else. I need you to sell your potential award, and any other financial benefit you may derive from the trial, to someone else before we even go to trial. Once it's out of your hands, you no longer have the power to settle the case. The one who purchases your rights will replace you regarding anything you may earn from the trial."

"But who would buy it?" she protested. "And how much is it worth?"

"I have a buyer for you. He will pay you two million dollars up front to be held in escrow until the end of the trial. The money is yours win or lose, as long as you carry through till the end. It's entirely yours. None of it goes to me. You can send your children to college and put away the rest for your retirement. It's a lot of money."

"Who is this buyer?"

"It's Rabbi Gutmacher's yeshivah. An anonymous donor has given him two million dollars for the purpose of buying your rights. If we win, the yeshivah will receive a large windfall. If we lose," I shrugged, "we lose. The donor is willing to take the chance. Isn't that so, rabbi?"

"Yes, it is, Mrs. Williams," said the rabbi. "I cannot reveal the donor's identity. All I can say is that he has deep pockets and that he believes strongly in what we are about to do."

"And he believes we will win?" asked Lavender.

"He believes we should try our best."

She turned to her husband. "Marvin, what do you say?'

"As I said before, a bird in hand. Two million is a lot of money. I say yes."

"So do I," she said. "I agree."

"In all fairness," I said, "I have to tell you that you have one more option. You can find a different attorney to represent you. You may make more money that way."

She shook her head. "No one in his right mind would take this case unless he was on a crusade. Mr. Taylor, you are our only option."

This was my last chance to walk away. I didn't.

Chapter Twenty-four

Undertaking a major enterprise, in my opinion, involves a substantial measure of self-delusion. For instance, a person opens a business after making a careful business plan. He knows he has his work cut out for him, but he convinces himself that, as long as he works hard, he'll find success. More often than not, however, the startup work and challenges exceed all expectations. He finds himself harried and almost overwhelmed. He doesn't have time to eat or sleep. Had he known what was coming, he might never have started. But he's already committed, so he hunkers down and perseveres.

All the cases I've ever tried required solid preparation. The more complicated cases required much more preparation. But they were rarely overwhelming. I didn't have to become a doctor to present medical evidence. But I quickly discovered that the Lavender Williams lawsuit was in a class of its own.

My first readings of the books Nancy Hannah had provided for me had been fairly superficial. I had just wanted to get a sense of the opposing views without getting into the weeds from which they drew their opinions. But now I had to examine all the evidence, and I quickly discovered that I could not present the evidence for the authenticity of the Bible or rebut the evidence against it without becoming something of an amateur expert on the Bible and its origins. The subject was too complicated to skirt the surface.

Fortunately, my partners at Cain, Schmidt, Barrow and Taylor were cooperative, and I was able to hand over my caseload to associate attorneys and concentrate on my research. I also commandeered Nancy Hannah Mikhail and Elliott O'Hara, two of the brightest young associates in the firm, to work with me full time. Paul Blake also joined our team. He would be needed to investigate potential expert witnesses and to do jury research when the time came. We set ourselves up in one of the small conference rooms and went to work in secrecy.

During the months of preparation, there were several small AIP rallies in different parts of the country and a few minor scuffles, but there was not much to distract us from our work. The AIP had clearly decided to keep a low profile for a while. The FBI investigation was unrelenting, not only in the manhunt for the killers but in the scrutiny of the AIP's seditious activities and its finances. Jordan Fowler, the special agent in charge of the New York office of the FBI, an old friend of mine, kept me abreast of developments in the case. He also informed me that the FBI was infiltrating additional undercover agents into the white supremacist groups that comprised the AIP.

The FBI is a great organization, and I had no doubt that they would bring the killers to justice and also expose the nasty underbelly of the white supremacist movement. They would weaken and contain the AIP, but they would not destroy it. As long as it remained neopagan, the movement would endure. If the Bible could be shown to be authentic, however, many white supremacists would return to their Christian roots. Although Christianity had a decidedly bloody history, it would not condone a race war. The Lavender Williams trial was a long shot, but it struck at the heart of the movement.

After months of intense effort, we were ready. We filed suit in federal court for violation of civil rights against the principal of the Cushman Middle School, the Board of Education and the City of New York. We asked for a jury trial. The trial was set for November in the Theodore Roosevelt Federal Courthouse, the United States District Court for the Eastern District of New York, at 225 Cadman Plaza East in downtown Brooklyn. The presiding judge was the Honorable Katherine Baker, who had a reputation for being tough but fair.

We still needed additional time for preparation, but by the trial date, we would be as ready as we would ever be. I called Lavender and brought her up to date. I reassured her that she would take the stand only briefly at the beginning of the trial. There was nothing else for her to do. Regardless of the outcome, she would be two million dollars richer.

The day of the trial was cold and rainy; it was a good thing I didn't believe in ominous omens. Nancy Hannah Mikhail and Elliott O'Hara were waiting for me in the hallway outside the courtroom. The client and her husband were also there.

"Good morning, Mrs. Williams, Major Williams," I said. "I'm glad you're on time."

"I'm never late to class, Mr. Taylor," she said. She was wearing a simple blue dress and a nervous look on her face.

"Then let's go in," I said. "Let's do this."

The courtroom was empty except for one woman sitting by herself in the last row of the visitor's gallery and looking at her phone. I recognized her as Jessica Davis, a reporter for the New York *Post* who frequented the halls of the courthouse in search of interesting cases. She was a small woman in her forties with short brown hair and restless brown eyes. Her eyes lit up when she saw me. She jumped to her feet and headed in my direction with her hand extended. I told my client to take a seat at the plaintiff's table along with my associates, and I braced myself.

"Congressman!" she gushed. "Fancy meeting you here."

"I could say the same. What are you doing here?"

"Well, I saw your name on the docket, and I thought the case might be newsworthy." She winked. "Maybe for a page past the centerfold."

"I'm flattered."

"Would you like to tell me something about your case?"

"I'm afraid not. I'm not looking to try the case in the media. If you're curious, you can sit and observe, but I'm not sure it's worth such a large investment of your precious time."

Actually, I did want the case to receive a lot of publicity, but not just yet. This was not a lurid murder trial. Too much premature publicity might lead to overexposure and a decline in public interest. That was the last thing I wanted. But Jessica Davis was the only reporter present, and if she was looking for a scoop, she was not likely to write about a wrongful termination suit if it might turn out to be much more interesting. She would hold off for a while.

"Listen, Congressman," she said. "Something is going on here. I can smell it. I'm sure you want favorable coverage, but obviously not just yet. I'll hold off if you promise me something."

"I'm listening."

"I want the inside track. This is my story, and when all the other media come barging in here, I'm first in line. Can you promise me that?"

I shook my head. "I can't make any promises, but I will definitely be more favorably disposed toward you."

This was tantamount to a promise, and she was satisfied. She went back to her seat and returned to her phone.

Chapter Twenty-five

Judge Katherine Baker was a thin woman in her fifties with snowy white hair, a very pale face, heavy mascara and crimson lipstick; when I looked at her, I thought I saw only eyes and lips on a white background. I'd known her for many years, and I've always found her fair and reasonable.

The attorney for the defendants was James Calabrese, the corporation counsel for the City of New York, a tall man with a patrician demeanor, pushing seventy, as am I. I'd known him for a long time. Although I wouldn't say we were exactly friends, we were more than acquaintances. Friendly colleagues might be a good way to put it. He was a decent man and a terrific lawyer. I did not have to worry about him playing Hamilton Burger to my Perry Mason. The trial promised to be science versus science. That's the way I wanted it. No histrionics. No posturing. Just an honest examination of the facts, a search for the truth.

Did I believe the Bible was the truth after all my research? It's hard to say. But I did come away convinced that there was at least a kernel of truth in it, that it was not a myth created about a thousand years after it claimed to have been written. I needed to show the jury what I had discovered and to convince them to see it from my point of view.

Before we went to jury selection, I asked the judge for a brief meeting in chambers with my client and opposing counsel. We could have had our conference in the courtroom, but I didn't want Jessica Davis, the reporter, to hear. She gave me a rueful look when we walked back to the judge's chambers, but I didn't feel bad for her. She would have plenty to report once the trial got under way.

Without removing her black robe, the judge took her place at her desk and asked us to sit.

"What's on your mind, Mr. Taylor?" she said.

I showed her the agreement between Rabbi Gutmacher's yeshivah and Mrs. Williams. It was all on a single sheet, short and to the point. She read it carefully and then read it again. She handed it to Calabrese and waited for him to read it.

"Why are you showing this to me?" she asked after he handed it back.

"I think you should be aware of the arrangement," I said. "It may or may not present an issue later, but I wanted to be up front with you."

"Do you have any problem with this, Mr. Calabrese?"

"Mr. Taylor has obviously done this," he said, "because he wants the trial to go through to completion. He wants to prevent Mrs. Williams from taking a settlement. But it seems legal, so I have no problem with this. I guess we'll just have to win with the jury."

"And one more thing," I added. "I want the agreement to be on the record to protect the interests of the yeshivah."

"Are you their attorney?" she asked. "That would be a conflict of interest."

"No, judge, I'm not. They have their own attorney. I'm not making any representations on their behalf. I just want to enter the agreement into the record. I can ask their attorney to come here if you wish."

She shook her head. "That won't be necessary." She looked at Lavender. "Mrs. Williams, you signed this agreement?"

"I did."

"Did you do so of your own free will?"

"Of course."

"You did not feel coerced? Did Mr. Taylor put any pressure on you?"

"Well, he said he wouldn't take the case if I didn't sign it, but that's his prerogative, isn't it?"

"It certainly is, Mrs. Williams. Are you satisfied with the terms of this agreement?"

"I am. I'll get two million dollars regardless of the outcome of the trial. All I have to do is see it through to the end. I just have to sit quietly at the plaintiff's table and let Mr. Taylor do his work. I'm more than satisfied."

"Then I have no problem with this agreement. Mr. Taylor, do you have a copy for me and for Mr. Calabrese."

"I do."

"What about the depositions? Are the records ready?"

"There are really no records," said Calabrese. "Almost all the testimony will be given by expert witnesses representing views expressed in different books. Mr. Taylor has given us copies of the books he'll be using, and we've given him copies of ours. There's nothing more to say." He shrugged. "If we ask an expert witness what he or she intends to say, they'll just say that they intend to answer our questions. I'm good with it. Depositions are a pain in the neck."

"Mr. Taylor?"

"He took the words right out of my mouth," I said.

She slapped her hands on the desk and stood up.

"Then we're ready to move ahead," she said. "Jury selection starts tomorrow."

Chapter Twenty-six

Jury selection is a critical phase of every trial, if not the most critical. You can make the strongest arguments until you're blue in the face, but if the jury is not impartial and open-minded, you're in dangerous waters. I was not looking for jurors who were religiously committed. It would defeat the purpose of the trial. A favorable verdict by such jurors would not strike a blow against the American Identity Party and the Church of Natural Humanism. Besides, Calabrese would probably reject them for cause, and he would be right to do so.

The prospective jurors were brought into the courtroom and took seats in the gallery. Judge Baker usually had prospective jurors called one by one to the witness box, where they were questioned in front of the other jurors. In this case, she decided that jurors would be questioned at a side bar. She was concerned that some of the questions would be of a sensitive nature and would give the other jurors time to formulate answers that were less than spontaneous. I thought it was a good idea. I wanted a clean jury.

She stepped down to the side of the bench right near the door to her chambers and motioned the attorneys over. Then she had the bailiff bring over one juror at a time. She allowed the defense to ask questions first.

The first seven prospective jurors were rejected for cause by one side or the other. The eighth candidate was an elderly

Korean man wearing an out-of-style suit and a white shirt open at the collar.

"Good day, sir," said the judge. "Can we have your name please?"

"Kim Kwan."

"And your place of birth?"

"South Korea."

"Are you an American citizen?"

"Yes. Ten years."

"Thank you, Mr. Kim. You may ask your questions, Mr. Calabrese."

Calabrese gave the man a reassuring smile. "What is your business or profession, sir?"

"I have a fruit store in Manhattan."

"Was that your profession in Korea as well?"

"No. I was a high school teacher."

"I see. What is your religion?"

"I am a Buddhist."

"Have you formed any opinions about the Bible?"

"I have no opinions about the Bible. I never think about it."

"Does it matter to you if the Bible is true or false?"

The man shrugged. "Why should I care?"

Calabrese smiled at him. "Why indeed. We accept Mr. Kim."

The judge looked to me.

"Mr. Kim," I said, "what did you teach in high school?"

"I taught geography, Chinese history and English."

"Thank you, Mr. Kim. The plaintiff accepts Mr. Kim."

The judge signaled for the next juror. Three more jurors were eliminated, and the judge called for a lunch break. The first juror after lunch was a slender man in his forties. His name was Jason Mandelbaum. He was born in the United States.

Calabrese went first. "What is your business or profession, sir?"

"I'm a chemist."

"What is your religion?"

"I'm a Conservative Jew."

"What do you think about the Bible?"

"Uh, I think it's a holy book."

"Do you know who wrote it?"

"I'm not sure. Some rabbis in our movement say that the Exodus never occurred and that the Bible was written many years later."

"And what do you believe?"

"Uh, I'm not sure. I don't know what to believe."

"Do you think you could accept that those rabbis are right?"

"I think I could."

"Would it cause you any problems in your personal life? You know, with friends, family, business associates and the like."

"No, I don't think so. It wouldn't change anything for me. Maybe they'd ask me to speak about the trial for study groups in the synagogue. After it's over, of course. But I wouldn't have any trouble, I don't think."

"We accept Mr. Mandelbaum."

"Mr. Mandelbaum," I began, "are you a religious man?"

"I already said that I'm a Conservative Jew."

"But are you religious? Does Judaism play a part in your life?"

"I suppose. I mean, we keep kosher in the house. We go to the synagogue as often as we can. We never miss the High Holidays."

"Do you believe in God?"

"Of course, I do."

"Do you believe Jewish people have a special relationship with God?"

He hesitated. "I guess. I mean, sort of. I mean, yes."

"The plaintiff accepts Mr. Mandelbaum."

The next prospective juror, a short black man with long arms and luminous eyes, took the stand. His name was Matthew Cooper.

"What is your business or profession, sir?" asked Calabrese.

"I'm a recording artist."

"What kind of music do you sing?"

"All kinds. Mostly soul, R&B and gospel."

"Are you a Christian?"

"Yes."

"Do you have any opinions about the authorship of the Bible?"

"I believe I have an open mind."

"What if it turns out the Bible is a fraud? Would you continue singing gospel music?"

"I don't know. I think I would. Music is music. I love gospel music."

"The defense rejects Mr. Cooper for cause."

After two hours of this, we had ten jurors. The next prospective juror was a slender young woman named Jane Li.

"What is your place of birth?" asked Calabrese. I suppose he asked people with Asian names where they were born. He meant no harm.

"Pasadena, California."

"And your parents?"

"My parents were originally from Shanghai. They immigrated to the United States from Hong Kong."

"What is your religion?"

She shrugged. "I'm not really religious. My parents weren't either. My grandparents back in Shanghai followed the teachings of Confucius, so I guess that makes us Confucianists, if there is such a word; is there?"

Calabrese smiled. "I really don't know. What are the teachings of Confucius?"

"You would have to ask my parents. I think it means you have to respect your ancestors or something like that."

"How about you? What do you believe?"

"I'm not very religious. I'm divorced with two young children and a job. I don't have the time or energy to think about those things. I suppose I'm a secular person."

"Are you against religion?"

"Not for or against. People should be free to worship as they please."

"The defendant accepts Ms. Li."

My turn. I was conflicted about this juror, but I felt she had potential. I knew she was an artist. Perhaps I could explore that. I thought for a moment before I began.

"Ms. Li, what kind of job do you do?"

"I'm a graphic designer."

"Are you familiar with ancient art?"

"Actually, I am. Strange you should ask. I love ancient art."

"What do you think of the people in the ancient world? Do you think they were less intelligent than we are today?"

"Oh, I don't think so. Actually, I think they were more intelligent."

"Really? How so?"

"Well, they didn't have the technology we have today or the knowledge about many different things. But they had the opportunity to think about life and things. They didn't watch television, and their phones weren't ringing all the time. And they weren't bombarded by advertising wherever they went. They had the time and peace of mind to sit under the stars and just think and get in touch with their inner selves and feelings. We can't really do that today."

"But aren't our advanced technology and scientific knowledge proof that we are more intelligent today?"

"Not at all. Technology and science are like a pile of bricks, each one based on the one below. They develop by steps. If we'd been born in those days, we couldn't make today's technology. And if the ancients had been born today, they'd do just as good a job as we do, if not better."

I was pleased. "The plaintiff accepts Ms. Li as our eleventh juror."

Fifteen minutes later, the bailiff called on a heavyset man with the rough hands of a manual laborer. The sleeves of his jacket strained against his biceps. He introduced himself as Mike Murdock.

"What is your profession, sir?" asked Calabrese.

"I'm an automobile technician, a transmission specialist."

"Are you a religious man?"

"Yeah. The wife and me, we go to church at least once a month."

"And what church is that?"

"Second Methodist Church on Bay Ridge Avenue in Bensonhurst."

"Do you read the Bible?"

"Not much."

"Do you know who wrote the Bible?"

"I think different people wrote it."

"Could you please explain that?"

"Sure. I think Moses wrote the first part. Jesus wrote the second part. And the last part, I think Billy Graham wrote it."

Calabrese bit his lower lip and tried to keep a serious face.

"The defense accepts Mr. Murdock."

It was my turn.

"Mr. Murdock, what kind of training did you receive in order to become an automobile mechanic?"

"I went to technical school for two years."

"Can you read schematics?"

"Sure thing. I was number three in my class in diagnostics."

"And how many were in your class?"

"Forty-six, I think."

"Do you read much now that you've graduated and have a job?"

"Well, depends on what you call much. I read all the computer magazines cover to cover, and I read *Popular Science* and *Popular Mechanics*. I read *National Geographic*, but mostly, I look at the pictures. And I read the sports section. I like to see how my Mets are doing. Sometimes, I read the front page, like if there's hot news from the Middle East or if there's a big election coming or terrorism."

"Sounds like you read quite a lot. And pretty heavy stuff, too. But you haven't really read the Bible, have you?"

"Nah, not too much. I hear the preacher read from the Bible when I go to church, so I know a little something about it. Like I said before, I only look at it when we're on a trip or something. The hotel room usually has a Bible, and I read it in the bathroom … sometimes. We don't have a Bible at home. Maybe we should get us one."

"The plaintiff accepts Mr. Murdock."

Chapter Twenty-seven

Jessica Davis, the reporter from the New York Post, had sat through jury selection and discovered that the trial would not hinge on wrongful termination but on the authenticity of the Bible. That in itself was newsworthy, but a former Congressman defending the Bible made the trial particularly intriguing. Shades of the Scopes trial with Clarence Darrow and William Jennings Bryan.

She reported on the case, including speculation about why I had taken the case, and posted it online that very same evening. Within an hour, the story had been picked up by numerous sites and stations; it was a feather in her cap. A few reporters called my office and left messages. I saw no need to return the calls. I would see them in person soon enough.

Soon enough came the very next day. Before I even entered the courtroom, I was assailed by reporters in the hallway. I deflected their questions and promised to hold a press conference in the near future.

Jessica's story had apparently received wide circulation. The courtroom was filled to capacity with journalists and members of the public. Lavender Williams was already sitting at the plaintiff's table next to my associates. Her husband sat directly behind her in the first row of the gallery.

At ten o'clock. the bailiff called out, "All rise. Court is now in session, the Honorable Katherine Baker presiding." Everyone rose and remained standing until the judge took her seat on the bench.

The judge instructed the bailiff to bring in the jury, and after they had settled in, she banged her gavel and addressed the court. "Learned counsels for the plaintiff and the defense," she said, "ladies and gentlemen of the jury, we are about to try the case of *Williams v. Youngblood et al.* Before we begin the trial with opening statements, I want to make a few remarks regarding procedure. As you have surely surmised from the questions you were asked during *voir dire*, this trial will examine the authenticity of the Bible. Considering the complexity of the issues and the unusual nature of this trial, I will allow the attorneys broad latitude in the presentation of evidence and in the lines of questioning.

"In addition, since a great deal of the expert testimony will be long and involved, I cannot expect the jury to remember it by the time cross-examination begins. I also don't want to have the court reporter read everything back to refresh your memories. It would take too much time. Therefore, I'll allow the attorneys to interrupt the testimony of an opposing witness at reasonable intervals, with my permission, for cross-examination and to present rebuttal testimony before the witness resumes his or her testimony. This will allow the jury to digest the evidence in smaller amounts. For the same reasons, the jurors will be provided with audio files and transcripts of the proceedings.

"You are instructed not to speak to anyone about the proceedings, not even with your families. I see many members of the media here, and I'm sure the trial will receive a lot of publicity. Please do not read or view reports in the media. You are on your honor, ladies and gentlemen of the jury, to protect the integrity of this trial. If anyone tries to influence you, report it to me immediately.

"One more thing, counsel for both sides feel it would be useful for each juror to have a Bible for reference. I agree.

Bibles will be provided at the end of the day before you are dismissed.

"Members of the jury, get ready for the long haul. Let's begin. Mr. Taylor, we are ready for your opening statement."

I took a deep breath. This was it, the moment of truth. I've tried many big cases in my lifetime, and I always get butterflies in my stomach when the trial begins. I feel like a gladiator stepping into the arena. With James Calabrese as opposing counsel, I was not expecting any grandstanding or clashes, but the trial by its very nature would be drama of the highest sort.

I took my copy of the Bible and walked to the lectern that had been placed some distance from the jury box. Unlike the way jury trials are portrayed on television, attorneys are not allowed to march around the courtroom or approach the jury box, lean on the railing and get into the faces of the jurors. The same goes for witnesses. We stand in one place and keep our distance. If we need to show something to the jury or a witness, we ask the judge for permission to approach.

I cleared my throat and began.

"Ladies and gentlemen of the jury, this is a civil lawsuit. My client, Lavender Williams, is a sixth-grade teacher. She was dismissed for using the Bible as a historical resource in her classroom. She is now suing for reinstatement and damages resulting from her wrongful termination. The facts of the case are clear. What is not clear is if her termination was indeed wrongful. Is the Bible disqualified from being a historical resource? Or can we glean significant information about the culture and history of ancient times, even if we disregard the supernatural parts?

"The critical question is, when was the Bible written? Was it written at more or less the time it claims to have been written, say within fifty years or so? Or is it a mythological tale concocted about a thousand years later? The plaintiff will argue that its origins are in deep antiquity, and we will present expert witnesses supporting that view. Defense will argue the opposite and present its own expert witnesses. You, ladies and gentlemen of the jury, will have to weigh the evidence and decide which position is more reasonable."

I picked up my copy of the Bible and held it aloft.

"This, my dear friends, is the true defendant in this trial. The holy Bible. I call it the holy Bible because it is definitely holy. Even its detractors, even the defendants and their counsel, would have to admit that the Bible is holy in the same way the Constitution of the United States is holy. It is holy because it has been revered and cherished by great numbers of people for thousands of years. No matter what anyone says about the Bible, it deserves our respect and reverence.

"You have all been provided with copies of the Bible, and I suggest you take some time to familiarize yourself with it. It's a book of many facets. It begins with a long narrative, but it's much more than a story. The Bible is a book of law, of morals, of ethics, of poetry, of wisdom for living, a book that explores and delineates the relationship between man and his fellow man and the relationship between man and God. To call it a great literary masterpiece is a huge understatement. The Bible is in a class of its own in its ability to move, inspire, inform, instruct and touch the heart and the soul. There is nothing remotely like it in all the literature of the world, from ancient times to the present day. Nothing.

"Ladies and gentlemen of the jury, this book has changed the face of the earth ... and it stands accused of fraud! This book is the cornerstone of Western civilization, the fountainhead of our morals and values, the champion of the sanctity of individual life and the inviolability of individual rights and liberties ... and it stands accused of fraud! This book has imbued human life with meaning, purpose and unlimited worth ... and it stands accused of fraud! Is it possible for a fake to come so close to the hearts and minds of billions of intelligent, thinking, caring people all over the world?

"I think not. So much truth cannot possibly come from a lie.

"My friends, in the course of this trial, you will be introduced to arcane subjects such as biblical scholarship, chronology, philology and archaeology. You will hear expert witnesses on both sides, and you will listen and evaluate. Don't let anyone tell you that you are not qualified to form opinions on subjects in which you are not experts.

"Remember, the Bible is innocent until proven guilty. If counsel for the defense accuses the Bible of deliberate fraud and misrepresentation, he should back it up with incontrovertible evidence. And you will see, my dear jurors, that this is impossible.

"I believe you will have no difficulty finding for the plaintiff."

Chapter Twenty-eight

James Calabrese put on a pair of gold-rimmed glasses, took a sip of water and stepped to the lectern to deliver his opening statement. He didn't usually wear glasses, but I suppose he thought they made him look more scholarly. Not a bad idea.

"Ladies and gentlemen of the jury," he began, "we all know there are tremendous stakes in this trial. Your verdict will be crucial to the future of free thought. Your unified voice will echo down the corridors of history long after we are all gone. Generations to come will remember your words, and they'll either praise you or berate you. The choice is yours. Their liberation is in your hands.

"The American people believe in God; they want a relationship with the divine. They want spirituality in their homes. They want to be exalted and uplifted. In the Western world, people have achieved this for thousands of years through the great monotheistic religions, Judaism, Christianity and Islam. These religions are critical to our society. They provide us with moral teachings and social values that are indispensable to our private and public lives. No one denies this.

"But at the same time, we have to realize that these religions come with serious baggage. These religions stem from the Bible, perhaps the most influential book in history. Yet the Bible tells a fanciful story about the birth of the Israelite people, the forerunners of the Jewish people today.

"Most of us are familiar with these stories, at least to a certain extent. We were brought up on them. We thought they were true. This gave everything in the Bible powerful authority. Everything it said, whether reasonable or not, had to be accepted as the word of the living God.

"However, modern science has held up the Bible to the light of reason and logic and exposed it as a fraud. Scholars have subjected the Bible to close analysis, and they've discovered that it was composed nearly a thousand years after it claims to have been written and that it was pieced together from a number of source documents. It's amazing how you can now look at a chapter or even a page of the Bible and clearly identify the different hands that wrote it.

"Before we go on, I have to point out that I'm talking about the Old Testament, sometimes called the Hebrew Bible, the foundation of all the sacred books of the Western religions. This is the book, or rather set of books, we'll examine in this trial. We'll prove beyond a doubt that the Old Testament is a fraud. The scientific world has known this for over a century. It's a well-established fact. It's now time we enlightened the world."

Calabrese went back to the defense table and took a sip of water. He glanced at the papers on the table and returned to the lectern.

"Ladies and gentlemen of the jury, I want to take you on a journey into history to a faraway land and a distant time. I want to tell you about a group of nomads who lived in the hill country of the area now known as Palestine-Israel, in the district now known as the West Bank. The story begins over three thousand years ago and is extremely relevant to us here today."

Calabrese went on to describe how these nomads banded together to form a tribe and then a loose, informal nation known as the Israelites, how they built villages and turned to agriculture. He spoke about their primitive religious beliefs. He spoke about how these people established two adjacent kingdoms that were sometimes allies, sometimes enemies and always rivals. He spoke about the evolution of their religion into a monotheistic cult with a central temple in Jerusalem. He spoke about the destruction of the northern kingdom by the Assyrian Empire and the ambition of the southern kingdom to rule over the remnants of its defunct cousin kingdom. And he spoke about how the priestly caste conspired to create a book that would give them virtual control over all the Israelites in both kingdoms.

"This is how the Bible was born. It was the child of political and economic expediency, the product of a conspiracy by a group of people seeking a permanent advantage for themselves and their offspring. They did a great job. They fooled the people of their times, and they have continued to pull the wool over the eyes of humankind for thousands of years.

"But evidence that surfaced in the last two centuries is overwhelming. Let me give you a little preview of this evidence. First, let's talk about the internal evidence. As you might expect, splicing together different documents is not an easy task if you want to pass them off on the public as an integrated document. Inevitably, a number of contradictions, redundancies, repetitions and anomalies will crop up in the text.

"In the beginning, the editor or editors who pulled off this incredible deception got away with it. At least, that's how it appears. We don't have records of people objecting to the authenticity of the Bible until quite some time after it was formulated. But after a period of time, the inconsistencies began to catch the attention of intelligent people.

"But the questions couldn't be buried forever. As we moved into the modern period, however, times were changing. The world was going through an intellectual revolution. People were no longer satisfied to accept on faith. The human mind in all its magnificent power was unleashed, and it was full of questions. The human mind wanted to know about the universe, about the natural world, about the relationship of humankind to the world. It put everything under the microscope of scientific investigation. It wanted to find its own answers and reach its own conclusions.

"Over the last two centuries, biblical scholarship has unlocked most of the mysteries of the authorship of the Bible. The pious fraud has been exposed. We can now identify the sources that thread through the Bible. We can pinpoint with amazing accuracy the time period when the sources were composed. We may even be able to determine the identity of the authors.

"There are many worthy ideas in the Bible. There's much to be learned about ethics and morality from the Bible, just as there's much to be learned from Homer and Shakespeare. But you're not bound by any of the dogma or any of the rules and regulations if they fail the test of modernity. Biblical scholarship has set humankind free. And I will show you exactly how during the course of this historic trial."

Calabrese went back to the defense table for another sip of water.

"Ladies and gentlemen of the jury," he continued, "please bear with me for a few more minutes. We're almost done. I want to tell you about the final nail in the coffin of the ancient myth of the Bible.

"Until this past century, the proof that the Bible is a pious fraud came from the internal evidence of the texts. Now it's our good fortune that a different branch of science has brought us confirmation. Over the last century, the remains of ancient civilizations, buried for thousands of years, have been excavated and analyzed. Archaeology has proved that the Bible is nothing more than a fantasy. We have no more reason to believe there ever was an Abraham or a Moses than to believe in the Abominable Snowman.

"My dear jurors, the task before you is daunting, even

frightening. It's fraught with emotion. Some of you will find it hard to accept the charges of fraud and misrepresentation leveled at the Bible. But the facts speak for themselves, and it's your responsibility to proclaim the truth as you see it.

"Do not worry that you might deprive millions of people of the security and comforts of religion. You will not. The people that want to believe will continue to believe whatever they wish to believe. I assure you that religion will not die after you bring in your verdict.

"Ladies and gentlemen of the jury, history is in your hands."

Chapter Twenty-nine

Our opening statements had not taken too much time, but the judge decided not to begin testimony until after lunch. There would be plenty of time to eat an unhurried lunch and still discuss strategy with my associates.

Just as I was leaving the courtroom, Jessica Davis approached me. Her reporting the previous evening had led to the large press contingent in the gallery, and now she was probably afraid of losing her advantage. I liked Jessica and decided to help her, but I wanted something in return.

She gave me her biggest smile. "Congressman! Can I ask you a few questions? I won't make you miss your lunch. I promise."

"How would you like to buy me lunch?" I said. "Then we can talk in private and at leisure."

She caught her breath. "That would be fabulous."

"Is it in your budget? You know that Congressmen eat expensive food, don't you? No hot dogs and pizza for me."

"Don't worry about it, Congressman, you can have caviar and lobster, even if I have to pay for it from my own pocket."

"There's one condition," I said. "Please don't call me Congressman. I don't like it."

"All right. Should I call you Adrian?"

"Let's keep it formal. Call me Mr. Taylor, and I'll call you Ms. Davis."

"Suits me. Where would you like to go?"

We went to the Mikonos Café, a Greek luncheonette five blocks from the courthouse with simple décor and terrific food. We ordered lunch and took a table far from the counter. I insisted we eat before we talked. Jessica picked at her food like a bird, but I ate all of mine.

"Do you mind if I record this?" she asked after we ordered coffee.

"Not at all."

"Great." She put a phone on the table and started recording. "Congressman, I mean Mr. Taylor, why did you take this case?"

"I'll be straight with you, Ms. Davis. It was for personal reasons."

"You never struck me as a particularly religious man."

I shook my head. "No, it was for my grandson. Did you ever hear of David Goldfield?"

The light of recognition appeared in her eyes. "Oh, I remember. I'm so sorry for your loss. I really am. It was such a horrible tragedy. I covered the funeral. Your eulogy really touched my heart." She took a deep breath. "So let me see if I understand this. Your grandson was Chabad, which means he believed in the Bible. So you want to justify his belief?"

"Not quite. I want to strike a blow against the people that murdered him. Have you listened to Sanford Johns?"

"Who hasn't? A real nut job."

"His followers don't think so. He preaches neopaganism, sounds a lot like Nietzsche. People should take their cues from nature. Might makes right. Survival is the only morality. The foundation of his so-called religion is that the Bible is a fraud, a hoax, fake news. There are no golden rules, no higher morality. Without the Bible, you can have a race war."

"I see," she said, drawing out the words. "You want to convince the world that the Bible is true. Do you want the world to believe that God spoke to Moses on Mount Sinai?"

I shook my head. "I'm not sure I believe it myself. I mean, I'm pretty sure something extraordinary happened back then. But I'm not sure what it was. I want people to believe the Bible was written when it claims to have been written, that it was not some hoax cooked up a thousand years later. If people were brought up as Jews or Christians or Muslims, I don't want their religion ripped away from them by people ridiculing their beliefs. Their religion protects us from the likes of Farragut and Johns."

"So, what exactly is your goal?"

"I want to prove that it's more reasonable to believe that the Bible is extremely old, that it was written in deep antiquity at about the time it claims to have been written. If I can prove that, it would be difficult to deny the basic truth of the monotheistic religions. If I can prove that, the clergy will convince those thugs that the AIP is the road to Hell."

"You're taking a chance. What if you lose? Then the verdict supports the claims of Sanford Johns."

I shook my head. "That's what I thought at first, but it's not really true. A verdict in my favor, I mean in favor of Mrs. Williams, would be wonderful, but even if we lose the verdict, we can still come out ahead."

"How's that?"

"That's where you come in, Ms. Davis. I told you I want something in return. I want your help."

"I don't understand. What can I do?"

"My goal is to bring the case to the people. I want to circumvent academia. Until now, the professors wrote their books and presented their opinions to the public as *fait accompli*. This is what you have to believe, they say, since we've proved it. The loudest voice wins. But did they really prove it? The people never examined the evidence and decided for themselves. Most people are intelligent. They're perfectly capable of hearing the evidence and making an intelligent determination. Just like the members of our jury."

"You mean just like in a murder trial."

"That's exactly what I mean. The detectives and the prosecutors collect and assemble the evidence, and based upon what they have, they conclude that such-and-such a person committed murder. The defendant offers a different view of the case. Then the jury hears the testimony, looks at the evidence and decides with whom they agree. The fate of the accused hinges on the decision of the jury. If they can't decide either way, they acquit. I want to prove to the jury, and by extension to the general public, that the case in favor of the Bible is as powerful as the case against it. More powerful in fact."

"And if you win, will people accept the opinion of the jurors over the opinions of the professors?"

"Don't forget that there are professors on both sides. But your point is well-taken. As I said, this where you come in."

"I still don't understand."

"I'll give you transcripts of the trial as it progresses, and I want you to post them on your website. Don't change a word, but you can condense them just a drop if you must. People will follow the actual trial on your website. They'll hear the evidence, and they'll discover a mountain of evidence in favor of the Bible. They may not read every single word, but they'll get the gist of it. They'll see the whole picture. You'll get a lot of traffic, Ms. Davis. More traffic than you've ever had. They'll read the transcripts, and they'll read your articles. Do a good job, and maybe you'll get a Pulitzer."

She took a sip of her coffee and gave me a long speculative look.

"You won't give the transcripts to anyone else?" she said at last. "I'll have an exclusive?"

"Only you."

She took a deep breath. "I'll do it. Thank you."

Chapter Thirty

My client met me in the hallway when I returned from lunch. She appeared agitated. Her husband stood beside her, ramrod straight, chin up, chest out, shoulders back, ready to defend his woman. The only thing missing was a weapon.

"Don't be nervous, Mrs. Williams," I said. "You'll be just fine."

"My stomach is tied up in knots. I didn't realize there'd be so many reporters. What if I mess up?"

"Don't worry. You won't mess up. Think of it this way. You have only a tiny part of this trial. Just tell the court the simple facts. Your testimony will not be in dispute. The trial is not about you. It's about the Bible. All you have to do is sit back and look intelligent and attentive."

"You see, honey?" said her husband. "That's what I told you. You don't have to worry about a thing."

She nodded and gave me a wan smile. "I'm good. I just want to get this behind me. I mean my testimony, not the trial. I'm looking forward to enjoying every moment of it."

We took our seats at the plaintiff's table. The bailiff brought the jury into the courtroom. The judge came in, and we were ready to begin.

"Let us proceed," she said. "Mr. Taylor?"

"The plaintiff calls Lavender Williams."

Lavender took her seat in the witness box.

"Mrs. Williams, what is your occupation?" I said.

"I teach sixth grade at Cushman Middle School in Bedford-Stuyvesant here in Brooklyn. At least, that's what I was doing until I was fired."

"Mrs. Williams, what exactly did you do that brought this on?"

"I taught the children historical material that appears in the Bible."

"Did you bring Bibles into the classroom?"

"No, but I assigned readings in the Bible. I assumed that most children had ready access to a Bible."

"What kind of material did you introduce to your classes?"

"It was historical. The origins of the Israelites. The captivity in Egypt and the Exodus. I should point out that I didn't mention any miracles described in the Bible. Whether you believe those or not is a matter of faith, and I wasn't teaching faith in my classroom. I was teaching ancient history. I taught them about the conquest of Canaan, the establishment of the Kingdom of Israel under King David and King Solomon and the downward spiral until the eventual exile of the Israelites to Babylon."

"And you never mentioned religion?"

"Only in the anthropological sense. I told them that the Israelites are especially important in history because they gave the world monotheism."

"And this does not violate the separation of church and state?"

"Of course not. Religious beliefs and customs are important to the study of different societies. I wasn't telling the children what to believe or not believe. I never promoted religion as a personal faith."

"Why did you think it was important to teach these things to them?"

"Because I wanted them to know the truth."

"And you believe the Bible is historically accurate?"

"Yes."

"Even though it tells miraculous stories?"

"We get a lot of historical information from ancient inscriptions, and most of them feature plenty of gods and miraculous tales. We don't chuck the historical stuff because we don't believe the religious stuff. I always felt the Bible deserved at least the same respect."

I paused a moment to let the jury digest this point.

"Now, Mrs. Williams," I continued, "did you realize that teaching this material could lead to problems for you?"

"Yes, I did."

"So why did you feel it was so important to teach this material? Why risk the wrath of your principal?"

"I felt it was important for the children to know the Bible was a valid historical record. Especially the children in my school in Bedford-Stuyvesant."

"Can you explain, please?"

"Of course. The most stable social force in black society has always been our Christian religion. Jesus gave us comfort when we were slaves, and he continues to give us hope as we struggle for genuine equality in American society. Our faith is important to us. Most of our great leaders are clergymen, from Martin Luther King on down. The children hear all around them that the Bible is a myth, and their faith is shaken. That's a bad thing."

"That's commendable, Mrs. Williams, but weren't you crossing the line into the area of religion?"

"No, I wasn't. I never talked to the children about their Christian faith. I never encouraged them to go to church or pray. I just taught them something that is true, something that is important for them to know. I taught them that the Bible is a valid historical record, as valid as anything else from ancient times. This is the opinion of many great scholars and scientists. I don't think the school has the right to dismiss the

Bible out of hand as a historical resource and send a message to the children that their religion is nonsense. It violates our freedom of religion and my right of free speech."

"But what if they could prove conclusively that the Bible is a myth?"

"That would be different. But there is no way they could prove that conclusively. On the contrary, according to the scholarly books I've read, the evidence points the other way. The school has no right to suppress that point of view and give the children the impression that only religious fanatics accept the historicity of the Bible."

"I see." I paused again. "Very well, let's move on to the facts of the case. What is your principal's name?"

"Wesley Youngblood."

I pointed to the defense table. "Is that Mr. Youngblood sitting over there?"

"Yes, that's Mr. Youngblood."

"Did you explain your position to your principal clearly and logically, just as you explained it to the jury now?"

"Yes, I did. In much greater detail."

"And what did he say?"

"He wasn't interested. He just wanted me to stop. Period."

"And when you didn't?"

"He fired me."

"Did you have an administrative hearing at the Board of Education?"

"I did."

"Did you explain yourself there?"

"I did. But it didn't do any good. They gave me an ultimatum. I could have my job back if I promised to stop. Otherwise, I was out."

"So, what did you do?"

"I stood by my principles and refused."

"Thank you, Mrs. Williams. I have no more questions."

The judge glanced over at Calabrese. "Your witness."

"No questions, your honor," said Calabrese, "but I would like to call a rebuttal witness at this time."

"Call your witness," said the judge.

Calabrese stood up. "The defense calls Wesley Youngblood."

The school principal was a tall black man, with high cheekbones and large solemn eyes. He carried himself with exaggerated dignity. He wore a three-button blue suit, a button-down white shirt and a yellow tie.

"Can we have your full name and occupation, sir?" said Calabrese.

"My name is Wesley Youngblood," he said with the slightest touch of a Caribbean accent. "I'm the principal of the Cushman Middle School here in Brooklyn."

"Mr. Youngblood, is Mrs. Lavender Williams in your employ?"

"She was. She taught sixth grade."

"And now she is no longer in your employ?"

"She was fired for teaching the Bible to the children in her class."

"And why didn't you want her to teach them the Bible, Mr. Youngblood?"

"Because it is a violation of the separation of church and state."

"Did you give her ample warning before you fired her?"

"I certainly did."

"Did she try to justify what she was doing?"

"Yes. She said she was teaching history rather than religion."

"And how did you respond to that?"

"I refused to get into a debate with her. I told her the Bible was not an acceptable historical resource for the classroom in a public school."

"And what did she say?"

"She called me a house nigger."

I jumped to my feet. "Objection! Irrelevant and highly prejudicial."

"Sustained," said the judge.

"Thank you, Mr. Youngblood," said Calabrese. "There will be no further questions."

"Do you wish to cross-examine, Mr. Taylor?" asked the judge.

"Yes, your honor, I do." Before getting up, I leaned over and whispered to Lavender, "Was that true?"

She shrugged and gave me a sheepish smile. "Yeah. I don't remember if I called him an Uncle Tom or a house nigger. Either one works."

"I'm not sure if that helps or hurts. Anyway, water under the bridge."

I walked slowly to the lectern.

"Mr. Youngblood, I objected to your telling the jury that Mrs. Williams called you a house nigger, and the judge sustained my objection. But the jury heard you. I might as well ask about that remark. Had she ever made such a remark to you before?"

"No, sir."

"Didn't this indicate that she felt strongly about what she was doing?"

"Objection," said Calabrese. "Calls for a conclusion on the part of the witness."

"Sustained," said the judge.

"Let me rephrase the question," I said. "Did you conclude in your own mind at the time that Mrs. Williams felt strongly about this issue?"

"Yes, I did."

"And yet you refused to discuss it with her."

"We did discuss it."

"But didn't you just say that you refused to get into a debate with her?"

"Well, yes. But we did discuss that she should stop doing it."

"I see. By discuss you mean you issued your orders. You didn't really listen, did you? Didn't you think she had a right to be heard?"

Youngblood's eyes narrowed. "I listened to her."

"Yes, we know how you listened." I glanced at the jury. "Let's go on. How long had she been teaching about the Bible in her classroom when you ordered her to stop?"

"I'm not sure. I'd say a few months, maybe close to a year."

"You knew about it for a year and did nothing?"

"Well … I didn't do anything right away."

"Why did you wait so long?"

"It was not on top of my list. The Cushman Middle School is in a disadvantaged neighborhood. We deal with many problems on a daily basis. Other issues took priority. Her classroom was functioning. Other teachers were not doing nearly as well. I let it ride for a while."

"A while being close to a year?"

"I suppose."

"What changed your mind, Mr. Youngblood? Have you solved all your other problems so that this was the only one that remained?"

"I wish that were true," said the principal with a throaty laugh. "I decided to put a stop to it. There were complaints."

"Complaints? From whom?"

"The American Conference on Educational Standards. They've been in the news lately because of their involvement in the fight against the Intelligent Design initiative. A.C.E.S. sent me a letter of complaint and said they would go to the attorney general's office if I didn't put a stop to it."

"And so, you told Mrs. Williams to cease and desist?"

"I did."

"Mr. Youngblood, you've known her for a while, haven't you?"

"Yes."

"Has she ever struck you as a religious fanatic?"

"No."

"Thank you. No more questions."

Youngblood vacated the witness box and returned to the gallery. He nodded to Lavender as he neared the plaintiff's table, but it was more an obligatory formality than an expression of friendship. He was clearly upset.

"Sorry for the trouble," Lavender said to him in a loud whisper.

He fixed her with a stern principal stare. "You do what you gotta do."

Lavender looked down at her hands. When she looked up, he was gone.

"The court is adjourned," said the judge. "We will resume Monday morning at ten o'clock. Ladies and gentlemen of the jury, please remember my instructions. Get a good rest over the weekend."

She stood up and disappeared into her chambers.

Chapter Thirty-one

Journalists have a nose for a developing story, but it often takes a while until they discover its sensational core. Jessica's reporting had drawn the media to the trial, but the excitement was still not there. A former congressman was representing a Brooklyn teacher who had used the Bible in her history classes. Interesting, but not quite front-page news. Nonetheless, the media attended the trial in force, just in case it became a major story. I was doing my best to make sure it would.

The posted transcripts of the opening statements of the trial had generated some interest but not enough. My goal was to promote the story of the trial in the media, which would drive traffic to Jessica's website, which would further raise the public profile of the trial, which would drive even more traffic to her website. And so on. If I wanted to strike at the AIP, that was what I had to do.

Friday night, June and I went out to dinner. We didn't take our cell phones, our usual practice when we're out together. Before we left, she lit two Sabbath candles, something she didn't normally do. She said it was in honor of David's memory. It brough tears to the backs of my eyelids.

There's a good kosher restaurant on Lexington Avenue, but we decided not to overdo it. David wouldn't have expected it of us. I really missed him, and I hoped that wherever he was he approved of what I was doing. It was for his sake, but also for my sake. His killers had hurt me deeply. Violence has many ripple effects, many victims, and all of us are entitled to vengeance. I didn't want to view myself as an avenger. I told myself I was a champion of truth and justice, but it was only partially true. The passion that drove me was the thirst for vengeance. I wanted to crush David's killers, just as they had crushed me, and June, and Margaret, and my poor father.

We ate in a steakhouse. After two glasses of wine, I felt the tension ooze away. I wasn't particularly hungry, but I ate all my food anyway. June once asked me why I finish everything on my plate if I'm not hungry, and I told her it was because people in India are starving. I used to think this was a cliché, that it wasn't true anymore, but it is. I was once having trouble with my computer, and I ended up spending some time on the phone with a Microsoft technician in New Delhi. I asked him what kind of safety net they had in India, and he told me there was none, that thousands of people died of starvation every year. I googled it later. I felt it was obscene to throw away good food when millions had little or nothing to eat. I felt that food deserved respect. If I couldn't find someone to take my leftovers, the least I could do was eat it myself.

After dinner, we went for a stroll hand in hand on the promenade by the East River. There was a hint of drizzle in the air, but we didn't mind. We sat on a bench and watched the joggers run by.

"How are you?" June asked. "Are you okay? I'm concerned about you."

I knew what she meant, but I asked anyway. "What do you mean?"

"You know what I mean! Sometimes, you look like you're going to explode. And the trial hasn't even started yet!"

"Don't worry. I have it under control."

"I'm sure the case is under control. But are you?"

"I'm trying." I smiled at her. "The wine, the river and my

beloved wife. That's a great combination for reducing stress."

She brushed the hair from her forehead and gave me a look. Then she smiled that enigmatic female smile and said nothing for a few minutes.

"Adrian, what's going to happen?"

"What do you mean?" This time I didn't know what she meant.

"You know, everything. The AIP. America. Our home. Our family. Where are we headed?"

"I don't know."

"Do you think the trial will have any effect? I mean, I know it's important to you. I know you're doing this for David. But do you really think it'll make a difference? Do you think it'll change anything?"

"I don't know. I wish I did. All I know is that I have to do what I can and hope for the best. I'm doing the best I can do. I can't think past that."

She folded her legs under her and stared at the languid river. "What drives these people? Why're they so full of hate?"

"People hate because they're deprived of something and afraid of something. Racism and bigotry aren't mysteries. If people were satisfied with what they have and confident that they wouldn't lose it, they'd be much happier, much more tolerant. But if they're worried about losing their jobs and their homes, and they see others who appear and sound different being successful, they become angry. If someone comes along and offers a solution, they're ready to listen."

"But how about the rich whites who fund organizations like the AIP? Are they feeling insecure as well?"

"Maybe. In a way. If they feel that the dominance of the white race is threatened, they feel threatened themselves. I suppose, there's some truth to what Sanford Johns was saying. We identify with our group. A threat to our group is a threat to each of its members."

"So, what's the solution?"

"It's not a race war. It's learning to see beyond race, to focus on what unites us rather than on what divides us. Sounds trite? Maybe it is." I paused. "What do you think? What's going to happen?"

"I'm hoping the government'll take down the AIP, just like they took down the Communist Party back in the day. I'm hoping the FBI infiltrates these groups and brings them to justice. I'm hoping for peace and goodwill on earth. I'm hoping that the trial brings you peace and closure and that the two of us will live together happily ever after."

"Amen."

"By the way," said June, "what's happening with the civil suit?"

I shrugged. "I'm not really involved. Last I heard, depositions were postponed for two months."

"Margaret must be getting impatient."

"No, not at all. She's hoping the FBI will find evidence that will help us in the civil suit."

"Makes sense."

When we got home, the first thing we did was check our phones for messages and missed calls; it was as if we'd stepped out of the world for three hours, and we had to know if we'd missed anything important. June made us some herbal tea, and we switched on the television.

There was a tedious report about the most recent polling in the next election, and then the familiar face of Sheldon Friedman, the reporter who had covered the demonstration at Tulane University, appeared on the screen. He was standing on a dark country road near a dirt track that led into the woods. The track was blocked by a heavy wooden barricade. Two black Suburbans, three police cars and a number of media vehicles were parked on the shoulders of the road. Overhead, a helicopter beamed a searchlight into the woods.

"We have a developing situation here outside the village of Yellow Brook in the Adirondack Mountains region of upstate New York, about forty miles from the Canadian border. After an intense manhunt for several months, FBI investigators believe they have tracked the Hesterville shooters to this lonely corner of Padunkee County. The FBI has identified the fugitives as Christopher Jones, John Paul Swift and Jerry Anderson. We have no more information about them at this moment."

He walked over to the barricade.

"I don't know if viewers out there can read the sign on the barricade, so I'll read it for you. 'Beware! Private property! Trespassers will be repelled with heavy arms. No exceptions for search warrants!' According to information provided by the FBI, this hundred-acre property belongs to Padunkee Investments, an offshore company headquartered in Aruba. It's a shell company owned by another shell company, whose ownership seems to be untraceable. Aerial photographs show a number of buildings on the property and quite a bit of human activity. An eight-foot chain link fence runs around the entire property.

"The FBI is reluctant to storm the compound, especially since there may be women and children on the grounds. They want to avoid a repeat of the Waco disaster nearly thirty years ago. They've sealed off the compound and are preparing for a protracted siege.

"This is Sheldon Friedman reporting from Padunkee County, New York. We will keep you informed as the situation develops."

Chapter Thirty-two

Monday morning was overcast and oppressively humid. The air conditioner in the cab that took me to the courthouse in Brooklyn wasn't working well, and my shirt was wilted by the time we arrived. A number of journalists were waiting for me on the courthouse steps. Jessica was among them.

"Congressman, why did you take this case?" asked Charles Bancroft, a reporter from the New York *Times*.

"That's an excellent question," I said. "It deserves a solid answer. Why don't you all meet me here after this afternoon's session, and I'll give something you can print."

The reporters looked at each other in puzzlement, but I could see that they would all be there in the afternoon.

The gallery was loud and full. The trial was clearly generating some interest. I was hoping that the interest would increase as the trial progressed. The bailiff brought in the jury, and we were ready to go.

The judge reviewed some papers on the bench.

"Good morning, everyone," she said. "Mr. Taylor, please call your next witness."

"Your honor, the plaintiff rests," I said, "but we reserve the right to introduce evidence at a later time if necessary."

For a moment or two, there was only silence. It was as if the courtroom was frozen in time. Then a hushed buzz ran through the gallery. The jurors turned puzzled faces to the judge. Calabrese just sat with steepled fingers.

"What is the meaning of this, Mr. Taylor?" said the judge. "Doesn't the plaintiff intend to present a case?"

"Absolutely, your honor," I said. "The plaintiff has just presented its entire case. We have proved that Mrs. Williams was dismissed for using the Bible as a historical resource. That has been firmly established. The defense has not disputed our contention. Therefore, we move for a directed verdict in our favor based on the principle of equipoise."

"Explain yourself, Mr. Taylor," said the judge.

"Your honor, according to the ruling of the Supreme Court in the case of *Schaffer v. Weast*, with Justice Sandra Day O'Connor writing for the majority, the general rule is that the burden of proof is on the party trying to change the status quo. If the evidence is in equipoise, meaning there is no clear indication to either side, the party calling for the maintenance of the status quo wins."

The judge stared at me in amazement. "I'm familiar with *Schaffer v. Weast*, counselor. How are you applying it here? As the plaintiff, aren't you the one seeking relief?"

"We are, indeed, your honor," I said. "However, this case is not about whether or not Mrs. Williams was dismissed. That is not in dispute. It is whether the Bible is or is not an acceptable historical resource. That is the question before the jury. Regarding this question, which is the crux of the case, the status quo established for thousands of years in Western society is that the Bible is a reliable historical document. That status quo has never been officially changed in the New York City school system. Books published by certain members of the academic community do not represent a change in the status quo.

"Therefore, the burden of proof falls on the defendants. They must prove that the status quo should not be allowed to stand. And if the evidence is considered in equipoise, the jury must find for the plaintiff. The plaintiff has proved she was fired for using the Bible as a historical resource and that her civil rights were violated. She should not be required to prove anything beyond that. If defense does not demonstrate that they did not violate her civil rights, plaintiff automatically wins."

Calabrese rose to his feet. "Your honor, this argument is unexpected. The defense requests a brief recess to consider its merits."

The judge frowned. "You're not the only one taken by surprise, counselor. Court will adjourn until two o'clock, at which time I will rule on the motion by the plaintiff."

At two o'clock, the judge returned to the courtroom. She looked around at the sea of expectant faces.

"Before I issue my ruling on plaintiff's motion," she began, "I want to explain the principle of equipoise to the jury and the context of the Supreme Court ruling.

"The case of *Schaffer v. Weast* involved individualized education programs (IEP) that schools are required by statute to provide for children with disabilities. The Maryland public school system designed an IEP for Brian Schaffer, a child with learning disabilities. Brian's parents were unhappy with the IEP. They placed Brian in a private school, after which they initiated a due process administrative hearing challenging the IEP and seeking compensation for the cost of Brian's private education. Who had the burden of persuasion? The Supreme Court ruled that they did."

The judge spent fifteen minutes explaining the background of the case and the principle established by the Supreme Court. She was being exceedingly careful, because she knew this ruling might be grounds for appeal; the defendant could argue that she had put her hand on the scale. But if the principle of equipoise were applicable and she didn't apply it, the plaintiff could appeal. It was a tough call.

"I've decided to allow the motion of the plaintiff," she declared. "It is unreasonable to assume that an opinion that prevails in academic circles, but is not unanimous, constitutes a *de facto* change of the status quo. Since there is no official school policy specifically forbidding the use of the Bible as a historical resource, the plaintiff's use of the Bible as an extracurricular resource would be justified unless the defendants can prove that the Bible is not a legitimate historical resource.

"The burden of proof, therefore, falls on the defendants. If the defendants present no case, I would be compelled to issue a directed verdict in favor of the plaintiff. The plaintiff would not be required to prove that the Bible is a legitimate historical resource. If the defendants do present a case, I will inform the jury that the burden of proof is on the defendants.

"I am assuming that the defendants intend to present a case. Is that correct, Mr. Calabrese?"

Calabrese stood up. "Of course, your honor."

"As I explained, the burden of proof is on the defense. Are you prepared to begin now?"

"Yes, we are."

"Then let us proceed."

I took a deep breath and let it out slowly. The equipoise ruling was a major step forward. It framed the trial properly in the minds of the jurors. It impressed on them that the true defendant in this trial was not the Board of Education. It was the Bible, and the burden of proof was on its detractors. This was not a legal trick. It was fair and just.

Calabrese called Dr. Charles I. Clayton. The battle was on.

Dr. Clayton had a ruddy face and a thick mane of white hair. He looked as if he would be most comfortable with a pipe in his mouth.

"Can we have your full name, Dr. Clayton?" said Calabrese.

"Charles Ingersoll Clayton."

"And what kind of doctor are you?"

"I am a doctor of biblical studies. I have been the Lindstrom Professor of Biblical Studies at Northwestern University for the last five years."

"Dr. Clayton, could you give us a little background about biblical studies? How old is your field?"

"Biblical scholarship is a textual science concerned with determining the Bible's origin. Who wrote it? Why? When? How much in it, if anything, is historical? We're interested in the message only insofar as it helps determine the identity of the authors and their motivation."

"You mentioned that you try to determine the identity of the authors of the Pentateuch. Not author, but authors. In the plural. Are you saying that there was more than one author?"

"Without a doubt. Biblical criticism has determined that there were at least four authors and that an editor formed the first five books of the Bible by combining the writings of these authors."

"How interesting. You say this is certain?"

"Oh yes. It's an established fact, one of the great accomplishments of Western science. It ranks right up there with Darwin's theory of evolution. No intelligent person would dispute it."

I could not allow this to pass. "Objection, your honor! This is offensive. Many millions of people would disagree with this witness, and I suspect that some of them might even be intelligent."

The judge nodded. "Objection sustained. Strike it from the record."

"Let me rephrase the question," said Calabrese. "Is there a general feeling in the academic and scientific community that multiple authorship of the Bible is so clear that no intelligent person would dispute it?"

I rose again. "Objection! Has the witness taken a poll?"

"I withdraw the question. Doctor Clayton, you say the field of biblical scholarship seeks to determine who wrote the Bible, why and when. Why is it so important to determine the identity of the author or authors?"

"In order to gain a full understanding of any work, it's important to know the identity of the author, when he wrote it, the social conditions, his personal life, his motivations and prejudices, all these give us a true picture of what he's saying and why he's saying it."

"Makes sense. I think that's beyond dispute. Why is it so clear to most biblical scholars that the Bible was not written by Moses?"

"The Bible claims to have been written about thirteen hundred years before the common era. But many indications in the text itself and modern discoveries of archaeology place the time of authorship at a much later date. Some of these clues point to a perfect fit for these texts with conditions in the Israelite kingdoms some six or seven hundred years later."

"How interesting."

"Believe me, it's fascinating. We call these anachronisms."

"What are anachronisms?"

"Anachronisms are statements of information that do not fit the times in which the Bible was supposedly written. For instance, an alleged eyewitness account of Napoleon's invasion of Russia in 1812 that describes Napoleon's arrival by helicopter at the siege of Moscow is obviously not authentic. The Bible is full of anachronisms."

"Could you share some anachronisms with the court and the jury?"

"Certainly. The most striking is the mention of camels in the time of the Patriarchs, which according to Biblical chronology was about 2000 B.C.E. The stories of the Patriarchs in Genesis are packed with camels, and yet we know that camels weren't domesticated until about 1100 B.C.E. Just to mention one instance, how could Abraham have sent his servant to find a wife for Isaac with a caravan of camels almost a thousand years earlier? It's like Napoleon flying in a helicopter. No, it's more like Julius Caesar flying in a helicopter."

"For the record, can you give us a source for

this information?"

"I suggest *The Bible Unearthed* by Dr. Israel Finkelstein."

"That is powerful evidence, Dr. Clayton. Are there any more anachronisms you can share with us?"

Clayton mention a few more, and then he came to the Philistines.

"The Book of Genesis reports that Isaac, the second Patriarch of the Israelites, had an encounter with Abimelech, the king of the Philistine city of Gerar," said Clayton. "Abraham is also reported to have visited Gerar. As I mentioned, these encounters supposedly took place about 2000 B.C.E. The problem is that the Philistines didn't arrive in the region until about 1100 B.C.E. There were Philistines in the writer's time, so he assumes there were Philistines in the times of the Patriarchs. How was he to know that the Philistines didn't arrive until nearly a thousand years later?"

Calabrese nodded. "It makes you think, doesn't it? Can you give the court specific citations about the Philistines in the Bible as well as some of the other anachronisms we discussed? You can give us chapter and verse."

Clayton produced a sheet. "It's all here," he said. "Citation and source."

"Permission to approach the witness," said Calabrese.

"You may approach," said the judge.

Calabrese took the sheet from Clayton and handed it to the judge.

"We have copies for the plaintiff and the jurors," he said.

"The bailiff will distribute them. You may proceed."

Calabrese returned to the lectern. For the better part of an hour, Clayton testified about anomalies in the biblical language and usage he considered indications of late authorship. Calabrese took him through his testimony meticulously, insisting on proper citations to support his testimony, both in the text and in critical sources.

"The evidence seems quite overwhelming, Dr. Clayton,"

said Calabrese after taking the witness through his paces. "What conclusion do you draw?"

I generally avoid interrupting with objections, but I felt I should make a point to the jury. I did not expect my objection to be sustained.

"Objection, your honor," I said. "I believe the jurors would like to draw their own conclusions from the witness's testimony. They are intelligent people and perfectly capable of doing so on their own."

"Your honor, Dr. Clayton is an expert witness," said Calabrese. "That's what expert witnesses do. They draw expert conclusions."

"Indeed, they do," said the judge. "Objection overruled. The witness will answer the question."

"Thank you, your honor," said Calabrese. "Dr. Clayton?"

"I draw the only reasonable conclusion possible –"

I got up again. "Objection! We've been through this before."

"Yes, we have, counselor," said the judge. "Objection sustained. Witness will refrain from making such incendiary statements."

"Dr. Clayton, your conclusions," said Calabrese.

"My conclusions. In my opinion ... uh ... it is clear that the Bible was not written at the time it claims to have been written. Therefore ... in my opinion ... it has no historical value. The stories of the Bible, especially the Pentateuch, the Five Books of Moses, are foundational myths and legends, concocted many centuries after the alleged events supposedly took place. They were meant to give the emerging Israelite nation a unifying history and a sense of antiquity and stability."

"Thank you for your expert opinion, Dr. Clayton. Now, the discovery of anachronisms doesn't solve the mystery of who wrote the Bible, does it?

Clayton smiled. "The questions were rhetorical. Biblical scholarship in the last one hundred and fifty years has discovered that the Bible is a composite of source documents. We've developed a set of ironclad criteria, and we can point with assurance at just about any passage, verse or verse fragment and identify the source document from which it was taken. This is called the Documentary Hypothesis."

"And this will help us discover who wrote the Bible and why?"

"It will. Since we have already established that it was not written at the time it claims to have been written but many years later, we can view the Bible in the context of the political situation in Israel at the approximate time of its composition, and we can see that the various source documents serve the political goals of the different parties."

"Thank you for your testimony, Dr. Clayton."

I stood up. "Your honor, counsel for the defense has covered a lot of ground with this witness regarding alleged anachronisms. I'd like to cross-examine the witness on his testimony and present rebuttal witnesses."

The judge nodded. "Motion granted. But the hour is late. Court is adjourned until tomorrow morning."

The press was waiting for me on the courthouse steps with television cameras and microphones. It was better than I had expected. They all started asking questions at the same time. I called on Jessica first.

"Can you tell us why you took this case, sir?" she asked. As she had promised, she did not address me as Congressman.

"As you all know, my beloved grandson was brutally murdered in Hesterville by members of the American Identity Party just a few months ago. His name was David Goldfield. He was twenty years old. Please remember that name and mention in your stories. As you also know, the FBI has cornered my grandson's killers in Yellow Brook up in Padunkee County. There's a siege going on there, but I'm confident the FBI will prevail and bring those bastards to justice.

"This trial is directly connected to Yellow Brook. They're both part of the struggle to save our beloved America from the evil designs of the American Identity Party. They're determined to start a race war and crush our democracy. They're armed with heavy weapons and a boatload of hate. They must be stopped.

"The FBI is going after the criminals, but that alone won't destroy the AIP. For each one they arrest and lock up, there may be two others to take their place. We have to strike at the ideological heart of the AIP movement. That's what this trial is all about.

"The American Identity Party is anti-Jewish, anti-Christian and anti-Muslim. They claim that the moral fabric of our society is a sham. They claim that the values of Western society, which are rooted in the Bible, are a fool's errand. They claim that the only meaningful values for human beings are might makes right and survival of the fittest. A society rooted in Judeo-Christian-Islamic values would not allow a race war. But if these values are the products of a grand hoax, all limits and restrictions are gone.

"I've taken this case because I want to prevent rivers of blood in our cities and towns. I want people to see that it's more reasonable to believe that the basic story of the Bible is historical, that its moral code is divinely inspired, than it is to call it a hoax. They can decide for themselves if they believe in the miracles, but I want them to know that God created human being in His image, that we are not animals in the wild.

"Remember David Goldfield!"

Chapter Thirty-three

The transcript was emailed to me later that evening, but I did not forward it immediately to Jessica Davis, as I had the transcripts of the opening statements. I didn't want her to post Clayton's testimony online before it was accompanied by my cross-examination.

On the newscasts that evening, clips of my press conference followed right after the reports from Yellow Brook. The late-night pundits picked up on the story of the trial. I couldn't stay up too late, but I caught a lot of it on the morning shows.

On MSNBC, Joe Bartholomew, a former Republican politician from Tennessee, went on a long rant in support of my assertion. One of the journalists he interviewed was Jessica Davis. She mentioned that people could read the full transcripts on her website. I also received a call from Joe's producers asking me to come on the show. Of course, I accepted.

When I arrived at the courthouse, there were a dozen demonstrators carrying placards with a variety of slogans. DEMOCRACY FOR ALL. HATERS BURN IN HELL. One of them was especially gratifying. REMEMBER DAVID GOLDFIELD! It was my battle cry.

Lavender Williams was waiting for me at the top of the steps, and we went up to the courtroom together. Back to the battlefield. I took my place at the lectern and faced the witness.

"Dr. Clayton, you testified yesterday – and here I quote you verbatim from the transcript – 'since we have already established that it was not written at the time it claims to have been written but many years later, we can view the Bible in the context of the political situation in Israel at the approximate time of its composition.' You also said that we can see how the various source documents serve the political goals of the different parties. Am I quoting you correctly?"

"Yes."

"In other words, the knowledge that the Bible was anachronistic lends impetus to the reconstruction of the Hypothesis, about which we will soon hear testimony. Is that correct?"

"Yes, it is."

"Thank you. Now, suppose we could demonstrate that there are no anachronisms. Suppose we could furthermore demonstrate that the Bible really is a document of great antiquity written at more or less the time it claims to have been written. What would that do to the Hypothesis?"

"The Hypothesis is a proven fact, sir. The anachronisms are facts."

"If the Hypothesis is a fact, why is it only a hypothesis?"

"It was a hypothesis originally, and the name has stuck. It's not important. The Hypothesis is a fact."

"Dr. Clayton, humor me. It's just a hypothetical. Suppose we could indeed demonstrate that the Bible is a document of great antiquity written at more or less the time it claims to have been written. What would that do to the Hypothesis the defense is about to present to the court? Would it basically demolish the Hypothesis?"

"Well, I don't know if it would demolish it, but it might create a need for some ... adjustments."

"I see. Adjustments. No doubt. Very well then, let's take a closer look at your alleged anachronisms. You mentioned camels, didn't you?"

"Yes, I did. The Bible speaks about extensive use of camels in the Patriarchal age, which is about 2000 B.C.E., but archaeology has established that camels were not domesticated until close to 1100 B.C.E."

"And this is conclusive proof of anachronisms in the Bible?"

"It is."

"Conclusive proof?"

"Yes."

"Let's talk about this conclusive proof, Dr. Clayton. Have archaeologists excavated the entire ancient world?"

"You mean every city, town and village?"

"That's what I mean. Have they excavated all these?"

"Of course not."

"How much have they excavated?"

"I don't know. A small part."

"Ten percent?"

"Less."

"One percent?"

"Probably less."

"So, we don't really know what the other ninety-nine plus percent would reveal, do we?"

"I suppose not. But we can project from the parts excavated."

"I see. Projections. So it appears that your definite statement that there were no camels in use before 1100 B.C.E. is a projection based on less than one percent excavation. How can you know that we wouldn't find camels if we excavate some more?"

"It's a reasonable assumption."

"I see. A projection based on an assumption. Are you saying that there is an assumption of conclusive proof based on a projection based on an assumption?"

"I'm saying there were no camels back then. It's a fact."

This is how it went for the rest of the afternoon. Supposed anachronism after supposed anachronism. I cross-examined Dr. Clayton about all the ones he had described. Most of the questioning involved intricate details of ancient Hebrew text and grammar. I have not included them in my story, but I attached the trial transcript all the way at the end for those who may be interested in the full picture. By the end of the day, we were done. I was ready to send the transcripts to Jessica Davis.

Chapter Thirty-four

As usual, I had turned off my cell phone when I came to court. I don't keep it on, not even on vibrate. because it's distracting. When I powered up my phone, I saw I had three text messages from Sylvia, my sister. The messages were an hour old, one minute apart. They all said the same thing. CALL ME, IMPORTANT. All caps means she was yelling. If she could text in bold, they'd have been in bold as well.

I called her as soon as the judge left. She picked up after the first ring.

"Adrian!" she almost screamed. "Listen, don't get worried."

Now, I was worried. "What happened, Sylvia?"

"It's Pop."

She was maddening. "What happened?" I repeated, trying not to shout.

"Pop had chest pains. George brought him to the hospital right away. I'm here with him now. Bernie is here too. I can't get hold of Alex. I left him messages."

"Is Pop all right? Did he have a heart attack?"

"He had an episode. I think he'll be okay."

"Can I talk to him?"

"They took him for tests. He should be back soon."

"Which hospital is he in?"

"Mountainside Medical Center in Hackensack."

"Why Hackensack?"

"Because I'm affiliated here. George has instructions to bring him here if there's time. It's only twenty minutes from my house. Pop didn't have a heart attack, Adrian. He just had mild chest pains. George did the right thing. I know the staff here. Pop will get the best care."

"Hey, Sylvia, you're the doctor. I'm sure you did the right thing. I'm on my way."

I asked Nancy Hannah to get me a cab while I called June.

Traffic was heavy on the Brooklyn-Queens Expressway and at the Verrazano Bridge. Staten Island was a nightmare. The shorter route through Manhattan and the Lincoln Tunnel or the George Washington Bridge probably would have been just as frustrating, if not more so. There is no easy way out of New York City during rush hour.

My father was back in his room when I got to the hospital. Sylvia and Bernie were at the nurses' station. My father looked a little pale, but I suppose everyone looks a little pale in a hospital bed. I hugged him and kissed him on the cheek.

"What's going on, Pop? You don't get enough attention?"

"Don't start up with me, boychik. My blood pressure."

"All right. How're you feeling?"

"Pretty good for an old geezer. I want to go home, but they want to keep me overnight for observation."

"Good. I'll visit you tomorrow in Montclair."

"I hope I'll be home."

"Tell me what happened, Pop."

He shrugged. "Nothing. I got a little kvetch in my chest. Didn't even hurt. I mean, maybe a little. George drags me into the car and shleps me to the hospital. Hey, where is the lovely June? Send her next time, and you don't have to come."

"I came straight from court, Pop. June's still with patients. She sends her love. I'll bring her with me when I visit you in Montclair."

"Is that a promise, boychik?"

"I promise."

"Good. I don't know why that lovely woman married a shlepper like you, but I'm happy she did."

"I'm worried about you, Pop. Why so much dialect? You sound like Jackie Mason."

"Oy vey. Okay, I'll stop. Seriously, how's the trial going?"

"I think it's going well. The judge ruled that the burden of proof is on the school board. I don't have to prove that the Bible is true. They have to prove that it isn't. I don't think they have a strong case. You can read the transcripts online. If you're interested."

"I've been reading the transcripts on Jessica Davis' website. And her articles. Good stuff. You're talking to her, boychik. Spilling your guts."

"I am. The idea is to drive the publicity. Raise the awareness."

My father raised both hands and beetled his brows like Bernie Sanders.

"Remember David Goldfield!" he declared.

"I see you've been watching television, Pop. Remember David Goldfield. That's what it's all about."

"You just be careful, boychik. You're messing with some really nasty people. Watch yourself."

Sylvia and Bernie came into the room. They looked a little somber.

"They're going to keep you another couple of days, Pop," said Sylvia. "They need to run some more tests."

"What for?"

"Just being cautious," she said. "You should be home by the weekend."

"I'll come by tomorrow, Pop," I said, "and I'll bring June."

"Nah, don't come tomorrow," he said. "Save your strength for the trial. I'm okay. They just want to run up the bills to Medicare."

I smiled. "I'll call you, and we'll visit you on Saturday."

Chapter Thirty-five

Judge Baker entered the courtroom late on Wednesday morning. Without addressing her tardiness, she instructed the bailiff to bring in the jury. She waited for them to settle in, after which she fixed the courtroom with a stern stare. Silence instantly reigned.

"Counsel for the plaintiff," she said, "you may call rebuttal witnesses."

I stood up. "The plaintiff calls Dr. Paulina Hernandez."

The witness was an intense, sharp-featured woman with black-rimmed glasses that dwarfed her face. She came forward with a purposeful stride, took her seat in the witness box and sat ramrod straight without touching the back of the chair.

"Dr. Hernandez, please describe to the court your field of expertise and your academic credentials."

"I'm a specialist in Semitic languages and in biblical linguistics. I'm a professor of biblical studies at the University of Southern California. For the current semester, I'm a visiting lecturer-in-residence at Harvard."

"Impressive. Would you agree with Dr. Clayton that scholars consider the Bible a work of fiction composed centuries after it claims to have been written?"

"Absolutely not. It's just one school of thought. I agree it has a considerable number of followers in academia, but there are numerous eminent scholars that disagree vehemently."

"Can you give us the name of a prominent scholar who opposes Dr. Clayton's views?"

"The most familiar name would be Dr. Kenneth Kitchen. He is one of the world's leading intellectuals. The breadth and depth of his scholarship are incredible. He is a prime authority on Egyptology, archaeology, Oriental history and ancient languages. He is fluent in cuneiform, hieroglyphics and hieratic script. More to the point, Dr. Kitchen's views on the Bible were set forth in two of his many books, an older one entitled *Ancient Orient, Old Testament* and a more recent one entitled *On the Reliability of the Old Testament*. He contends that the Bible is more or less as old as it claims to be."

"I don't understand, Dr. Hernandez. You say that Dr. Kitchen is such a towering intellectual figure, and yet he does not command the following of some of the lesser intellectual lights in the anti-Bible school of thought. Can you explain this phenomenon?"

"It's not so difficult to understand. The anti-Bible school, as you call it, is highly skilled at getting publicity. It packages itself as the liberal view and portrays Dr. Kitchen and the scholars that share his views, me included, as conservative and reactionary. Liberal is a good label in the academic community. Conservative is death. So, it's no wonder young doctoral students seek out the anti-Bible mentors."

"Are you indeed conservative, Dr. Hernandez?"

"I'm conservative in the sense that I'm not prepared to tear down the Bible on the basis of anomalies that can be readily explained. I'm conservative in the sense that I'm not prepared to tear down the Bible given the mass of evidence that supports its extreme antiquity."

"Go on."

"In my opinion, biblical studies should be a search for the truth, a quest for the factual. Unfortunately, that's not always the case. It's fashionable these days to tear down the Bible.

Therefore, it's also popular."

"I see you care deeply about intellectual integrity in your field, Dr. Hernandez. Let's move on. Dr. Clayton testified under cross-examination that archaeologists have uncovered a small fraction of one percent of the ancient world, but that they're nonetheless justified in making generalizations based on what they find or do not find. Do you agree?"

"I do not agree. You can make cautious generalizations based on what you find, especially inscriptions and drawings, but you have to be wary of making broad generalizations based on what you don't find. Negative evidence is notoriously unreliable."

"I see. Dr. Clayton also testified, quoting from Dr. Finkelstein's book, that the Bible anachronistically mentions the use of camels in the Patriarchal age, which was about 2,000 B.C.E., although camels weren't domesticated until about 1100 B.C.E. Do you agree with that testimony?"

"I do not. This is an excellent example of the shortcomings of negative evidence. If you draw a conclusion from something you did not find, you stand a good chance of being proven wrong."

"Would you please explain?"

"The idea that there were no camels in the Patriarchal age originated with the late Dr. William Foxwell Albright, one of the preeminent giants in the field of archaeology. Finding hardly any traces of camel bones among the bones of other domesticated animals in archaeological digs until late in the second millennium B.C.E., he declared that the mention of camels in the Bible was an anachronism. But as it turns out, he was wrong."

"How so?"

"More recent discoveries in archaeology reveal plenty of evidence of the use of camels in the Patriarchal age and quite a bit earlier as well."

"Really? Could we have a few examples?"

"Sure. Dr. Kitchen brings evidence from ancient livestock registers listing 'sheep, cattle and camels' and from a Sumerian text from the city of Nippur dated around 2000 B.C.E. that mentions camel's milk. You would assume that milk comes from domesticated animals. You should try milking a wild animal. Not a good idea."

This brought some laughter. A little comic relief.

"Please go on," I said.

"There's more. Dr. Joseph Free describes an Egyptian clay camel head and a scene of camel riders on a terracotta tablet, both dated to pre-dynastic Egypt, about 3150 B.C.E. He also found camel artifacts from the first dynastic period, about 3000 B.C.E., the fourth dynastic period, about 2500 B.C.E., and the sixth dynastic period, about 2200 B.C.E."

The witness gave many more examples, each fully supported by the meticulous mention of citations. I stole a glance at the jury and sensed they were approaching overload.

"Shall I go on?" said the witness. "There are more."

I smiled. "No, I think that will be enough for now. Dr. Hernandez, maybe you can clear up a mystery for the court. Apparently, archaeologists from earlier generations assumed, based on the near absence of camel bones in archaeological digs, as you told us, that camels were not domesticated during the Patriarchal age. And yet, as time went on, plenty of evidence was discovered to support the use of camels during that time, as the Bible reports. So how do you explain the lack of camel bones?"

Dr. Hernandez frowned. "Are you asking me to speculate?"

"Yes, I am. Expert witnesses are allowed to speculate."

"All right," she said. "I assume that camels in early times were not in such common use among the general population. They may have been a novelty, like royal elephants in India and the Far East. They may have been the luxury conveyance of the rich, like fancy Italian sports cars. You won't find the remains of too many Ferraris, Lamborghinis and Maseratis in your average neighborhood junkyards, would you?"

"No, I don't think you would."

"Now listen to this. The first mention of camels in the Bible is when Pharaoh gives Abraham a parting gift. What does he give him? Assorted livestock ... and camels! The first mention of camels is as part of a royal gift. And this was a truly royal gift. The ancient equivalent of a Rolls Royce. Abraham was probably the first on his block to have camels. These animals were a luxury form of transportation, but they were not commonly used by the people. That's why there are inscriptions and drawings but hardly any bones."

"Doesn't the Bible tell us that Abraham sent his servant Eliezer with ten laden camels to Harran to find a wife for Isaac?"

"Exactly. But when the sons of Jacob go to Egypt to buy food during a famine they travel on donkeys. No mention of camels. Abraham sent camels to Harran to impress the prospective in-laws. For their own transportation, his family used donkeys."

"Makes a lot of sense."

She spent the next few hours rebutting Clayton's testimony about his other supposed anachronisms. The proofs she had brought effectively demolished the supposed anachronism of the missing camels. The other supposed anachronisms could not be so easily demolished. Nonetheless, her testimony had demonstrated very reasonable alternate explanations. I hoped that the jury would at least understand that there could be two different interpretations depending on point of view. Equipoise would then give the Bible the benefit of the doubt.

"Now, Dr. Hernandez," I said, "I'd like to talk about the Philistines."

"The Philistines will have to wait, counselor," said the judge. "Court is adjourned until ten o'clock tomorrow morning."

Chapter Thirty-six

Friday morning arrived at last. It had been a grueling week for everyone, the judge, the litigants, the attorneys, the jurors, the media. Even though I had a heavy schedule for the weekend, a little respite would be welcome. I could visit my father.

At ten o'clock, Dr. Hernandez returned to the witness box for the conclusion of her rebuttal testimony.

"I'd like to explore one more issue with you," I began. "Dr. Clayton testified that the mention of Philistines in the time of Abraham and Isaac, who lived close to 2000 B.C.E., is anachronistic, because the Philistines did not appear in Israel until about 1100 B.C.E., almost a thousand years later. Do you agree with that argument?"

"I do not."

"All right. Let's go over this carefully. Is it true that the Philistines came to Israel about 1100 B.C.E.?"

"It is, and it isn't."

"I'm confused. Is it or isn't it?"

"Look, let's start from the beginning. We have inscriptions from the time of Ramses III, an Egyptian pharaoh from the twelfth century B.C.E., in which we get a vivid description of the invasion of the Philistines, also called the Sea Peoples. The Philistines were apparently a marauding people who migrated from the island of Crete, just south of Greece in the Mediterranean Sea, and settled on the southwestern coast of Israel."

"Is it an established fact that the Philistines came from Crete?"

"Yes. It's also confirmed by the Bible. The prophet Amos states in the name of God, 'Haven't I brought forth Israel from Egypt and the Philistines from Kaphtor?' One of the Hebrew names for the island of Crete is Kaphtor. The prophet Jeremiah states that 'God has destroyed the Philistines, the remnants of the isle of Kaphtor.' There seems to be no question that the Philistines came from Crete."

"But when did they come?"

"Aha! Good question. The Egyptian sources indicate they came in the twelfth century B.C.E. And once again the Bible seems to corroborate this."

"Wait a minute, wait a minute," I said, holding up my hand. "How can the Bible corroborate that the Philistines came in the twelfth century B.C.E. and at the same time talk about Philistines in the time of the Patriarchs many centuries earlier?"

"The answer to this question will explain how some people mistakenly see an anachronism in the mention of the Philistines. Look, the Philistines are known to Biblical history as the implacable enemies of Israel, the nemesis of Israel for centuries. The two nations fought many wars. Perhaps it would be more accurate to say that they were in a state of perpetual war."

"A hot and cold war."

"Yes, that's a good description. Unending hostilities with periodic eruptions of fighting. These aggressive Philistines lived in a confederation of five garrison cities on the coast of Israel – Ashkelon, Ashdod, Gaza, Ekron and Gath – each ruled by a *seren*, a military commander. But strangely, there is no mention of any these five cities in the Five Books of Moses. We first hear mention of these cities in the Book of Joshua, which begins with the conquest of the Land of Canaan."

"But if the Philistines didn't arrive until the middle of the

War of Conquest," I said, "why were they there in the time of Abraham and Isaac?"

Dr. Hernandez leaned forward. "Those were not the same Philistines. Abraham goes to the Philistine city of Gerar, the site of the royal palace of King Abimelech. His son Isaac also goes to Gerar. A number of other cities are mentioned in the encounters between the Patriarchs and the Philistines. None of these cities is ever mentioned in connection with the coastal confederation of later years, nor are any of the cities of the coastal confederation mentioned in connection with the Patriarchs. The only city mentioned in the context of both is Beersheba."

"But how do you know that Gerar wasn't in the Philistine lands? Maybe it was a smaller town eventually eclipsed by the bigger cities."

"Because the Bible places Gerar further south," said Dr. Hernandez. "The Book of Genesis states that 'Abraham traveled from there to the Negev and settled between Kadesh and Shur, and he lived in Gerar.' Kadesh is in the northern Sinai Desert. The Book of Genesis places Shur near Egypt, as does the Book of Exodus. We can safely assume that Gerar is somewhere in the northern Negev or the Sinai Peninsula."

"Who then were these Philistines? Where did they come from?"

"We should call them the Gerarites just to avoid confusion. They were different from the coastal Philistines. Gerar was a rather large country ruled by a king. The coastal Philistines, on the other hand, were a confederation of city states under military rule. The coastal Philistines were warriors. The Gerarites were shepherds and farmers. The Gerarites were reasonably friendly; they forged a covenant with Abraham and renewed it with Isaac. The coastal Philistines were belligerent. Their arrival in Israel was a disaster. It meant the loss of the fertile coastal plain for centuries. Constant warfare and strife. No hint of the possibility of rapprochement. Kill or be killed.

These are not the same people as the Gerarites."

"In a nutshell, the Bible differentiates between the Gerarite Philistines and the coastal Philistines. Is that correct?"

"Yes. The Bible makes the distinction explicitly in the Book of Genesis. Listen to the words, 'And the Pathrusites and the Kasluchites, from where the Philistines emerged, and the Kaphtorites.' The Philistines that Genesis knows emerged from Kasluchia, or whatever that land was called. They are distinct from the Kaphtorites; they did not come from Crete."

"Outstanding. You've really cleared up the mystery for the court. So let's get to the bottom line. Is the mention of Gerarites in the Patriarchal age an anachronism?"

"Not at all. There is no anachronism. On the contrary, the references to the Philistines in the Bible are a powerful proof of its historical accuracy."

"How so?"

"Because, as I explained, the Bible clearly knows that the coastal Philistines arrived after the Conquest was already under way, which dovetails nicely with the information we have from Egyptian sources. Now, if the Bible were created many centuries later, how would the writers have known this information? Did they have access to ancient Egyptian hieroglyphic inscriptions? That's more than a little absurd."

The rebuttal testimony proceeded with numerous precise citations and additional highly detailed information. Calabrese's cross-examination on the Philistines was cursory. I suppose he saw no drawback in conceding the point. Dr. Hernandez did not finish her testimony until well after the lunch break. The judge adjourned the court until the after the weekend.

Chapter Thirty-seven

Saturday brought some respite from the trial. I still had preparation work to do, but I also had time for relaxation. After a leisurely lunch in an Italian restaurant on Madison Avenue, June and I drove to Montclair to visit my father. We found him sitting in his recliner, his eyes glued to the television.

He looked up and smiled when he saw us.

"Hello, boychik. Hello, bubaleh." That's a Yiddish term of endearment he uses for June. "Come sit here with me. They're talking about New Jersey politics now. Boring stuff. But national news is next."

I kissed him on his right cheek, and June kissed him on his left. Then we pulled up chairs and stared at the television. New Jersey politics is really mind-numbing stuff, but thankfully, it did not last too long.

"This is Latoya Alcindor at the national desk," said the newscaster. "In Padunkee County, New York, the standoff continues between the FBI and heavily armed members of the Waco-Ridge Coalition. According to the latest intelligence, it is unlikely that there are women and children in the Yellow Creek compound, but as it has not been completely ruled out, FBI agents are reluctant to storm it. The siege goes on.

"We have more information about the three fugitives the FBI has identified from surveillance camera footage." She put up a picture of a gaunt-faced man with a shaven head. "This is Christopher Jones, thirty-four years old, a delivery truck driver from Shreveport, Louisiana." She put up a picture of a corpulent man with a large beard who looked like Charlie Daniels. "This is Jerry Anderson, age twenty-seven, an insurance salesman from Biloxi, Mississippi." Then she put a picture of a barrel-chested man with stringy blond hair and a tattoo on the side of his neck. "This is John Paul Swift, age thirty-two, a security guard from Baton Rouge, Louisiana. This is all we know about the three fugitives at this time. We will keep you updated."

June and I jumped up and pointed at the third picture.

"That's him!" June shouted.

"That's him!" I echoed. "That's the bastard that murdered David."

"Are you sure?" said my father.

"Positive."

"How about you, bubaleh?"

"I'm pretty sure. He was a big guy with long blond hair and a tattoo on the side of his neck. I didn't get a good look at his face, but it feels like it's him."

"How about you, boychik? Are you sure enough to testify at his trial? If they take him alive."

I shrugged. "Maybe, maybe not. They probably have plenty of evidence even without my testimony. We saw him from the roof. There were many people on the street who got a much better look at him. But I'm telling you, it's him. He's the one. I hope he rots in Hell."

"So do I," said my father. "So do I. But he's just a tiny cog in a big machine. You're attacking the machine in the courtroom, and you're doing a good job. I'm proud of you, boychik. How about you, bubaleh?"

June smiled at me. "I'm very proud of your boychik, Pop."

"Are you going to the trial, bubaleh?"

She shook her head. "I can't. I have patients. But I read the transcripts every night. Maybe I'll take off for the closing arguments and the verdict."

"Yeah, that's a good idea. I also read the transcripts. Maybe I'll also come to court for the end of the trial."

"Let's hope you're up to it, Pop," I said.

"I'll be up to it. Don't worry. Are you following the polls?"

"A little. I don't have time to pay much attention."

"Well I do. All I have now is time. I'll give you rough numbers. Sixty percent of the country think the trial is important. Twenty percent think that it's not important. Ten percent are undecided, and ten percent have never heard about it. That's pretty damn good. Ninety percent are aware of the trial. Yellow Brook is a blessing for you. All you have to do now is win."

"That would be great, but it's not critical. The main thing is to get millions of people to follow the trial through the transcripts. If the public sees the evidence, they'll realize that the case against the Bible is far weaker than the case in favor of the Bible. The public will reach its own verdict, and I believe they'll agree with our side. Of course, it would be great if the twelve jurors reach the same verdict."

"That's a good fallback position. But listen to me, boychik, you need the jury's verdict to go your way. Make sure it happens."

Chapter Thirty-eight

We stopped for an early dinner in Teaneck. Traffic was light on the George Washington Bridge, and we got back to Manhattan before eight. We had three notifications awaiting response. We usually ignored messages from unrecognized numbers, but that night, for some reason, June checked the messages.

The first message was a recording telling us that this was an important call and we should not hang up. That's as far as it got before June deleted it. The second voice message was delivered by a sinister male voice. It was not a recording

"Hey, Jew lawyer, this is a warning. If you know what's good for you and your wife, drop this dumb trial right now. Walk away. This is your first and only warning."

June sank onto the sofa, the color drained from her face. My heart was pounding. We listened to it again, and I pressed the save button.

"What are we supposed to do, Adrian?" Her voice was jittery. "How did he get our number?"

"I don't know. We need protection. I'll call the police commissioner. We go back a long way. I'll ask him to provide police protection for both of us for the duration of the trial."

"What are they going to do? Park a police car in front of our building? Station a police officer in my office waiting room?"

"That would be a good start. I'll also call the FBI. This death threat is a hate crime. We saved the message. Maybe they can trace the call. Or maybe they can identify the caller by voice recognition software."

"We need bodyguards, Adrian. Full time."

"You're right. I'll call Paul Blake. Let's see what he can do."

Paul came an hour later. He listened to the message several times and copied it to a flash drive. The call log provided the time of the call and the number from which the call had been placed. Paul dialed the number. He got a busy signal. He tried several times and kept getting busy signals.

"All right, Mr. Taylor, Dr. Taylor," he said. "This is what we'll do. I'll arrange for bodyguards from the time you leave the apartment until you're back home and locked down for the night. You'll be fine. In the meantime, I'm going to track down this call."

"Your man will follow me into my office?" asked June.

"Actually, the bodyguard I had in mind for you, Dr. Taylor, is a petite woman. Believe me, she is more than qualified for the assignment."

"And whom do you have for me, Paul?" I said with a smile.

"Someone good. We'll see. Do you want the bodyguard next to you all the time?"

"Can it be avoided?"

"Sure, I'll have him shadow you. Keep you in sight."

"That'll be fine."

"Maybe we should get protection for Lavender Williams and her family," said Paul. "They could threaten her to drop the case. There'd be nothing you could do."

"You're right. Please take care of it."

"Okay, I'll be going. Make sure you lock up tight and put the chain on." He opened the door to leave, but then he turned around. "Looks like you've got the AIP worried, Mr. Taylor. It means you're on the right track and doing a good job."

"You think this is connected to the AIP?"

He gave me a wry smile and touched his fingers to

his forehead.

"Talk to you in the morning," he said and closed the door behind him.

Chapter Thirty-nine

Sunday was a beautiful day. Paul came by to report on his progress. He had traced the telephone call to a pay phone in a bar on the corner of Eighth Avenue and Forty-ninth Street in the Hell's Kitchen neighborhood on the West Side of Manhattan.

The bar's closed-circuit cameras did not cover the pay phone, but they did show many patrons. The caller might be one of them. Or maybe one of them had seen the caller and could identify him. The investigation, Paul told us, was proceeding. He also told us that he had assigned two bodyguards to the Williams family.

An hour later, our bodyguards arrived. June's bodyguard was a wiry black woman named Charlotte Finchy. She looked like an explosion waiting to erupt. I could see that June liked her. My bodyguard was a squat man with a gray ponytail named Caleb Garcia. He walked like a dancer. I could see him excelling in a dojo. He was satisfactory.

The bodyguards gave us their numbers and said they would be nearby if either of us wanted to go out. Paul double-checked our locks and left.

Ordinarily, June and I would have gone for a stroll alongside the East River on a beautiful Sunday afternoon and then to a restaurant for dinner. But that would have required calling the bodyguards, and we were not in the mood for that. So, we watched a movie, then I helped June with dinner.

At eight o'clock, Lavender called on my cell phone. My heart jumped.

"Is everything okay, Mrs. Williams?" I said.

"Well, not exactly. I just had a call from a man named John Smith who says he represents Senator Farragut. The senator wants to talk to me."

"Really? John Smith?"

"Yeah. Maybe it was John Doe. Farragut wants to make me an offer."

"Really? Interesting. And what did you say?"

"I asked him what kind of offer. He said it had to do with the trial, which was obvious, of course."

"What did you say?"

"I said I wouldn't do anything without my lawyer. He said this has nothing to do with my lawyer. I said anything connected with the trial has to do with my lawyer."

"Did he threaten you?"

"Not really. Paul Blake told me about the message on your voice mail. Horrible. But this guy didn't threaten me. He was just pushy. Maybe they thought they could buy me off and didn't have to threaten me."

"That's a possibility, but you have to be careful anyway. How are your bodyguards? Are you okay with them?"

"I guess. We're not used to bodyguards. They seem fine."

"Good. So how did you leave it with John Smith?"

"He said I should give it some really serious thought and call him back. He gave me a number."

"You did great, Mrs. Williams. Let me have the guy's number. If he calls you again, tell him he'll be hearing from your lawyer. Any offer he wants to make has to be made in front of your lawyer. Tell him that you'll only speak with him in my presence."

"Got it." She gave me the number and ended the call.

This was an unexpected development, and I had to give it

some thought before I proceeded. Why would Farragut think she'd be open to an offer? Did he know about the agreement between her and Rabbi Gutmacher's yeshivah? Did he know she was guaranteed two million dollars, win or lose, as long as she saw the trial through to its end?

Lavender was not going to back out of the trial. I was sure of that. She didn't have that option. So how could I turn this unexpected offer to our advantage? I was sure there was a way.

Chapter Forty

When the trial resumed Monday morning, Calabrese seemed in good spirits. I watched him chatting with his next witness, a dapper man with twinkly eyes, before the judge entered the courtroom. We had done our research on the witness, and we expected him to be formidable. Five minutes later, we were ready to begin.

"Call your next witness, Mr. Calabrese," the judge said.

"The defense calls Dr. Evan Winemaker."

Calabrese shuffled some papers before approaching the lectern.

"Can you give us your full name and occupation, sir?"

"My name is Dr. Frederick Winemaker. I'm a professor of biblical studies at the University of Wisconsin."

"Dr. Winemaker, the court and jury have heard the Documentary Hypothesis mentioned a number of times during the course of the trial so far, but it hasn't really been explained. Could you enlighten us?"

"Of course. The term Documentary Hypothesis is a bit heavy; it makes it sound more complicated than it really is. To state it as simply as possible, biblical scholarship has proven that the Bible was pieced together from a number of source documents."

I couldn't let this pass. "Objection, your honor. It has not been proved. Let the witness present his proof. Let counsel for the plaintiff cross-examine. Then the jury can decide whether or not it has been proved."

"Sustained."

Calabrese bowed his head slightly. "Dr. Winemaker, please rephrase your statement."

"Of course. The dominant view among biblical scholars is that the Bible was pieced together by an editor or editors from at least four different source documents. Biblical scholars have further identified the approximate historical period during which this work was done."

I was back on my feet. "Objection! They haven't proved or identified anything. They've theorized, and they've surmised. Nothing more."

"Sustained. The witness will be more careful with his choice of words."

"I will, your honor. Although there are different opinions as to which source came after which, the consensus is that they all came from the same general historical period."

"When is that period?" asked Calabrese.

"The middle of the first millennium B.C.E. Say between 700 B.C.E. and 400 B.C.E."

"What are the proofs for the existence of different source documents?"

"There are a number of them," said the witness. "Each proof is a strong indicator on its own, but when taken all together, the conclusion is abundantly clear. We are looking at different works by different authors."

"Would you please explain?"

"Let's begin with the most basic indicator, the appearance of numerous doublets in the Bible. The term doublet refers to the same story being told twice in the Bible. There are two different stories of the creation; two different stories of the forging of a covenant between God and Abraham; two different stories of Abraham sending away Hagar, his Egyptian concubine; two different stories of the naming of Abraham's son

Isaac; two different stories of Abraham presenting his wife Sarah to a foreign king as his sister; two different stories of Jacob making a journey to Syria; two different stories of God speaking to Jacob at Bethel; two different stories of Jacob's name being changed to Israel. This is just to mention a few. It is quite clear that these are two different sources presenting two different versions of the same story."

"I see. What other proofs are there?"

"There's the crucial matter of the divine names. Investigators have discovered that sometimes the Bible identifies God as Elo-him. We call that the E name. Sometimes God is identified by the Tetragrammaton, the name composed of the letters *yod*, *heh*, *vav* and *heh*. We call that the J name."

"Why is that name called J when it starts with a *yod*, the Y sound?"

"Technically it should indeed be called the Y name. However, most of the early Biblical scholars were German, and in German the J has a Y sound. Anyway, as I was saying, the scholars identified the doublets I mentioned before, and they noticed that in most cases of doublets, one version used the E name and the other used the J name. This led them to conclude that there were two different source documents, the E source, which spoke of God as E, and the J source, which spoke of Him as J. This is strong proof that there were at least two sources."

"You say at least two. Are there more?"

"There are. Based on linguistics, style and interest, scholars discerned a third source, which is the largest of all. It contains most of the legal matter of the Bible and is much concerned with matters relating to priests. Scholars called it the Priestly Codex, the P source for short. It is austere and dry. The P writer is concerned with legal matters and details, such as genealogies, statistics and measurements. He views God as a transcendent distant figure."

"That's three. Are there more?"

"At least one more. Scholars discovered that the language, style and tone of Deuteronomy are markedly different from the rest of the Bible, indicating that it was composed by a fourth author. They called it the D source. So that's where we are. We have reached the stage where we can point to any page in the Bible and identify one or more of the four basic sources. Although it may have been written with good intentions, scholars nonetheless refer to it as a pious fraud."

"Is there any evidence to support this view?"

"Oh yes, lots of it. Scholars have discovered contradictions among the source documents."

"Interesting. You mention differences in language?"

Calabrese led the witness through a long litany of differences among various parts of the Bible. Finally, the witness paused to drink some water.

"My throat gets dry when I talk so much," he said.

Calabrese smiled. "You've really given us a lot of information here, Dr. Winemaker. Thank you, Dr. Winemaker. I have no more questions."

Chapter Forty-one

Evan Winemaker looked relaxed as he chatted with Calabrese at the defense table during the lunch break. He did not seem concerned about facing my cross-examination, but I was confident I could punch gaping holes in his testimony.

"Dr. Winemaker, you called the Bible a pious fraud," I began. "Strong words. Fighting words. You can't say something like that unless you're prepared to back it up."

"I believe I've backed it up."

"Have you backed it up with evidence or with assumptions?"

"Solid evidence, sir."

"We'll see. Let's begin. Dr. Winemaker, in the entire history of the world, has there ever been a case of another book – any book – that was put together in this way? I mean, we know that some ransom notes are made this way. Some kidnappers snip a couple of words from one magazine and a couple of words from another and send it to the family. But has there ever been a single recorded case of an editor taking four different books, cutting them up with a pair of scissors into big and little pieces, pasting them together into one book, publishing this mishmash as a unified book written by a single author?"

"Well, it's not so –"

"Yes or no?"

"No."

"You say that there are four source documents."

"I do."

"Isn't it true that recent scholars have identified many more source documents?"

"Yes, it's true."

"As many as fifteen or twenty?"

"Perhaps. But that's just speculation."

"You don't subscribe to those views?"

"No, I do not."

"It seems absurd that editors spliced the Bible together from over a dozen sources, wouldn't you say?"

"It's a little far-fetched."

"But four documents is not far-fetched? Do you expect the jury to believe that the only book ever put together in this bizarre manner became the most widely read, admired and beloved book in the history of the world?"

"Well, as I –"

"A yes or no answer, please."

"Yes, sir. I do."

"Yes you do what?"

"I expect the jury to believe it."

"Based on your … um … arguments?"

"Yes."

"Dr. Winemaker, this pious hoax pulled off by an unidentified editor, how could such a thing have happened? How did he fool everyone?"

"I really don't know. My field of expertise is the biblical text, not social conditions at the time it was introduced."

"I see. Well, let me ask this question another way. If you'd been living in the land of Israel at the time the Bible was introduced, do you think you'd have accepted the Bible as genuine?"

Calabrese stood up. "Objection. The question calls for speculation on the part of the witness."

"Your honor," I said, "aren't expert witnesses allowed to speculate?"

Calabrese shook his head. "Counsel is not asking this expert witness to speculate within his field of expertise. He is asking for personal speculation. How is the witness supposed to know what he would have done or believed under those circumstances?"

"Your honor," I said, "I suggest that, if the witness claims the Bible was put together as he contends, the likelihood of public acceptance is relevant to his thesis. He should not be allowed to disregard that issue. Furthermore, the point of my question is to establish bias on the part of the witness."

"Is counsel suggesting," said Calabrese, "that Dr. Winemaker is anti-Semitic or anti-Christian?"

"Not at all," I said. "I have no doubt that Dr. Winemaker is a fine, upstanding person of goodwill, a seeker of truth. However, I believe he has a bias against people of the ancient world. I believe he considers them less intelligent and less sophisticated than people of modern times. My question is meant to determine if he considers the ancients equals or inferiors."

"Mr. Calabrese?" said the judge.

"I still think the question is unfair. If he had been in the pagan world, he might have been a polytheist, but now he knows better."

"Mr. Taylor?"

"Mr. Calabrese's point about polytheism is well-taken. Nonetheless, my question is not ideological. I just want to know if, in his opinion, the alleged editors could have pulled the wool over his eyes. Or to use another metaphor, could they have sold him a pig in a poke? Does he think he's a more evolved human being?"

The judge didn't respond right away. I could see her thoughts playing across her pale face. She did not want to get it wrong and risk having the verdict overturned on appeal.

"I'll allow it," she said at last. "Objection overruled. The witness will answer the question."

"Dr. Winemaker," I said, "do you want the court reporter to

read the question back to you?"

He shook his head. "I remember the question."

"And? Would you have accepted the Bible as genuine?"

"I think ... I would have seen through it."

I had to give the man credit for telling the truth.

"Here we have ancient Israel, a country of several million people," I said, "or at least several hundred thousand, and all them fell for the hoax. Were they boors?"

"I really don't know." He shrugged. "Anything is possible."

"Do you think the authors and editors of the Bible were talented?"

"Yes, of course."

"Could a society of boors produce such people?"

"I suppose."

"Could a society of boors produce Shakespeare?"

"Perhaps not."

"I understand." Time to stop beating a dead horse. "Dr. Winemaker, is there a shred of external evidence that corroborates the existence of different source documents, assorted writers and unidentified editors? Is there a single inscription in any ancient archive or on a stone or a piece of pottery that even hints at such a possibility?"

"None has been discovered yet."

"I see. So, we've established that, as of now, the theory is not supported by a single shred of external evidence, that it rests entirely on a reading of the text. Let us now examine your reading of the text."

I stepped to the plaintiff's table, took a sip of water and returned to the lectern.

"I would like to begin with two of the criteria you mentioned. Interest and style. Let's talk about interest first. You stated that P is concerned with legal matters and dry details, such as genealogies, statistics and exact measurements, while J and E are more focused on narratives. This indicates that there are different writers at work here. Is that correct?"

"Basically."

"Now, if the Bible is intending to tell the story of the development of the Israelite people, their encounter with God and the code of laws He gave them, wouldn't you expect the interests to vary? Is there any reason why the Bible has to behave only as a novel or a history book?"

"It's not normal," said Dr. Winemaker, "for a book to be so varied."

"Let me put it to you another way. If you were writing a biography of Albert Einstein, for instance, would it be reasonable for you to devote twenty or thirty pages to a general description of the theory of relativity?"

"I suppose it would."

"Now if Albert Einstein was descended from Maimonides, the great Jewish philosopher of medieval Spain, would you include that information in your biography?"

"Probably."

"And if you had birth records and other genealogical information that traced Einstein's lineage to Maimonides, would you include them in the book?"

"I would imagine so."

"So would a professor who came across your biography of Einstein be justified in assuming that it was written by three different people because part of it was a story, part of it was physics and part of it was genealogy?"

"It's not the same."

"Just answer the question, sir. Would he be justified in making such an assumption about your biography of Einstein?"

"No."

"You claim that the styles are different. I believe you said that the P writer was austere and dry. The implication being that the E and J writers are warmer. Is that correct?"

"Yes."

"Let's go back to your biography of Einstein. You have chapters on his early life, his struggles, his triumphs, his family. And you have chapters on the theory of relativity and his genealogy. Would your styles of writing be different in these chapters? Would you be warm and even passionate in the narratives and dry in relating the scientific information and the genealogies? A yes or no answer, please."

"Yes."

"Just to be clear, are you saying that the style of such a biography would be varied?"

"So listen to this. You decide to create a measuring stick called interest and perceive different documents simply on the basis of different subject matter. Then you discover that the different documents have different styles! You have confirmation of your theory! Don't you think this is circular reasoning?"

"I do not."

"During your testimony, you implied that your case was overwhelming. Do you still contend that interest and style are reliable criteria for establishing that the Bible was written by different writers?"

"They may be weaker than some of the other ways."

"Are prophetic visions one of the ways you differentiate E from J?"

"Yes. In J, God reveals Himself to people in corporeal form and speaks to them directly while they are wide awake. In E, God speaks to people through dreams and visions by night."

"I refer you to Genesis 15:1, which reads as follows, 'After these things, the word of J came to Abram in a vision.' Here we have a vision and the J name is used. How do you explain this?"

"It's a mistake," said the witness. "The word vision should not be there. It's a scribal error that fell into the text during the copying and recopying."

"How do you know it's an error?"

"It has been proved by earlier scholars. I couldn't tell you exactly."

"Does the name Hermann Gunkel mean anything to you?"

"Yes. He was a great biblical scholar."

"How did he prove that the word vision was a scribal error and should be removed?"

The witness was silent.

"Should I refresh your memory?"

"Please do."

"Here is Gunkel quoted by Dr. Umberto Cassuto in *The Documentary Hypothesis*, and I quote, 'Gunkel justifies the textual emendation on the ground that theophanies in dreams and visions are characteristic of E.'" I turned to the jury. "I'd like to explain for the benefit of the jury that theophanies are visions of God. Gunkel claims that theophanies are characteristic of the E writer. " I turned back to the witness. "Have I refreshed your memory?"

"You have."

"Let me understand this. You create a rule for differentiating between documents by the mention of visions, and when you find a mention that is out of place according to your thinking, you just change the text. Is that intellectually honest? Doesn't it occur to you that you may be wrong?"

Calabrese rose to his feet. "Objection, your honor. Counsel is badgering the witness."

"I withdraw the question," I said. "Dr. Winemaker, I refer you to Genesis 26:24, and I quote, 'And J appeared to him that night and said, I am the God of your father Abraham ...' Here is another case of a vision in the night that appears in a J document. What do you do with this one?"

"The verse is deleted."

"The entire verse?"

"Yes."

"Why?"

"Because it's out of place."

"How did it wander there in the first place? Scribal error? Did a scribe copying the Old Testament scrolls happen to include by accident an entire verse of twenty-two words plucked out of thin air?"

"I can't explain it."

"Very well, let's go to doublets. I won't belabor the jury by taking you through all the ones you cited. Let's talk about only a few of them. You mentioned two stories of God forging a covenant with Abraham. Yes?"

"Yes. The first is J. The second is E."

"Are the two identical?"

"Almost."

"Isn't it a fact that the second covenant features two important new elements, Abram's name being changed to Abraham and the introduction of the covenant of circumcision?"

"That's true."

"Are you telling me that the J writer never knew that Abram's name was changed to Abraham and that he continued calling him Abram?"

"Of course not. I'm sure he was also aware of the change. He just never describes the actual act of changing it."

"How about circumcision? I believe you said the J writer was from Judah. Were the people in Judah circumcised?"

"Perhaps not. The J writer doesn't mention the custom."

"But isn't circumcision a major element of Judaism?"

"It is."

"It's universally practiced by observant Jews and by most non-observant Jews as well, is it not?"

"It is."

"Are you saying that it was only practiced in the northern kingdom but not in the kingdom of Judah?"

"Perhaps circumcision was practiced in Judah, only the J writer didn't mention it in his document."

"Is it reasonable that the J writer would fail to mention the very mark of an Israelite, the sign of the eternal covenant with God?"

"I don't know. Perhaps he did. Perhaps the editor removed it."

"Why would the editor remove it? Because it was redundant since E had already written about it?"

"Perhaps."

"So why didn't the editor remove all the other apparent redundancies you claim to have found in the Bible?"

"I don't know."

"You mentioned two different stories of Jacob making a journey to Syria after he cleverly appropriates his brother Esau's birthright. Yes?"

"Yes."

"I refer you to Genesis 28:7-12, and I quote, 'And Jacob listened to his father and to his mother, and he went to Paddan Aram. And Esau saw that his father Isaac disapproved of the daughters of Canaan. And Esau went to Ishmael and took Mahalath the daughter of Ishmael the son of Abraham, the sister of Nebaioth, as his wife. And Jacob left Beersheba and went to Harran ... And he came upon the place and stayed there all night, because the sun had set ... And he dreamed, and behold, there was a ladder set upon the earth with its top reaching into the heavens ... and behold, angels of E were ascending and descending on it.' It's a little condensed, but that's the gist of it. So where is the doublet? Is it the first mention that Jacob went to Paddan Aram?"

"Yes."

"When the Bible goes on to say that he went to Harran, which is a city in the province of Paddan Aram, and tells the story of his experiences on the journey, that is a doublet?"

"Yes."

"Amazing. So, the first is a J story, and the second is an E story?"

"Yes. You see yourself that the E name is used."

"So we read in this E story that Jacob went to sleep and had a fantastic dream. Then he got up in the morning, and I quote again, 'And Jacob awoke from his sleep, and he said, "Surely J is in this place, and I didn't know it."' Hey, this sounds like a J document. Can you imagine? Jacob fell asleep in an E story but woke up in a J story. He must have been disoriented."

There was a burst of laughter in the courtroom. Even the judge could not suppress a smile. The judge banged her gavel several times, and the laughter subsided.

"Very amusing," said Dr. Winemaker. "I admit there are exceptions to the rule. But most of the time, the J name does not appear in E."

"If you don't mind my asking, why don't you just snip out that J name and say it was a scribal error?"

"I've never heard that it was a scribal error."

"Dr. Winemaker, let me present to you a modern-day doublet that will puzzle future historians. They will read two stories that were not identical in all their details but took place at about the same time and were quite similar. An American president named George W. Bush put together a coalition to fight a Persian Gulf war against Iraq, whose president was a man named Saddam Hussein. One story is said to have taken place in 1991. The other is said to have taken place in 2002. Are these two stories a doublet? Are they really one and the same story told by different writers?"

"Of course not. Many of the details differ. For one, the first president is George H. W. Bush and the second is George W. Bush."

"Perhaps the extra H is a scribal error."

Laughter interrupted the proceedings again until the judge quelled it with her gavel.

The witness smiled. "Touché. They differ in numerous details. One took place in 1991 and the other in 2002. One was triggered by the Iraqi occupation of Kuwait and the other by the destruction of the Twin Towers in New York. And many others."

"I see. One of the doublets you identified is the two stories of Abraham sending away his concubine Hagar. But aren't there important differences? One story takes place soon after Abraham takes the concubine into his house because his wife Sarah cannot conceive. Hagar quickly conceives and becomes insubordinate to her mistress Sarah. Abraham sends her away, but when she submits to her mistress, he takes her back. The second story takes place some twenty years later. Similar to 1991 and 2002, isn't it? Hagar's son Ishmael is already a young man. Sarah has given birth to Isaac thirteen years after Hagar has Ishmael. Young Isaac is growing up under the malevolent influence of Ishmael, and Abraham sends Hagar and Ishmael away for good. Have I told the stories correctly?"

"Yes, you have."

"And don't you think these are important differences? Do you still think they should be considered a doublet?"

"Perhaps if you examine every little piece you can explain it away, but when you take it all together ..."

"It's all right. Let's move on. Let's talk about the most basic of your criteria, which is the variation of the divine names. The E name denotes one writer, and the J name denotes another. In fact, according to what I heard you say, they lived in two different kingdoms. Yes?"

"That is correct."

"Very well, let me read to you a passage from I Samuel 4-6. I have copied it out in condensed form and made copies for the benefit of the court and the jury."

I stepped to the plaintiff's table and picked up the papers.

"May I approach?" I said.

"You may."

I gave a copy to the witness, another copy to the judge and a dozen copies to Jane Li, who was serving as the forewoman, to distribute to the jurors. Then I dropped a few copies on the defendant's table and returned to the lectern.

"Do you see what I have done here, Dr. Winemaker?" I said. "I've printed the divine names in bold and color so that they stand out when you look at the passage in total. Now let me read this passage to you. "And the elders of Israel said, 'Why has J smitten us today before the Philistines? Let us fetch us the ark of the covenant of J from Shiloh.' The people sent to Shiloh and they brought from there the ark of the covenant of J ... And there were the sons of Eli with the ark of the covenant of E ... And it happened when the ark of the covenant of J came into the encampment ... And the Philistines ... knew that the ark of J had come into the encampment. And the Philistines were frightened, for they said, 'E has come into the encampment ...' And the ark of E was taken ... And the Philistines took the ark of E ... to the Temple of Dagon ... Behold, Dagon had fallen onto the ground before the ark of J ... And the ark of J was in the fields of Philistia seven months ..."

I put the paper down and looked at the witness.

"Did you notice, Dr. Winemaker, that the writer of the Book of Samuel alternates back and forth, back and forth, back and forth between the J and the E names? Would you say that this passage was spliced together from two different source documents?"

"No, I wouldn't."

"Of course not. It would be absurd. So, don't we see here that the Bible uses the divine names interchangeably?"

"In this passage, it apparently does."

"After all that we talked about this afternoon, are you still as convinced as ever that the evidence for different source documents is strong?"

"Absolutely."

"But why?"

"Because that is the academic consensus."

"Isn't this exactly what this trial is about – whether academic fundamentalism and the truth are one and the same thing?"

Calabrese was on his feet again. "Objection, your honor. Is counsel asking a question or is he making his closing arguments to the jury?"

"Never mind," I said. "I withdraw the question."

There was much more ground to cover, but I felt I had gone the distance with this witness. I could have made all these points with rebuttal witnesses, but then the jury would have wondered what Winemaker would have said in response to them. This way I gave them a sampling of Winemaker's responses. The rebuttal witnesses would pick up from here.

"Thank you, Dr. Winemaker," I said. "I have no more questions."

Chapter Forty-two

My first rebuttal witness was ready to testify, but the judge decided that the hour was late and adjourned the court until the next day. Before I went back to my office, I asked Lavender to call Farragut's man and hand the phone to me. I didn't want to call him myself, because I didn't want him to have my number.

We waited until the courtroom was empty. Lavender put her phone on speaker and dialed. The man picked up after two rings.

"Hello," he said. "Who's this?" I thought it might be the voice from my message, but it wasn't. It was thin and high-pitched.

"Mr. … um … Smith? This is Lavender Williams."

"Ah, you've reconsidered. Excellent. We have to meet."

"I'm here with my lawyer. He'd like to speak with you."

She handed me the phone, and I took it off speaker.

"Mr. Smith," I said.

"Mr. Taylor," he replied.

"I understand that Senator Farragut wishes to meet with my client."

"He does."

"Let him call me in my office in two hours. We will discuss it."

"Senator Farragut wishes to have a private conversation with Mrs. Williams. You have no involvement."

"But I do have involvement. I'm her attorney."

"Not in this matter, sir."

"I advise and represent Mrs. Williams in all matters."

"Senator Farragut disagrees."

"That is his prerogative. Mrs. Williams will not communicate with you or with him unless I am present. If she picks up the phone and you're on the line, she will hang up. If Senator Farragut wishes to have a conversation with my client, he should call me in my office in two hours."

There was a long moment of silence, and then he said, "I will give him the message, sir."

"Does he have my office number?"

"If he doesn't, he can find it. I'll give him the message."

I returned the phone to Lavender. She had a frown of concern on her face, as if being caught in the middle between a former Congressman and a former Senator was not something she relished. I reassured her that there was no need for concern. Her husband put his arm around her shoulders and led her out of the courtroom.

Two hours later, Farragut called me in my office.

"You asked me to call you, Congressman," he said. "Here I am."

"You asked for a meeting with my client."

"I did. I understand that you are standing in the way."

"Just as my grandson was standing in your way?"

"That was an inappropriate remark, Congressman. Your grandson's death was unfortunate, and I am sorry for your loss. I was not responsible."

"That will be for a jury to decide in the civil lawsuit."

"There are no grounds for that lawsuit. My remarks in Hesterville on the Fourth of July are a matter of record. They're available online. Go to YouTube. There was no incitement to violence."

"I think you're a despicable human being, Senator, but I'm not going to argue the civil case with you now. After the FBI arrests John Paul Swift, there may even be a criminal case against you."

"I don't know any John Paul Swift. I never heard his name before the FBI announced it. No one will even connect him to me."

"Perhaps not. But there may be a chain that leads directly to you."

"We will see. But enough of that. I want to meet with Mrs. Williams. Do you insist on preventing such a meeting?"

"My client will meet with you if you wish. But you will accomplish nothing. She's determined to stay the course."

"Regardless," he said. "I would like to speak with her."

"Can you meet tomorrow evening?"

"I can."

"There are conditions to the meeting."

"I'm listening."

"The meeting will take place tomorrow evening in my office at seven o'clock. It will be on the record. There will be a stenographer present. We will meet in one of the conference rooms. You may bring John Smith and whomever else you wish, and we will bring staff and interested parties with no restrictions. Is that acceptable?"

"On the record?"

"On the record."

"Do you suspect me of attempting something nefarious?"

"You have a track record," I said.

"Of doing things nefarious?"

"I'd call the American Identity Party something nefarious. I'd call Hesterville something nefarious. I'd call this approach something underhanded and nefarious."

He did not immediately respond.

"You are being exceedingly hostile, Congressman. I accept your conditions. We'll be there at seven tomorrow. I have just one request."

"I'm listening."

"Can we keep the hostility level low and just concentrate on business?"

"I'll see you tomorrow at seven. Coffee and tea will be served."

Chapter Forty-three

Bruce Halliday was my first rebuttal witness to Evan Winemaker's testimony regarding the Documentary Hypothesis. It took all my powers of concentration to block out thoughts of the meeting with Farragut and focus on the witness and his testimony.

Dr. Halliday was a large man with thick white hair, a bow-tie and an expansive manner. After he was sworn in, he settled himself comfortably. He took a pair of half glasses from his pocket, polished them with a handkerchief and put them gingerly on his nose. Then he lowered his head slightly and peered around the courtroom over the top of his glasses.

"Dr. Halliday," I said, "what are your academic credentials?"

"I teach biblical studies and ancient Semitic languages at Yale."

"Were you present in the court when Dr. Winemaker gave his testimony?"

"I was."

"I'd like you to comment on some statements he made. Let's start with the issue of doublets. Dr. Winemaker told the court that the two divergent accounts of the creation story represent a doublet. Do you agree?"

"I do not. This literary form is common in ancient Near Eastern inscriptions, which begin with a general statement and then zero in on specific aspects. Many inscriptions from

Urartu, for instance, begin with a paragraph that describes a military victory achieved by the chariots of the god Haldi, followed by a description of the same victory achieved by the king. Does that mean we should separate the inscription into the H source for Haldi and the K source for the king?"

"Obviously not."

"In Genesis as well," he said, "the account starts with a description of creation in the broadest terms, and then it reviews the creation in closer focus. The minor duplications are meaningless. You see, the Germanic style of telling a story is linear, in a straight line. The Hebrew style – in fact, the prevalent style in the ancient Near East – was to tell a story in a sort of spiral, circling in on the story in ever narrowing circles."

"Interesting. How about the difference in the order of creation? Why does the first account speak of plants, animals and humans as the order of creation and the second as humans, plants, animals?"

"That's easily explained. The first account gives the chronological order of creation. The second gives the order of importance, which begins with humans, of course, followed by plants, which provide food for the humans. Animals are last, since humans were forbidden to eat meat at that point."

"And why does the first story say that 'male and female were created,' which implies that they were created together, while the second story tells of the woman being created after the man?"

"Here again, we see the distinction between general and specific. In the first story, which is general, we're given the bare fact that man and woman were both created on the same day. In the more specific story, we spiral in on the details and discover that they were created in sequence. All the discrepancies can easily be resolved in this way. Moreover ..."

"Yes, Dr. Halliday?"

"Well, in the first place, it seems unreasonable that this hypothetical editor splicing together these strips of parchment would begin his work with two contradictory creation stories. This hypothetical editor must have considered them complementary, so why should we think otherwise?"

"Indeed," I said. "Basically, you're saying, 'What was this guy thinking by starting his book with two contradictory stories back to back? Did he think no one would catch on?' Is that correct?"

"Well, yes. But I'm looking at it from a more scholarly angle. If the alleged editor, for whatever reason, considered them complementary, how can we use that as proof that there are two contradictory sources?"

For over an hour, I led the witness through a rebuttal of some of Winemaker's testimony regarding other discrepancies.

"Now let's talk about the divine names," I said. "Is there a problem with the Bible sometimes using the E name and sometimes the J name?"

"None at all. In fact, other divine names are also used. Should we designate sources for those as well? It's elegant variation. Anyway, if you have even the most basic knowledge of ancient inscriptions, you would see that different names are used all the time in the same account. For instance, the Berlin Stela –"

"Excuse me, Dr. Halliday, but could you tell us what a stela is?"

"Of course. It's a stone slab or a pillar carved or inscribed to commemorate an event or a person. This particular stela is an Egyptian stone that uses five different names for the god Osiris. In addition to Osiris, we read Wennofer, Khent-amen-tiu, Neb Abydos and Nuter. No one in his right mind would suggest that these revealed the hands of O, W, K, NA and N writers. The same phenomenon of multiple divine names occurs in Mesopotamian, Canaanite, Hurrian and Hittite inscriptions. The use of multiple divine names should not ring any alarm bells."

"Are there any guidelines for when the one is used or

the other?"

"Different ideas have been advanced. The Midrashic solution is that the E name is used when God is manifesting the attribute of strict justice, while the J name is used to indicate the attribute of merciful judgment. Also, Dr. Cassuto has quite an elaborate set of rules that seem to work well, the central rule being that the J name, which is specific, is used when God is relating to the Israelites, while the E name is used when God is relating to all the nations of the world. Do you want me to elaborate on this?"

"No, we get the idea," I said. "Let's go on. One final point. Dr. Winemaker seemed to believe that religions develop by an evolutionary process, and therefore, he felt compelled to view the alleged sources as representing the different stages of the development of Judaism. What is your opinion?"

The witness shook his head. "Again, we come into contact with nineteenth century German thinking that refuses to be dislodged from the academic community. According to Friedrich Hegel, everything proceeds slowly toward higher stages of development, primitive to advanced. There are no radical changes. But history has shown us otherwise, especially the history of the ancient world. Three times Egypt rises, falls dramatically and rises again – after the Old, Middle and New Kingdoms. In Mesopotamia, we witness the successive flowering in full-blown form of Sumerian, Babylonian and Assyrian civilizations. We find evidence of drastic change in all aspects of civilization – political, social, economic and religious."

"So the historical argument is not valid?"

"It is not."

"Do you see any signs of erosion in the support for the Hypothesis in the academic community?"

"Actually, I do see some movement away from it. It's encouraging."

"Let's sum up. Is there reason to doubt the Bible was written by one author at more or less the time it claims to have been written?"

"None."

"I have no further questions. Thank you very much, Dr. Halliday."

I returned to the plaintiff's table. The judge jotted down a few notes and looked over at the defense table.

"Counselor," she said, "do you wish to cross-examine?"

"Yes, your honor. I do."

"Do you need much time?" said the judge. "If you do, we'll take a break now. If not, we'll just push through and then adjourn for the day."

"I don't need that much time, your honor," said Calabrese.

"Very well. Go ahead and cross-examine."

Calabrese pursed his lips and stepped to the lectern.

"Dr. Halliday, who do you think wrote the Bible?"

"I'm convinced it was written by one author in deep antiquity, because it reflects the ancient world in the second millennium B.C.E."

"Do you think Moses wrote it?"

"That's as good a choice as any. The Bible says Moses wrote it, and I have no scientific reason to doubt it."

"Dr. Halliday, you had all sorts of explanations for the anomalies in the text that lead scholars to the conclusion that the Bible is a composite of different source documents. But how do you explain that the criteria seem to coincide? You will find that the E source uses the E name and is also consistent in the language it uses, its attitudes, its interests. And the same consistency goes for the other sources. How do you explain that?"

Dr. Halliday laid both hands on the rail of the witness box. "If I were a physicist testing a theory, I'd only consider it proved if it worked all the time. I would reject it if it only worked most of the time. Most is just not good enough. As a scientist investigating the Bible, I demand the same standards. I have no patience for theories like the Hypothesis that have so many exceptions and emendations of the text when it violates the rules imposed on it. I do not approve of explaining all those exceptions as scribal errors or editorial changes. That is not sound scholarship."

"Dr. Halliday, are your views representative of the views of most scholars in the field of biblical studies?"

"No, but there are –"

"Are you accusing the majority of scholars in your field of unsound scholarship?"

"It is not their scholarship that is unsound, it is the assumptions –"

"Dr. Halliday, please give me just a yes or no answer."

The witness took off his glasses and polished them again. "If truth were determined by a majority vote, we'd all be Chinese."

"You're saying that most biblical scholars are mistaken?"

"I am."

"I have no more questions for this witness."

Calabrese returned to his place, and I stood up.

"Your honor, I have one more witness in rebuttal of Dr. Winemaker's testimony."

"Please call your witness."

"The plaintiff calls Dr. Sadhu Singh."

A tall Sikh with fierce eyes, a white turban and a long black beard came forward.

"Can we have your full name and occupation, sir?"

"My name is Sadhu Singh." He spoke in heavily accented English. "I'm Professor of Statistical Mathematics at Massachusetts Institute of Technology in Boston."

"Are you aware of a statistical study of the authorship of the Bible?"

"I am. A group of scientists at the Technion Institute in Haifa, Israel, headed by Yehuda Radday and Haim Shorr, did a statistical analysis of the Old Testament. It was published as *Genesis: An Authorship Study*."

"Can you give us a brief synopsis of their work?"

"The scientists involved applied objective scientific and mathematical methods to linguistic studies. They analyzed each word in the sample and recorded the absolute forms of nouns and verbs, word length, numbers and gender, prepositional prefixes, position in the verse. Samples were drawn from fairly homogenous texts. No poetry or legal material was used, so they were checking for the authorship of the supposed E and J sources. Instead of saying that the two sounded alike or different from each other, as many scholars have done, they limited themselves to objective criteria."

"Who were the scientists participating? Were they secular? Religious? Were they all Israelis? Europeans?"

"All kinds. One religious man, mostly seculars. Some Israelis. A German. Dr. David Noel Freedman, Professor of Religious Studies at the University of Michigan, a respected biblical scholar, wrote the preface."

"And what were the results of the study?"

"The evidence was overwhelming that J and E were written by the same author. The similarities were substantially greater than the internal similarities of the works of Kant and Goethe, which had internal similarity of twenty-two percent and eight percent respectively. The internal similarity percentage of the J and E documents was eighty-two percent. Stunning."

"Do you agree with the results, Dr. Singh?"

"It is hard to disagree. The mathematics is brilliant."

"On the basis of the mathematical analysis, are you convinced that J and E are one and the same document?"

"Absolutely."

"Thank you, Dr. Singh." I turned to Calabrese. "Your witness."

Calabrese stepped to the lectern.

"Dr. Singh, are you a religious man?"

"I am a religious Sikh. I have no interest in the Bible whatsoever. It means nothing to me one way or the other."

"This is a bit of a radical study, isn't it? An unconventional approach?"

"Yes."

"The study was published about thirty-five years ago, yes?"

"Yes."

"Has it gained wide acceptance in the academic community?"

"No. But –"

"A simple no is enough, Dr. Singh. Thank you. No more questions."

Chapter Forty-four

arragut arrived at my office ten minutes early accompanied by a man with a sloping forehead, a receding chin and thick glasses. On our side, we had Lavender and Marvin Williams, Nancy Hannah, Paul Blake, Jessica Davis and Rabbi Gutmacher. A stenographer sat at the end of the table.

"It looks like we're outnumbered," said Farragut.

"Are we on a battlefield?" I responded.

"I was just making conversation, Congressman. As I requested, let's keep the hostility level low."

"Very well, let's begin," I said. "This meeting is on the record. Everything said here will be recorded. For the record, let me state who is present at this meeting. The two principal parties to the meeting are Senator Frederick Farragut and Mrs. Lavender Williams. Also present is Major Williams, Mrs. Williams' husband. I am Adrian Taylor of Cain, Schmidt, Barrow and Taylor, Mrs. Williams' attorney. Ms. Mikhail is an associate at our firm. Mr. Blake is an employee of our firm. Ms. Davis is a neutral observer. Rabbi Gutmacher is an interested party."

I only gave first names for the principals, because I didn't want to give Jessica's first name. Farragut might have recognized the name Jessica Davis as the journalist of the trial and objected to her presence, but the common surname Davis raised no alarm bells. I was reasonably sure that he did not know what she looked like. I gave her name and identified her as a neutral observer, which she was in her professional capacity.

"Senator Farragut has brought a companion," I continued. "Sir, please identify yourself."

"My name is John Smith," said the man without a brow or a chin. "I am Senator Farragut's attorney."

"Is your name really John Smith?" I said.

He grinned. "It is indeed. John Smith is the most common name in America. There are tens of thousands of us. But when people meet one of us, they almost always think it's an alias. Would you like to see my identification?"

"That won't be necessary, sir." Despite myself, I decided that I liked him. "For the record, we have Senator Farragut's attorney, whose name is really John Smith. Very well, let's begin. Senator?"

Farragut cleared his throat. "Congressman, you've done a great job at the trial. But you've done an even greater job generating public interest in the trial. This creates an embarrassing situation for the American Identity Party. You've succeeded in linking us with this trial, and therefore, your successes are viewed as our failures. They undermine our message."

"But isn't that legitimate? Isn't the discrediting of the Bible the basis of the teachings of Sanford Johns?"

"Sanford Johns is an extremist. I consider myself a Southern gentleman and good Christian. I don't think Jesus wants us to surrender the country to Jews and blacks. Or any other mongrel race. But our rank and file members believe that Jesus wants us to love every damn human being. They have to be told that the Bible is false, and that Jesus and Mohammed were just a couple of fools taken in by the hoax."

"What do want from Mrs. Williams?" I said.

He turned to Lavender. "I want to make you an offer. Drop your lawsuit, and we will pay you five million dollars."

"Why would I accept five million dollars from people who are out to destroy the blacks and other mongrel races, as you called us?"

"Mrs. Williams, I have no quarrel with you. You are obviously a charming and gracious lady. I would be honored to be your friend. Our party is fighting for the survival of our race, just as you people are fighting for the survival of your race. What you do here in this trial, one way or the other, will have no effect on the outcome of the struggle, but it may cause us some temporary discomfort. Avoiding this discomfort is worth five million dollars to us. And five million dollars is a lot of money. It will definitely have an effect on the outcome of your family's personal struggles. It will change your life for the better. Your attorney is on a quixotic mission to avenge his grandson, but you have no skin in the game. Why not take the money?"

"Mrs. Williams is not at liberty to accept your offer," I said.

"And why is that?"

"Because she has assigned her settlement rewards to Rabbi Gutmacher's yeshivah."

"We are aware of that agreement, Congressman," said John Smith. "However, that applies only to a settlement offered by the defendants. This is an offer by an independent party. She is free to accept it."

"Have you seen a copy of the agreement, Mr. Smith?"

"I have."

"The agreement states clearly that Mrs. Williams has assigned her potential award, and any other financial benefit she may derive from the trial, to Rabbi Gutmacher's yeshivah."

"A settlement offer by the defendants is a financial benefit that derives from the trial. An independent offer cannot be considered a financial benefit derived from the trial. The connection to the trial is only circumstantial."

"I understand your argument, and we disagree. If Mrs. Williams accepts your offer and fails to see the trial through to completion, she'll forfeit the money paid by the yeshivah, which is being held for her in escrow. But she will not be able to collect the five million you're offering. The yeshivah will fight it in court. Isn't that so, Rabbi Gutmacher?"

"Absolutely," said the rabbi.

"Do you represent the yeshivah, Congressman?" said Smith.

"I do not. The yeshivah has its own attorney."

"Give us a minute. I want to confer with my client."

Farragut and Smith held a whispered conference for five minutes.

"Congressman, you are being obstructionist," said Farragut. "You have a responsibility to your client, and you are acting against her interests. We are on the record. If you continue to be unreasonable, we will file a complaint with the Bar."

"That's an empty threat, Senator. The yeshivah is entitled to pursue any moneys to which it feels entitled. I am not the yeshivah's attorney. It is not in the interests of my client to forfeit a substantial guaranteed payment in the questionable hopes of receiving an even larger payment after a long, difficult and expensive lawsuit."

Farragut sighed. "We have another offer, Mrs. Williams."

"I'm here."

"We have connections with a publishing house that is offering you a book deal. They want you to write a book about your experiences during this interesting episode. You will receive an advance against royalties in the sum of five million dollars."

I shook my head. "Same problem. The yeshivah would go after the five million dollars from the publishing company."

"A book advance," said Smith, "would certainly not be considered a financial benefit derived from the trial. If a company were to buy the rights to a litigator's financial benefits from the trial, and five years later, the litigator published his or her story, could the company sue for the royalties from that book? Certainly not. We are offering Mrs. Williams a book deal. The five million dollars are an advance against royalties."

"You could argue that in court, Mr. Smith," I said. "We would argue otherwise. The five million dollars are not for her story. The y're conditional on her dropping the lawsuit against the school board. We can let the courts decide. Mrs. Williams would be ill-advised to take the risk."

Farragut put his hand on Smith's arm and shook his head. It was clearly useless to argue further.

"Mrs. Williams, listen to me carefully," he said. "No matter what your attorney is telling you, it is in your best interest to drop this lawsuit and step away. Listen to my words. Do not pursue this lawsuit. Take our offer and step away."

"Did I hear a threat, Senator?" I said.

"There was no threat," he said. "John, did you hear a threat?"

"No, sir," said Smith. "I heard no threat. Just some good advice."

Paul Blake stood up and walked over to Farragut. He pulled himself to his full impressive height and leaned down until his face was just inches from Farragut's face.

"You listen to me, you worthless piece of horse dung," he said. "If you dare threaten anyone again, I will kick your *tukhes*, as they say in Yiddish. If anyone associated with you or your movement, with your knowledge or without, harms one hair on anyone in the Williams family or anyone in the Taylor family, I or one of my boys will break every single bone in your body. Your body! That is not a threat. It's a solemn promise. You had better make them untouchable. Do you hear me?"

Farragut did not respond.

"Do you hear me, scumbag?" he shouted directly into Farragut's ear.

"I hear you," Farragut muttered.

Smith stood up. "I think we're done here."

"I'd like to say something to the Senator," said Lavender, "while we're on the record. If you had offered me a hundred million dollars guaranteed, I would have had one response to you. No way in Hell!"

Chapter Forty-five

Rabbi Gutmacher and I moved to my office after the others left. We hadn't spoken for months. When I had called to invite him to the meeting, he mentioned that he was following the trial online, and I wanted to hear his comments. I was also eager to hear some more about David.

Fifteen minutes later, there was a light tap on the door, and Jessica stuck her head in.

"Am I disturbing?" she said. "I decided to come back. I just need a minute or two."

"Sure," I said. "Come on in and sit down. You can speak freely in front of Rabbi Gutmacher."

She gave him a smile and sat down.

"Hello, rabbi," she said. "It's nice meeting you. I covered David Goldfield's funeral in Crown Heights. Your eulogy was amazing."

"Thank you," said the rabbi. "And I'm following your wonderful coverage of the trial. Mr. Taylor was telling me that he thinks you should be up for a Pulitzer. Today's session should help."

She grinned. "Talk about amazing. The meeting couldn't have gone better. Mr. Taylor, you trapped Farragut in the web of his own words. Before I write the story, I just have a few questions."

"Fire away," I said.

"Was there anything unethical about what we just did, either for me or for you?"

"Well, I don't know how this could be unethical for you. You were introduced as a neutral observer. I think we can safely say that you are."

"I'm supposed to be."

"There was no misrepresentation. You were not obligated to tell him that you are a journalist. He agreed to go on the record. He never claimed confidentiality."

"But if he had known I was a journalist, he would never have spoken on the record in front of me."

"That was his fault. Everyone was introduced to him with an explanation of their standing at the meeting. You were introduced as a neutral observer. He should have asked more about your standing. He failed to do so. You were not required to correct his mistakes."

"Okay. That's what I thought." She paused. "Now let's talk about you. I really appreciate what you've done for me these last few weeks, and I want to be careful not to write anything that'll hurt you."

"You don't need to worry about me. Write the story exactly as you saw it. The meeting was a trap, but I did not give him misleading information. I just failed to mention that you're a journalist. I don't think I had a responsibility to do so. We were on the record with a stenographer present."

"Were you taking a risk? Could this come back to bite you?"

I shrugged. "I'm on a campaign to hurt these bastards, and I can tolerate a little risk. But what's my risk? A lawsuit? I don't think so. What would he claim? That I played him for a fool? It would cause him way too much embarrassment. A complaint to the Bar Association? Maybe. I wouldn't get disbarred. At the most, I'd be reprimanded. I can handle it."

"Can I report on this conversation or is it on background?"

"You can report it. The main points of the story, it seems to me, are that Farragut has no confidence in the case against the Bible, although the American Identity Party claims the Bible is clearly a hoax; that he begged Mrs. Williams to drop the lawsuit and even made veiled threats; that he called Sanford Johns an extremist and claimed to be a Christian. That's good stuff."

"It sure is," she said, "but this little caper of yours adds a lot of spice to it. It makes it sensational. Farragut will be a laughingstock. One more question. How many of the others at the meeting were privy to your plan?"

"No one else. I wanted everyone to act naturally. Words, facial expressions, body language. The only one I told was you."

She stood up. "Perfect. Thank you very much, Mr. Taylor. Nice meeting you, rabbi."

"Same here," said the rabbi. "When this is over, Ms. Davis, you should come to Crown Heights and write interesting stories about Chabad. I'd be happy to show you around."

She gave him a speculative look. "I might just take you up on that, rabbi. Good night!"

I was pleased that she had come back. It showed her thoroughness and her attention to detail. I really wanted her to be considered for a Pulitzer, partly out of gratitude, and partly to draw more attention to the trial and to the memory of my grandson. Remember David Goldfield! That was my slogan.

I texted June that I would miss dinner, then I ordered sandwiches from the kosher café on Lexington Avenue. We had coffee and soft drinks in the office. Rabbi Gutmacher and I discussed the testimony at the trial for over two hours. It was basically a post-mortem; there was nothing I could do about the previous testimony. I did give him a preview, however, of the evidence I would present on the subject of archaeology.

"I want to ask you a question," I said. "Chabad people believe the Bible is historical."

"Almost all observant Jews believe that."

"Are you sure?"

"As sure as a person can be."

"What makes you so sure? I read somewhere that it's because that's what you've been taught by your fathers, and fathers never lie to their children. Is that why you believe it?"

"Come on. Do you really think fathers never lie to their children? Have you ever lied to your children?"

"I have only one child. Have I ever lied to Margaret? I'm sure I have. So why then do you believe it? Do you accept it on faith?"

"I'm not sure I understand your question. Are you asking if we accept it on blind faith, even though there's no rational reason to accept it?"

I rubbed my eyebrows, as I usually do when I feel discomfort. "I suppose that's kind of what I'm asking."

"It's all right. We call it *mesorah*, which means tradition, or *emunah pshutah*, which means simple faith. Not blind faith. Simple faith. It has a deeper meaning." He paused to stroke his beard; maybe that's what he usually did when he felt discomfort. "You're a lawyer. Tell me, are all Americans obligated to abide by the Constitution?"

"Of course."

"But why? Who in this generation signed on to the Constitution? The Constitution was signed over two centuries ago. Why should people in this generation be obligated by the commitment of people who are long dead?"

"That's an excellent question. It's because the obligation devolves on the society as a whole, and all who are part of the society must honor its obligations."

"Exactly! We all have dual personalities. We're individuals, but we're also cells in the corpus of society. Cells come and cells go, but the corpus never changes. A murderer cannot demand to be released after ten years in prison because just about all his cells have been replaced. The person is still the same. Only the cells have changed. It is the same with society. The society as a whole is unchanged. Only the worn-out cells have been replaced. If we're a part of society, we're obligated."

"I agree. That is basically what I was saying."

"Tell me, was there a civil war? Were the blacks enslaved?"

"Of course."

"How do you know?"

"I don't understand," I said. "We have mountains of evidence."

"But aren't there mountains of evidence about the Holocaust? Oceans? And Holocaust deniers still find ways to dispute the evidence. Testimonials are lies. Films and photos are doctored." He paused. "Most evidence is not absolutely conclusive. Nonetheless, you know there was slavery in the United States with absolute certainty, don't you?"

"I do."

"Are you absolutely sure?"

"Yes, I'm absolutely sure. Why don't you explain it to me?"

"I will. The only evidence that cannot be disputed is memory. If one person remembers something, the memory may be mistaken; eyewitness accounts are notoriously unreliable. But if a hundred people remember the same thing, you can be sure it's true."

"But who remembers slavery?"

"The collective remembers it. As you said, society assumes collective obligations that survive its individual members. Society incurs collective guilt. Society develops collective personality traits. Society also has a collective memory that survives long after its individual cells are replaced. The United States remembers slavery, because race is perhaps the biggest part of our social consciousness today. The memory is driven by powerful emotions. Hatred. Bigotry. Resentment. It's passed down from generation to generation in a thousand ways, not by testimony but by shared experience. When a white child hears his parent ranting against the blacks, or a black child hears his parent railing against the legacy of injustice, those emotions and the memories that drive them are passed along to the next generation. And to the one after that.

Our society remembers slavery collectively, and as a member of our society, as a cell in its corpus, you share that memory."

"I see where you're going."

"I'll give you a good example. In 1999, after the collapse of the Yugoslav confederation, there was a war in Kosovo. Once they were set loose, the Serbs avenged themselves on the Kosovars for their defeat at the Battle of Kosovo. When did that battle take place?"

"I don't know. 1700?"

"1389! Six hundred and thirty years later, the memory of that stinging defeat is still very much alive. No one individual remembers it, but the society does. A Serb child hears his parent saying, 'If I get my hands on a Kosovar, I'd rip out his throat,' and the memory instantly passes into him.' He is absolutely certain that the defeat took place. And if Serbs and Kosovars kill each other over it in 1999, I am also absolutely certain. Collective memories don't lie."

"So how does all that relate to you?"

"Collective memories are usually driven by seething emotions. We remember Lincoln and slavery. Perhaps we remember George Washington. But we do not remember Columbus. We only know him from the history books, and you know what they say. The victors write the history books. I believe Columbus existed, because I have no reason to doubt it, not because I'm objectively sure of it. The Jewish people have a collective memory of the Exodus, not because we're driven by the thirst for revenge but because the Bible ritualizes the memory, connecting it to every aspect of our daily lives and our calendar cycles. Observant Jewish life keeps the collective memory alive. We don't need external evidence. We know our life, and we know that the memory is true. That, in my opinion, is the meaning of tradition and simple faith."

I looked at him with wonder. "Are you saying that you are living archaeological stelae, that the memories were inscribed on the Jewish collective thousands of years ago and that they are still there to be read?"

He gave me a broad smile. "That's exactly what I'm saying."

"And what about David? Would he have shared this memory? After all, he wasn't brought up observant."

"It doesn't matter. Anyone who becomes integrated into a collective assumes all the features of the collective. Immigrants to the United States, after they've been here for a while, share the collective memory of slavery. Anyone who converts or becomes observant shares the collective memory of the Jewish people."

Chapter Forty-six

The trial was heading for the archaeology phase. Calabrese's next witness was a short, rail-thin man with a deeply sunburned face. His eyes flitted around the courtroom as he walked to the witness box. He took his seat and ran his fingers through his sparse hair.

"Good morning, sir," said Calabrese. "Please state your name and occupation."

"Dr. Jamison Potemkin," said the witness in a surprisingly deep voice. "I'm professor of biblical archaeology at the University of Rhode Island."

"Dr. Potemkin, I understand that archaeology can be a technical and arcane field. Is that not so?"

"It can be for amateurs. For the true archaeologist, all the minutiae are exceedingly interesting."

"No doubt. Most of us here in this courtroom are just amateurs, so I'll ask you to couch your answers in layman's terms."

"I'll do my best."

"Very well. Based on your knowledge of biblical archaeology, would you say the Bible is a reliable historical source?"

"When you say the Bible, you're covering an exceedingly long period, from the creation story until the destruction of the Jerusalem Temple in 586 B.C.E. and beyond. Your question has to be more specific."

"That's fine. I'll ask specific questions. Before we go on

to talk about archaeology, however, two quick points about chronology. First, the Bible states that Pharaoh Shishak went up against Jerusalem in the fifth year of the reign of King Rehoboam, son of King Solomon. In what year did Shishak conduct his campaign against the Kingdom of Judah?"

"It was 925 B.C.E."

"That means that Solomon died in 930 B.C.E. Is that consistent with the conventional chronology?"

"Yes, it is."

"Does anyone in the academic community question the conventional chronology as you've explained it to this court?"

"No, sir. It's universally accepted."

"Thank you. Now let's go on to more serious issues –"

I stood up. "Your honor, Counsel has introduced new testimony. I'd like to cross-examine."

"Go ahead, counselor," said the judge.

I turned to the witness. "Dr. Potemkin, how do we know that Shishak invaded Judah in 925 B.C.E.?"

"It's an established fact."

"But how was it established? Isn't it true, that this is one of the points of synchronicity by which Egyptian chronology is established? Isn't the date for Shishak's campaign derived from the conventional chronology of Israel and Judah rather than the other way around?"

"Yes."

"All of ancient chronology is a muddle, isn't it?" I said.

Calabrese stood up. "Objection, your honor."

"I withdraw the question." I went back to my seat. "You can continue, Mr. Calabrese."

Calabrese riffled through some papers on his table and scribbled notes. Finally, he put down his pen and returned to the lectern.

"Dr. Potemkin, you were making a distinction between different parts of the Bible. Please continue with the point you were making."

"I was saying that ... Look, if we limit ourselves to Israelite history and start with the Patriarchs, the Bible covers a period of well over a thousand years. Some radical minimalists deny all Israelite history, saying it was all invented during the Hellenistic period under the Greeks. I do not subscribe to that school of thought. Nor do most moderate archaeologists."

"All right."

"As we come closer to the modern era, we find corroboration of the biblical account from extra-biblical sources. Aramean, Moabite and Assyrian inscriptions mention Israelite kings. We have coins, seals and other remnants of what we call the material culture."

"From excavations?"

"Yes, of course. But as you go back further, there is practically no outside corroboration of the Biblical account. There was a time when archaeologists believed archaeology would confirm the biblical story. In recent generations, however, we've come to the conclusion that archaeology supports the view that the early accounts of the Bible are pure fiction."

"You mean there was no Israel in ancient times?"

"We know there was an Israel in 1207 B.C.E. The famous Merneptah Stela mentioned an Israel in the Judean hills."

"And what is the Merneptah Stela?"

"It's a large stone monument commissioned by Pharaoh Merneptah. The monument is densely inscribed with Merneptah's glorious military victories. Other than that, we hear nothing about Israel in the Egyptian record. There is no mention of the settlement of a patriarchal Israelite family in Egypt."

"I see."

"It's also preposterous that an Israelite named Joseph would become the second most powerful person in Egypt. There is absolutely no mention of the bondage of Israelites in Egypt. There's no record of an Exodus. There's no record of many travels and encampments in the desert for forty years."

"How about the War of Conquest under Joshua?"

"There's no record of a military conquest of Canaan. No record of a wide-scale destruction of Canaanite cities. No Israelite inscriptions from this period confirming any of the Bible's claims. In fact, we've never found any Israelite inscriptions, although we've found inscriptions from just about every nation in the area; it certainly shows the lack of sophistication of any Israelite kingdoms that may have existed in ancient times."

"It does make you think, doesn't it? Go on."

"Yes, where was I? Ah, yes. The Bible reports that the Israelites besieged and destroyed the city of Jericho, but the archaeological record, according to the prestigious archaeologist Dame Kathleen Kenyon, shows that Jericho was not inhabited at that time. That discovery was the last nail in the coffin of the maximalists such as William Albright and his school."

"You've made many provocative points, Dr. Potemkin. I'd like to review them one by one, if you please. You say it's unlikely that an Israelite such as Joseph would rise to a position of supreme power in Egypt."

"Pure fantasy. Romantic fiction."

"And you say there's no record of Israelites enslaved in Egypt?"

"According to the Bible, Israelites in large numbers, perhaps hundreds of thousands, were enslaved in Egypt. Now, the Egyptians kept meticulous records. They left huge archives that include records of government affairs, military records and business. One would expect that the enslavement of hundreds of thousands of people would be recorded. But it isn't. Not a trace of their being there, not a trace of their escape into the desert."

"And you said something about no records of their encampments."

"That's right. According to the Bible, the Israelites camped at forty-two places in the desert before entering Canaan. We found no trace of such an encampment anywhere. You might argue that we can't be sure of the exact locations of these camps. Two of the places, however, can be identified with reasonable assurance – Kadesh Barne'a and Etzion Geber. Yet in neither of these has a single thirteenth century pottery sherd been found."

"And the Biblical story of the conquest of Canaan?"

"The archaeological record shows there was no violent conquest. The Canaanite city of Hazor was destroyed. That's true. But there's no record of thirteenth century destruction for the other cities recorded as conquered in the Book of Joshua. As for the colorful story of the siege of Jericho and the sounding of the ram's horn that brought its walls tumbling down, there's no archaeological record of habitation in Jericho at that time."

"Tell me, Dr. Potemkin, is there a record of an increase of population in Canaan during the thirteenth century?"

"Yes, there was apparently a significant increase in population, mostly in the Judean hill country. But even so, the population was nowhere near the hundreds of thousands reported by the Bible. According to archaeological data, the population of Canaan in the thirteenth century B.C.E. was approximately 45,000 in 250 sites. By the eight century B.C.E., the total population of Judah and Israel was about 160,000 in 500 sites."

"Not very great numbers indeed. Obviously, the Bible's figures cannot be taken seriously. But nonetheless, as you have said, there was undeniably a significant population increase in these lands in the thirteenth century. How do you account for that increase?"

"There are different opinions among archaeologists. All agree there was an influx of a different population group, because the luxury implements and fine ceramic pottery of the sophisticated Canaanite cities were replaced by rough and primitive implements and ceramics.

"Who were these new people?"

"The German scholar Albrecht Alt suggests that the new arrivals were the result of peaceful infiltration of peoples from surrounding areas. George Mendenhall suggests there was a peasant revolt in the Canaanite cities. This theory was dismissed, because no archaeological evidence supports it. Israel Finkelstein suggests they are the result of the resedentarization of nomads."

"The what? Please explain."

"Of course. Dr. Finkelstein suggested that, because of difficult times, many city people abandoned urban life and became nomadic shepherds. Then, in the thirteenth century, they decided to settle down again to a sedentary life. Thus, we find a sudden increase in population. Nomads do not register in the archaeological record, but cities, towns and villages do. I subscribe to this point of view. The Israelites were originally Canaanites."

"Interesting. One more question. The Bible reports that King David and King Solomon ruled over a large and glorious kingdom. Does archaeology support or contradict this view?"

"The Bible reports that King Solomon rebuilt the northern cities of Megiddo, Hazor and Gezer. In all these places, archaeologists uncovered monumental palace remains. They also had characteristic city gates that had three chambers on each side. These came to be identified as the Solomonic architectural style."

"Was that corroboration?"

"It didn't turn out that way. At first, there was some excitement, as many thought they'd found corroboration for the Bible. But it was a false alarm. The sites were tested with carbon-14 dating, and it was discovered that the ruins were over a century younger, well after the time of David and Solomon. It appears that Israel under David and Solomon was at best a backward mountain kingdom."

"Please sum up for us, Dr. Potemkin."

"Archaeology has demonstrated that Israel began modestly in the hill country of Judah and did not reach the level of a respectable regional kingdom until late in its history. The Bible is a fantasy."

"Thank you, Dr. Potemkin. No more questions."

It was my turn. I took a deep breath and walked to the lectern. When we were discussing the anachronisms, doublets, source document and all the rest of the textual analysis, I felt we were on solid ground. The evidence and simple logic militated against the notion of a flawed composite document spliced together by editors. Archaeology would prove a more difficult task. The archaeological evidence against the Bible was mostly negative evidence, which is notoriously unreliable. But the waters were murky at best. We had worked hard to prepare for this phase of the trial. The time had come to implement our research.

"Dr. Potemkin, you've made a blanket statement," I began, "that there was no significant Israelite presence in Egypt. Your basis for this sweeping generalization is that there's no record of it. Would you consider this negative evidence?"

"I suppose."

"Isn't it a rule in archaeology and in general that absence of evidence is not evidence of absence? Isn't it generally assumed that negative evidence only proves that you have not found anything but that you very well may?"

"This is true. Nonetheless, you would expect to see some record."

"Where would you expect to find such records?"

"On papyrus rolls from Egyptian archives."

"And since the Israelites were in the Nile Delta, isn't that where you would expect to find such records? Like in Heliopolis or Pi-Ramesses?"

"Yes."

"Now we know that such archives existed from tomb records in the dry sands of Saqqara, isn't that so?"

"Yes."

"What happened to those archives?"

"They have not survived."

"Why not?" I said.

"Because the climate is wet, and the ground is muddy."

"I see. How many papyri from these archives have survived?"

"None."

"Nothing? Not even a scrap?"

"Not even a scrap."

"So, there could have been volumes of records of Israelites in those archives that disintegrated in the heat and the mud. Isn't that so?"

"Who knows what was in those archives? There could have been anything. But just because the archives were destroyed doesn't prove that there were Israelites mentioned there. If the biblical narrative is true, you would expect to see some record somewhere. Just something. Anything."

"Are there records for Semitic people infiltrating Egypt in times of drought and famine, as the Bible recounts?"

"Yes."

"Do Egyptian inscriptions identify different Semitic groups?"

"No, they're all called Semites."

"And there are inscriptions in the tomb of the vizier of Thutmose III of Semites making bricks, aren't there?"

"Yes. But they're described as prisoners of war."

"But don't we have a basis for Egyptians using captive Semites for forced labor? Doesn't the Bible speak of an *erub rab*, a mixed multitude, joining the Israelites in the Exodus? Couldn't these have been other captive Semitic peoples as well as disgruntled Egyptians?"

"Anything could be. We don't believe it."

"Dr. Potemkin, this court is not interested in your beliefs. We're looking for facts. And you've given us hardly any facts. You say the Joseph story is romantic fiction, that it would have been impossible for a Semite to rise to such power in Egypt. Is that correct?"

"Yes, that is correct."

"How about Aper-El, vizier to Amenhotep III and Akhenaten? Wasn't he a Semite?"

"Maybe. His name would indicate he was."

"So, if Aper-El could be vizier, why couldn't Joseph? In fact, didn't Jaroslav Cerny observe that during the Ramesside era it became quite common for men of foreign origin to serve in high office at court?"

"It's unclear. Anyway, the Joseph story supposedly took place before the Ramesside era."

Time to switch gears.

"Let's move on to Solomon's construction projects in Megiddo, Hazor and Gezer. You say these projects are dated more than a century after King Solomon. When did King Solomon live?"

"In the late tenth century B.C.E. That is almost 1000 B.C.E."

"How do you know that?"

"We can date it back from the destruction of the Temple he built. According to the Book of Kings, the Temple stood for four hundred years. Since it was destroyed in 586 B.C.E., it must have been built around 990 B.C.E. Those palaces in Megiddo, Hazor and Gezer were built in the mid-800s B.C.E."

"I see. You're using the conventional chronology. But if you follow the Talmudic chronology – that the Temple was destroyed in 420 B.C.E. – everything falls into place neatly, doesn't it? The Exodus and Conquest take place exactly when the Bible claims they took place, and Solomon's construction projects take place exactly when the Bible says they took place. Isn't that so?"

"What do you want me to say? I think that chronology is wrong."

A quick glance at the jury told me that my point had registered. There was no need to belabor the point. It would only be counterproductive.

"All right," I said. "Let's talk about the significant increase in population in Canaan in the thirteenth century. If the Bible is fiction, how did the Bible writers, supposedly writing seven hundred years later, know exactly when to place the Israelite influx into Canaan so that it would coincide with a sudden and rapid growth in population? Were they archaeologists?"

"I have no answer to that question. Perhaps they had a tradition."

"A tradition? They remembered nothing factual about their history, but they knew exactly when they arrived. Tell me, was there anything unusual about the remains from these thirteenth century Israelite habitations?"

"What do you mean? Their pottery and implements were relatively primitive, as I mentioned before."

"Was there anything unusual about their eating habits? You know ... about the kind of meat they ate?"

"Oh, yes, of course. No pig bones were found in these settlements."

"Were pig bones found in the habitations of the Canaanites, the Philistines and the other peoples of the area?"

"Yes, many pig bones."

"But no pig bones in the Israelite habitations?"

"None."

"How do you explain that?"

"We have no explanation for it. It's a mystery."

"Isn't it a strange coincidence that the Bible forbids pig meat? Could that have been the reason for the absence of pig bones?"

"It couldn't have been, because the Bible did not exist at the time. The Israelites probably decided not to eat pigs and then wrote it into the Bible."

"Why would they do such a thing? Pigs are a good source of meat. They're also easy to feed, because they'll eat anything. Why would a people struggling to eke out a livelihood deprive themselves of pig meat? Is there any other instance of a people deciding not to eat pig meat?"

"I know of no other instance, and I cannot speak for the motivation of the early Israelites. They may have felt that abstaining from pig meat would make them stand out among their neighbors. Who knows? They may have considered abstinence from pig meat a sign of distinction."

"That is your thesis?"

"I do not have a thesis. As I said before, it's a mystery."

"I see. I have no more questions for this witness, your honor. I'd like to call my next rebuttal witness."

Chapter Forty-seven

My next rebuttal witness was a rotund man with round rimless glasses, gray-streaked brown hair, a gray jacket and a gray turtleneck sweater. That's what John Lennon would have looked like, I thought, if he'd lived to grow older and fatter. I'd spent a lot of time with this witness. I'd also told him about my own discovery of evidence for the Exodus in the archaeological record. He wanted to use it in his testimony, but I'd asked him not to reveal his source for that information.

"Please state your name and occupation, sir," I began.

"My name is Dr. Kyle Webster. I'm professor of archaeology and ancient Near Eastern history at the University of Pennsylvania."

"Dr. Webster, let's start with the Joseph story. Is it plausible?"

"Oh, yes. Eminently plausible. There are numerous indications of its authenticity. Scholars with specialized training in Egyptology have long recognized the powerful Egyptian elements of the story. I refer you to Dr. Kenneth Kitchen, one of the greatest scholars in the world, head and shoulders above everyone else in Egyptology and comparative Near Eastern studies. Specifically, I recommend his latest book, *On the Reliability of the Old Testament*. It is totally authoritative."

"Any others?"

"Many. I would also recommend Dr. James K. Hoffmeier's

Israel in Egypt, an excellent piece of scholarship. Dr. Alan R. Schulman, quoted by Hoffmeier, claims that the writer of the Joseph story must have had an exceedingly intimate knowledge of Egyptian life, literature and culture."

"Can you give us details of this intimate knowledge?"

"There are many. I'll try not to overload you. First, there's the average price of slaves. At the time of the Joseph story, it was indeed twenty shekels, as the Bible reports, but then it rose sharply. It's highly unlikely that later writers could guess the price of a slave centuries before."

"And the price of slaves at that time was discovered in the archaeological record?"

"It was."

"Would you consider that archaeological evidence for the early authorship of the Bible?"

"Most certainly. It's irrefutable evidence. At least for the Joseph story."

"What about the name Pharaoh?" I asked.

"Scholars are frustrated that the Bible does not mention the name of the Pharaoh of the enslavement or the Exodus, as the Bible does in the Books of the Prophets where we read about Pharaoh Necho or Hofra or Shishak. But not in the Books of Genesis and Exodus. Why the omission?"

"Why, indeed?"

"There's a good reason. Pharaoh means 'the great house' in Egyptian. It wasn't used as a title for the king until the middle of the second millennium B.C.E., about 1450 B.C.E. For the next five hundred years or so, the king was known just by the name Pharaoh without the addition of a personal name. If the Books of Genesis and Exodus were written during these five hundred years, they would not have identified an Egyptian king by any name other than Pharaoh, which was the accepted Egyptian custom. Afterward, personal names began to be added, and they indeed appear in the later books of the Prophets."

"Interesting. Anything else?"

"You already mentioned during your cross-examination of Dr. Potemkin that Semites did indeed reach high office in Egypt. That's an important piece of evidence, because how would a later writer have known such a thing? There is much more evidence. Would you like me to go on?"

"I think you have made a powerful case for the authenticity of the Joseph story, Dr. Webster. Let's move on to the Exodus."

"As you pointed out during cross-examination," he said, "the archives in the Nile Delta have not survived, but we do have a lot of indirect evidence for the presence of the Israelites in Egypt and the Exodus, some of which you have already covered yesterday during your cross-examination. Take for instance the Bible's statement that the Israelites asked for permission to go into the desert to worship their God. Strange request, wouldn't you say? Yet there is plenty of evidence that it was customary for laborers in Egypt to be given time off for religious observances. How would someone writing centuries later know this?"

"How, indeed? All right, let's talk about the desert travels of the Israelites. Dr. Potemkin seemed to feel that there should have been some trace left over, at least a few broken pieces of pottery. How come there is no trace of any habitation at any of those places at that time?"

"Well, Dr. Potemkin should not have been expecting to find traces of pottery. He himself said that nomads do not register in the archaeological record. People on the move, even if they're traveling at a leisurely pace, are not likely to bring along heavy ceramic pottery. You only go shopping for ceramics after you settle down. As long as you're on the road, you make do with leatherwork or skins. You see?"

"I do. So you're not disturbed by the absence of evidence of habitation at these sites?"

"Not at all. On the contrary, I believe the absence of habitation is actually strong proof to the authenticity of the desert itinerary."

"Really? How is that?"

"Look, it's common sense. The Israelites traveling through the desert would not have encamped at a spot already occupied by other people. They needed empty, uninhabited spots. That's obvious. Now if archaeologists had found that some of these purported sites of encampment had houses and pottery at the time, it would really raise questions about the itinerary. But as it is, everything works out perfectly. All forty-two camp sites were uninhabited at the time, so the Israelites had room to encamp. Now, could a writer living hundreds of years later have guessed that every single one of the forty-two places he picked out of a hat would be uninhabited back then, especially since some of them were inhabited during his own time?"

"Let me understand this. Are you saying that the mention of forty-two uninhabited places is actually proof of the antiquity of the Bible?"

"Exactly."

"How about the lack of evidence of the destruction of the Canaanite cities mentioned in the Conquest list of the Book of Joshua?"

"The Bible does not say they were destroyed but that they were smitten. Smitten does not mean destroyed. Why would they destroy the Canaanite cities? They weren't some foreign invaders who would burn, pillage and go back home. They were invaders, immigrants. They intended to live in this land. Moses had promised them they would live in houses other people had built. They weren't about to destroy their future homes. That's why the Conquest took so long. They couldn't just attack and destroy. They had to fight house to house, door to door, so that they wouldn't destroy the valuable property. Only a couple of cities, such as Hazor, had to be destroyed to break the resistance."

"How about there being no signs of habitation in Jericho at that time?"

"According to archaeological evidence, Jericho was destroyed by fire about 1550 B.C.E. and then was uninhabited for two hundred years. As Dr. Kitchen explains, when a new city is built on the ruins of the old, the ruins are preserved. But when the site is left uninhabited, the remains are destroyed by erosion and by scavenging for building materials. During these two hundred years, erosion wiped out almost all traces of the old Jericho. What we know of the old settlement is based on a few fragments. Then the city was resettled in 1350 B.C.E. When the Israelites destroyed the city again about a hundred years later, they established a taboo against rebuilding the city. As a result, it was uninhabited for another four hundred years. During that time, erosion and scavengers erased every trace of the city, as expected."

"Let's talk about the increase in population in Canaan during the thirteenth century B.C.E. What do you think of Dr. Potemkin's theory that the early Israelites were local Canaanites?"

The witness shook his head. "The archaeological evidence is clear that this is when the Israelites arrived on the scene. The archeological evidence also shows they were different from the indigenous population. Different implements and ceramics. Different architectural styles. Different dietary customs. Twist it as hard as you wish, you cannot make a reasonable case for them coming out of the local woodwork."

"What do you mean by architectural styles?"

"Their villages were oval, patterned after desert encampments."

"What does this prove? Why couldn't they have been nomads who were settling down, as Finkelstein claims?"

"Because this theory is unsound. Dr. William Dever takes it to pieces in *Who Were the Early Israelites and Where Did They Come from?* He points out that Finkelstein himself admits that nomads in Palestine in all periods up until the present comprise no more than ten to fifteen percent of the population. Yet during the thirteenth century B.C.E., the population of the hill country of Judah tripled. If all the nomads settled down and became farmers and villagers, you still wouldn't come close to accounting for the tremendous increase in population. If you don't accept the historical authenticity of the Bible, it's an insoluble mystery."

"Dr. Webster, I would like to talk to you about population. Yesterday, Dr. Potemkin testified, based once again on Finkelstein, that the population of the hill country of Judah in the thirteenth century was about 45,000 and that there were about 160,000 people in Judah in the eighth century. Do you agree?"

"No, I most emphatically do not. Let's just look at extra-biblical sources. According to the Sennaherib Stela, King Sennaherib of Assyria claimed to have exiled over two hundred thousand people from Judah to Assyria. According to Finkelstein, that's more than the total number of people who lived in Judah during that time. Not only does he disregard the information in the Bible, he also disregards the ancient inscription record."

"Well, Finkelstein didn't just make up those figures, did he? How did he arrive at those figures? Where did he go wrong?"

"Finkelstein arrives at his figures by using something called the Population Density Coefficient. It sounds complicated, but it's not. They measure the population density in modern-day settlements that feature primitive conditions without the benefits of modern technology. Life hasn't changed so much for these people in the last few thousand years. The population density in Jerusalem in 1918, as in Aleppo and Tripoli, was 51 people per dunam, which is about a quarter of an acre. But Finkelstein uses the figure of 25 people per dunam. Dr. Isaac Maitlis, an Israeli archaeologist, disputes these figures in *Excavating the Bible*. He bases his projections on population density figures for the Jewish Quarter of Jerusalem in 1870, which was 157 people per dunam, six times Finkelstein's number."

"Do you have any population density data a little further back in time than the last couple of centuries?"

"We most definitely have. The Book of Nehemiah lists 2,872 heads of households returning to Jerusalem from exile in Babylon. If we use the conservative figure of four people per family, that means about 12,000 people. The archaeological data show that Jerusalem at the time measured about 120 dunams, which give us a density of about 100 people per dunam. I suggest we work with the conservative figure of 100 people per dunam for ancient Israel and Judah."

"Can we use this to get an idea of the total population?"

"We can. I'll make a long story short. Archaeological studies have shown that in ancient times between three and seven percent of a country's population lived in cities, settlements that measure fifty dunams or more. This means that about ninety-five percent of the population lived in small villages in the countryside. Let's say it's only ninety percent, just to be on the safe side."

"You're saying that ancient societies were rural. Only ten percent urban. Correct?"

"Correct. According to Dr. Yigal Shilo, there were sixty settlements of fifty dunams or more west of the Jordan River during the time of the Kingdoms of Israel and Judah. At the density coefficient of one hundred per dunam, that means that each of these settlements had about five thousand, for a total urban population of at least three hundred thousand people. Since cities held only ten percent of the population, that iniicates a total population of at least three million people and probably more, not even counting the settlements east of the Jordan River."

"And this is in keeping with the figures in the Bible?"

"Very much so. It also fits perfectly with the information on the inscriptions of the Sennaherib Stela in Assyria."

"This is illuminating. Perhaps you can help us clear up another matter as well. Yesterday, Dr. Potemkin testified that there are no inscriptions on stelae and monuments in Israel and Judah such as are found in all the neighboring countries. He said that this raised questions about the sophistication of these kingdoms. Can you enlighten us about this matter?"

"My pleasure. You know, archaeologists love inscriptions. As much as you can potter about in the pottery, you're really just groping in the dark. But inscriptions! Ah, what a pleasure. Names! Places! Stories! The ancient world opens up. But in Israel ... no inscriptions. The problem is not that we haven't found any yet. Apparently, no Jewish kings, not even Herod the Great, who lived during the last century before the common era, left stone inscriptions. If not for Josephus, we wouldn't know who built Caesarea."

"Why didn't they leave inscriptions?"

"The Bible looks askance at victory inscriptions. You have to understand the Biblical culture of ancient Israel, their world view. The ancient Israelite kings ascribed their successes to God and considered raising monuments to their own glorification presumptuous. This attitude of royal humility became so ingrained in the Israelite culture that no kings, not even the idolatrous ones, dared raise monuments to their own glorification."

"Extraordinary. The Bible actually demands humility of the king, doesn't it?"

"It certainly does. The Bible forbids the king to take too many wives, accumulate too much money or have too many horses. And it commands him to carry a scroll of the Law with him at all times."

"Thank you, Dr. Webster. No more questions."

After the lunch recess, the trial resumed with Calabrese's cross-examination. Sometimes, he tried to undermine the testimony itself. Sometimes, however, he did not address the testimony in a substantive way. He just tried to undermine the credibility of the witness. Just as he had done with Dr. Singh. He didn't even bother to discuss the mathematical study. He just pointed out that the study was thirty-five years old and still not accepted by the academic community. I suppose this is one way to discredit the witness. It's certainly easier. I wondered how he would cross-examine Dr. Webster. I hoped he would give him the Singh treatment.

Calabrese stepped to the lectern.

"Dr. Webster, have you adequately explained why there's no trace of Jericho? Do you expect us to believe that a whole city with massive walls could vanish without a trace?"

"You can believe what you choose, sir. Four hundred years is a long time. It is perfectly reasonable to believe that erosion removed a good part of the traces. You also have to understand that people scavenge the stones and bricks of abandoned ruins, which are right there for the taking, to use in their homes and buildings. After hundreds of years of exposure, every stone and brick would have been removed by people in the area. As for the scraps left over, erosion would easily take care of them."

"I will not debate the point with you. But it must certainly seem a far-fetched scenario to any reasonable person. Let's talk about population."

"By all means."

"According to your ... ah ... calculations, you arrive at a population in the millions in ancient Israel. How could the land support so many people?"

"Where's the problem? According to a census taken by the Roman Empire, eight million people lived in ancient Israel in the first century B.C.E. They were eating well and living a fairly decent life."

"But seven or eight centuries earlier?"

"Customs didn't change so fast in agriculture in the ancient world. If the land could support eight million people in Roman times, it could support three million people in deep antiquity."

"Dr. Webster, what is the consensus in the academic community? Are your views shared by the mainstream?"

The witness pursed his lips. "They're shared by many academics."

"I understand. I have no more questions for this witness, your honor."

Chapter Forty-eight

Early Friday morning, my father suffered a heart attack and was taken to Mountainside Medical Center in Hackensack. June and I got there at half past six. We found him in intensive care. Sylvia and Bernie, both of whom lived in New Jersey, were already there. Alex had called to say he was on his way.

My father was on oxygen. He was conscious but could not speak much. I squeezed his hand and kissed his cheek. I called Nancy Hannah and told her what had happened. I told her I might be late and that she might have to cover for me.

The doctors were familiar with my father's case from his earlier episode. They were concerned about his condition but guardedly hopeful. It was arranged that George, my father's assistant, would stay with him most of the time. An aide from an agency would stay with him during the night so that George could go home and get some rest.

My siblings and I sat in the waiting room and chatted about stuff and nonsense. George got us coffee and snacks from the cafeteria. He went to sit by my father's bedside, and we settled in for the long haul. I suggested to June that she go back to her patients in Manhattan. I promised to keep her updated, but she was reluctant to leave.

An hour later, George reported that my father had asked if I was there. He wanted to speak to me.

My father's eyes were closed, and I thought he was asleep. But they fluttered open when I came near his bed. He crooked his index finger, signaling me to come closer. He was saying something, but I couldn't understand him.

"What are you saying, Pop?"

He made a great effort and said, "Why … you … here?"

"My father's in the hospital. Where should I be?"

"You … be … court."

"Nancy Hannah is covering for me, Pop."

He was agitated and shook his head. "Im … por … tant … you … please."

"Will it make you feel better if I go?" I asked.

He nodded.

I took his hand in mine. "All right, Pop. I'll go. I'll be back as soon as I can. I love you, Pop. Stay strong. We need you. Don't you dare leave."

I arrived in court fifteen minutes late. Nancy Hannah was explaining to the judge that I was delayed because my father had suffered a heart attack. I hurried to the plaintiff's table and took my seat.

"I'm happy you could make it, Mr. Taylor," said the judge. "I trust your father is better."

"He's in intensive care in New Jersey," I said. "He insisted I come to court to finish the case. He considers it important."

"As does everyone else," said the judge. "We all wish him a speedy recovery. You may call your next rebuttal witness."

I called my final rebuttal witness. After his testimony, the presentation of evidence phase of the trial would draw to a close. That is, unless Calabrese chose to call more witnesses, but I didn't think he would. Both of us were trying to keep it fairly simple for the benefit of the jury. A plunge into thickets of minutiae would not be helpful.

I stepped to the lectern.

"Your honor, the plaintiff calls Dr. Allen Graves."

An old man with sparse white hair and sparkling blue eyes

that were anything but grave ambled to the witness box and smiled at the jury.

"Can we have your full name and occupation, sir?"

"Allen Pinkerton Graves. I am Professor of Ancient Oriental Studies at McMaster University in Toronto, Ontario. That's in Canada."

"Dr. Graves, how old is the field of Ancient Oriental Studies?"

"Oh, I'd say about a hundred years old."

"Is the field of biblical studies older?"

"Yes, quite a bit. The hypotheses of the Bible critics were fairly full-blown when ancient Oriental studies were still in their infancy. They knew little about the life and customs of the ancient world."

"Did this lack of knowledge influence their perception of the Bible?"

"Without a doubt. You see, the more we learn about the ancient world in the second millennium before the common era, the more we realize we're looking at the world of the Old Testament. The spirit, the customs, the way of life, the feel of the times, they all point straight at the Old Testament. I'd venture to say that much of the dry information we have derived from other sources comes to vivid life in the Old Testament. Yes, without a doubt the Old Testament has the resounding ring of truth."

"I would like you to explain to the jury how this lack of knowledge of the ancient world affected the development of biblical studies."

"Well, you see, the early biblical scholars were working in a vacuum, so to speak. They found anomalies in the Bible, and according to their nineteenth-century German perception of literature, they concluded that they were looking at an anachronistic amalgam of different source documents spliced together centuries after the fact. They didn't recognize the literary style and standards of the Patriarchal era. They didn't understand the language in the context of the other languages of the time, because they knew nothing about them."

"And this is all wrong?" I said.

"It's not just wrong," said the witness, "it's scandalous. They showed no respect for the ancient texts." He pulled an index card from his pocket. "This is the certification at the end of an Egyptian funeral papyrus from about 1400 B.C.E., quoted in Cerny's *Paper and Books in Ancient Egypt*. '[The document] is completed from its beginning to its end, having been copied, revised, compared and verified sign by sign.' See the meticulous care with which Egyptian scribes prepared a simple funerary papyrus. Do you think Hebrew scribes were less careful with the preparation of their sacred literature? Is it conceivable that they put together the Bible without copying, revising and comparing it letter by letter? Horsefeathers!"

"But when the flow of information from ancient Oriental studies increased," I asked, "why didn't these biblical scholars abandon their earlier theories?"

"Because they were accustomed to their ingenious reconstructions. They were mentally conditioned in one direction. As you phrased it during your cross-examination of Dr. Winemaker, many of them became academic fundamentalists. They saw only one pathway, and they followed it blindly. But you'll be happy to hear that in recent years the old discredited preconceptions are slowly crumbling into the ash heap. Where they belong."

"Do you think the study of the ancient Near East corroborates the historicity of the Bible?"

"I do. William Albright wrote in *Archaeology and the Religion of Israel* that 'the Mosaic tradition is so consistent ... so congruent with our independent knowledge of the religious development of the Near East in the late second millennium B.C.E. that only hypercritical pseudo-rationalism can reject its essential historicity.'"

"Those are strong words."

"And more recently, Dr. Henri Blocher wrote in *Révélation des Origines: Le Début de la Genése* that 'the critics, when they judge the internal phenomena [of the Bible], project into it their customs as modern Western readers and neglect all we know today of the writing customs of biblical times. The taste for repetition, the structure of a global statement, repeated with development, the replacement of a word by its synonyms, especially the change of a divine name in a text, such as the previously mentioned names of Osiris on the Ikhern-ofret stele, are well-attested characteristics of ancient Middle Eastern texts ... The biblical text, as it is, agrees with the literary canons of its time.'"

For the next hour, I led Dr. Graves through a number of striking reflections in the Bible of ancient cultural mores long forgotten by the middle of the first millennium B.C.E.

"Would you sum up for us, Dr. Graves?"

"With pleasure." He faced the jury. "You see, the more we learn about the ancient Near East, the more we see how perfectly the Bible fits into that setting – in the customs, the laws, the lifestyles, the treaties and covenants, the language, the historical picture. The Old Testament transports us back to the second millennium before the common era, and the times and societies come alive before our eyes. For scholars in my field, and even for laypeople, it is an incredibly exciting journey of discovery. In my opinion, the Bible is one the most priceless historical treasures in existence."

"Thank you, Dr. Graves. No more questions."

The judge wrote something down and then looked up at Calabrese.

"Do you wish to cross-examine?" she said.

I wondered how he could dispute the points Dr. Graves had made.

"Yes, your honor," said Calabrese.

He clasped his hands behind his back and stepped to the lectern.

"Just a quick point. You quoted Dr. Henri Blocher's opinion that the Bible conforms to the literary canons of its time. Does Dr. Blocher teach in a university?"

"He is a professor at Wheaton College in the Boston area."

"Biblical studies or archaeology or ancient Oriental studies?"

"He's a professor of theology."

"Theology? Is Wheaton a Christian college?"

"Yes, it is."

"And you accept his opinion as objective and unbiased?"

"Of course, I do. I don't discriminate against religious scholars. I evaluate their work on its own merits, and Dr. Blocher's work is excellent."

"No doubt. I have no more questions for this witness."

Chapter Forty-nine

There was important news from Yellow Brook over the weekend. On Friday night, several FBI agents had made a clandestine reconnaissance incursion into the Waco-Ridge compound, and they had reported that there were no families there, only armed men and women fighters.

On Saturday morning, the FBI stormed the compound. Using rubber bullets and tear gas, agents subdued seventeen defenders. There were no casualties on either side. The defenders, including Christopher Jones, John Paul Swift and Jerry Anderson, were taken into custody. According to reports, all the defenders of the compound asked for lawyers and refused to talk to the authorities.

The prosecution of the suspects promised to become a drawn-out affair. The government would move slowly and methodically to build the cases, but in the end, I believed the killers would be convicted. I hoped they would be denied bail as they awaited trial, but who could tell? At least, the resolution of the siege without casualties was a victory of sorts.

June and I spent most of the weekend in Hackensack with my father. All my siblings were there, as were Margaret and Gerald. He was showing signs of improvement, and they had moved him out of intensive care to a private room. That was much better. We didn't have to worry about disturbing the other gravely ill patients. We retold old family stories and looked at pictures and videos. My father could not participate to the extent he usually did, but he was right in the middle of the mix.

We watched the FBI raid on the newscasts, and when they brought out John Paul Swift, we recognized him immediately. My father stared at him and let loose with a string of curses, most of them in Yiddish. But I could see that he was pleased.

I've never quite understood the psychology of it, but it is well-known that the capture of the killer is cathartic for the family of the victim. Perhaps they feel that the victim may have lost his or her life but at least they got justice. In my opinion, justice is no substitute for life. It's a substitute for vengeance. I wanted justice, because I wanted vengeance. I had gotten a small measure of revenge against Farragut at that meeting in my office. I wanted more.

Sunday afternoon, my father took a turn for the worse. He didn't go back to intensive care, but we could see that the doctors were concerned.

"Listen, boychik," he said. "Tomorrow you make your closing argument. Are you prepared?"

"I am."

"Do you want to share it with me?"

"I don't." I never share my speeches and remarks with anyone beforehand. It takes away from the fire building inside me.

"I know," he said. "Makes sense. Will the other guy make his argument tomorrow as well?"

"It's possible."

"And then it goes to the jury."

"Right."

"Do you think they'll return a verdict tomorrow?"

"You never know," I said, "but I don't think so."

"I want you to stay in court until they have a verdict or go to sleep. Don't come running here when the case goes to the jury."

"Why not, Pop? My associates can be there with the client.

There's really no need for me there."

"Yes, there is, boychik. If you win, this is a victory for David. You have to be there. You have to talk to the media. You have to say, 'Remember David Goldfield!' You can come here later if you wish."

"All right, Pop."

"But don't forget to call me the second they have a verdict."

Chapter Fifty

The judge was late on Monday morning. I had put everything I had into my closing argument, and the delay was burning a hole in my stomach. The door to her chambers didn't open until ten thirty. She apologized for her lateness; she'd been caught in traffic. She called the court into session and invited me to make my closing remarks.

I stepped to the lectern that had been set up near the jury box.

"Good morning, ladies and gentlemen of the jury," I began, "I want to tell you a story about a famous Egyptian boy king named Tutankhamun, popularly known as King Tut. Tutankhamun lived about three and a half thousand years ago. But the story I'm about to tell you is not about his life. It's about his death."

I paused for effect.

"At first, the Egyptian pharaohs were entombed in the pyramids; the pyramids are mausoleums. The tombs of the pharaohs were filled with works of art, gold, precious stones and all manner of magnificent treasures meant to accompany them into the hereafter. But after graverobbers started looting the tombs, they buried the kings in a bleak and remote desert in southern Egypt, known as the Valley of the Kings. The tombs were dug into the mountainsides and concealed. Even if the graverobbers could make their way to this valley, they would not find the tombs. And indeed, they didn't.

"Tutankhamun's multi-chamber tomb surpassed all other tombs in magnificence and funerary treasures. The king's mummified body was laid to rest in the main chamber in a golden sarcophagus – that's a coffin – with a stunning golden death mask attached to his face. Tutankhamun's tomb was legendary, but its location was unknown.

"Early in the twentieth century, British archaeologists discovered the tomb after years of search and excavation. Over a period of ten years, they removed five thousand precious artifacts and shipped them off to Cairo. They also moved the sarcophagus to Cairo and displayed it in a museum. They opened the sarcophagus, removed Tutankhamun's death mask and studied his mummified body.

"This was considered one of the greatest discoveries in the history of archaeology. Over the years, exhibitions of artifacts from the tomb toured the museums of the world, and millions came to view them. You can catch one of these traveling exhibitions if you look out for them, and you can even check out Tutankhamun's body if you visit Cairo.

"So, let me ask you a question. How are these archaeologists different from the graverobbers? What gave them the right to disturb the rest of the dead? What gave them the right to take the body of the dead king out of his grave and put it into a museum? Is there a statute of limitations on the sanctity of the grave? Are the dead fair game after thousands of years?

"So, they'll say they do it in the interest of science rather than for greed. What science? Did disturbing the grave of Tutankhamun help them save lives? Did it help them find cures for diseases? Did it help them relieve poverty? Of course not. It only increased our knowledge of the culture and history of ancient Egypt. So, if archaeologists were studying American history in the eighteenth century, would it be acceptable to dig up George Washington and check out his wooden teeth? Is academic curiosity about ancient times a valid excuse for violating the sanctity of the grave?"

I paused.

"Would you want your body dug up? Maybe you'd be okay with it if it helped save lives. But in the interests of learning about the culture of the twenty-first century? I don't think you'd want your grave disturbed for that. The dead deserve the sanctity of the grave. Why then was it acceptable, even exciting, to dig up Tutankhamun and put him into a museum?

"Now, don't get me wrong. I'm in favor of archaeological studies of ancient ruins that teach us about ancient civilizations. But with boundaries! Why can ancient graves be disturbed? Makes you think, doesn't it?"

I paused for a few moments before giving them my answer.

"Let me tell you what I believe. Modern academics do not relate to Tutankhamun as a person but as an ancient artifact. The passage of time has dehumanized the ancients in the modern mind. Certainly, the people of the ancient world – at least some of them – were brilliant and talented and creative, but they were not Us. They were an earlier version of Us, an earlier stage in the evolution of civilized humankind. They were our ancestors, our antecedents, but they were not Us, and they do not deserve the respect we extend to full-fledged fellow human beings.

"Counsel for the defendants would have you believe that the Bible, one of the greatest literary masterpieces in history, was a pious fraud spliced together from different source documents in an extremely sloppy manner. To mention just one example, one of his proofs is that the Bible begins with two contradictory creation stories. But why would these hypothetical splicers have done such a thing? Why not include just one? Didn't it occur to these hypothetical splicers that people would find that strange?

"If you recall, I asked Dr. Winemaker if he would have been taken in by the hoax, and he said that he would have seen through it. But he still insists that the ancients would not have seen through it. Do you know why? Because they were not Us. If they are not Us, we can acknowledge their talent and brilliance in putting together a masterpiece such as the Bible, and we can still cluck our tongues at their bumbling clumsiness. You really couldn't expect much more from the unfinished prototypes of the model that would one day become Us.

"But you, the members of the jury, know that this is not true. During jury selection, one of you said that – and I quote – the ancients were more intelligent, because although they were lacking our technology and knowledge, they had the opportunity to think about life and things. They didn't watch television, and their phones weren't ringing all the time.

"The literature of the ancients is sophisticated and complex. They were just as intelligent and as shrewd as we are. They were Us living in deep antiquity. You couldn't pull the wool over their eyes so easily. The style of the Bible is unfamiliar to us, but as we have shown, it accurately reflects the literary style of its time. And as we have also shown, the contents of the Bible reflect the customs of the second millennium B.C.E., customs that were forgotten by the first millennium B.C.E. and remained forgotten until they were discovered by archaeologists in the last two centuries. The Bible could not have been written nearly a thousand years after it claims to have been written. It comes to us intact from deep antiquity, and as such, it is as reliable a source of history as Merneptah's stela."

I paused before going into the next segment of my closing arguments.

"Ladies and gentlemen of the jury, I didn't take this case because I'm a religious man. On the contrary, God and religion played hardly any role in my life. I accepted the academic orthodoxy that the Bible is myth without giving it much thought. It didn't matter to me.

"Why did I take this case? Because, as some of you may know, my beloved grandson, my only grandchild, was murdered in Hesterville by thugs from the American Identity Party, the party that justifies race wars by claiming that the Bible is a fraud and that its moral teachings are irrelevant. They view people as intelligent animals and believe that survival is the only morality. I took this case, because I wanted to strike a blow against the ideological foundation of their movement.

"If you recall, at the beginning of the trial I claimed equipoise, and the judge ruled in our favor. That means that the burden of proof regarding the historicity of the Bible is on the defendants. The Bible has been accepted as historical by billions of people for thousands of years, and if the defendants claimed it was unhistorical, they would have to prove it. I felt I could weaken their case enough to get a favorable verdict based on equipoise.

"But as I dove into a deep study of the Bible and the academic literature, I discovered that the evidence in favor of the Bible was extraordinarily strong, far better than the evidence against it, and I hope I have presented the evidence to you clearly.

"But if the evidence for the Bible is so strong, you might ask, why is there so much opposition to the Bible in the academic community? The answer is that it stems from German scholars in the nineteenth century who wanted to free Germanic society from the shackles of the Bible. A strong strain of anti-Semitism and anti-Christianity runs through the writings of Wellhausen, the father of the Documentary Hypothesis.

"But how could he extricate people from the grips of the Bible, which was so deeply ingrained in their hearts and minds? The Bible had to be exposed as a hoax. The authorship had to be moved up about a thousand years so that its historicity could be discredited. Because if the Bible were written when it claims to have been written, it would be hard to argue that there was never an encounter with the divine, that the Ten Commandments and the Golden Rule had no validity.

"Under the cloak of academic scholarship, they dissected

the Bible and added layer upon layer of unsupported speculation. With the passage of time, those unsupported speculations became academic orthodoxy and were accepted as fact. Biblical studies in universities used the manufactured facts as the starting point of their teaching. Students were not invited to question the underlying assumptions. Rather, they pored over the biblical text in search of ever more source documents until the Bible was rendered a ridiculous patchwork of scraps and pieces. It didn't matter that no other book was ever produced this way. The Bible had to be relegated to myth.

"But I believe we've demonstrated, ladies and gentlemen of the jury, that the Bible is not a work of fiction but a work of magnificent history of the highest importance. Whether or not you choose to believe the miracle stories, the basic historicity of the Bible cannot be denied, just as the historicity of the Merneptah stela cannot be denied, despite its miracle stories."

I paused again.

"Ladies and gentlemen of the jury, this trial is not about the separation between church and state. Our society permits people to believe whatever they wish about God, even nothing at all. Mrs. Williams was not teaching religion in her classroom. She was teaching the history of the ancient world, which is wonderfully preserved in the Bible.

"The school board has no list of approved supplementary texts that can used in the classroom. Teachers can bring in any history book of their choice, many of which are much less reliable than the Bible. Mrs. Williams chose to use the Bible, and she was fired. Her civil rights were violated. I hope you will agree that the defendants are guilty as charged.

"Thank you, and God bless you."

I returned to my seat and just stared up at the ceiling. I was exhausted. I caught sight of June from the corner of my eye. She blew me a kiss. I noticed that Margaret was sitting next to June. She gave me a slight nod of the head. I did not respond to either of them. The jury was watching me, and I wanted to maintain the gravitas on my face.

Lavender touched my arm and whispered, "Wow! That's all I can say, Mr. Taylor. Wow!"

I nodded gravely. The jury was still watching.

"We've reached the lunch hour," said the judge. "Mr. Calabrese, are you ready to make your closing arguments after we break for lunch?"

"I'm ready, your honor," he said.

Chapter Fifty-one

Calabrese walked slowly to the lectern near the jury box. His face was grave and solemn. He made eye contact with each of the jurors individually. Then he leaned forward and began his presentation.

"In a short time, you'll be making the most important decision of your lives, outside of your personal affairs. You'll go down in the annals of history. You have a tremendous responsibility, and I implore you to vote with your heads rather than with your hearts.

"You have listened to countless hours of expert testimony about whether or not the Bible is a reliable historical record or a beautiful collection of inspiring myths and legends. I'm sure you'll be relieved to hear that I don't intend to review all the material today. The proofs we've presented are just the tip of a vast iceberg of evidence that the Bible is a brilliant creation of writers and editors living many centuries after it claims to have been written.

"No one has disputed in this trial that the overwhelming majority of biblical scholars in the world have reached this conclusion after studying the Bible intensively. They have analyzed every verse, every phrase, every word. Faced with the overwhelming mass of evidence, they have reached the inevitable conclusion – that the Bible was composed in the middle of the first millennium B.C.E., many centuries after it claims to have been written. The references are all from the later peri-od. The historical context is the later period. The style of the language and the vocabulary are from the later period. As you have seen, the evidence from the text itself is crystal clear. And then we have the archaeological evidence, which only corrob-orates the conclusion the scholars have already reached.

"I cannot expect you to become Bible experts in such a brief period of time when the experts have toiled for many years. But I can expect you to get a sense of the mountain of evidence that exists on the authorship of the Bible. You should recognize that a consensus exists among Bible scholars, not on every piece of the evidence, but certainly on the overall conviction that the Bible – specifically, the Five Books of Mo-ses – was not written in the second millennium B.C.E. In fact, the consensus among scholars is that there never was a Mo-ses, nor an Abraham, nor an Isaac, nor a Jacob, nor a Joseph. These are all mythical figures, larger than life, the stuff of leg-end, the products of the creative genius of the composers of the Bible. Such is the verdict of science.

"At one time, humankind lived in a world governed by su-perstition and magical thinking, when faith ruled supreme and reason was disdained. But we've progressed since then. We've become enlightened. The human intellect has been lib-erated. Reason now rules supreme. Who among you is ready to sacrifice your reason to faith? I venture to say that not one of you would do so. Your presence on this jury is an affirma-tion of the rule of reason. You are here to make a rational evaluation of the facts, not to promote some spiritual ideal or irrational faith."

Calabrese walk back to the defense table and took a sip of water.

"My friends," he continued, "the science of biblical studies does not reject the Bible, nor am I asking you to do anything of the sort. The science of biblical studies rescues the Bible from the prison of ignorance, obscurantism and blind faith and allows its pure light to shine forth and illuminate the world. Do we have to believe that great novels such as Stendhal's *The Red and the Black* and Maugham's *Of Human Bondage* are true stories in order to appreciate their insights into the inner crevices of the soul? Don't we recognize literature as one of the highest forms of creative art? We should also recognize the Bible as one of the greatest masterpieces of literature in the history of the world. Nothing less. Nothing more.

"To restrict the Bible to the narrow confines of a true story is to rob it of its universal power. It's not important to insist that Abraham and Moses existed; it's important to recognize the ideals they represent. We need to embrace the messages of compassion, social responsibility, liberty and justice found in the Bible; they're the enduring truth. If all of humankind were to embrace these ideals, this world in which we live would be a far better place. But it's ridiculous to confuse the Bible's legends and myths with history. Too many people have done so over the centuries and brought untold tragedy and misery on the world.

"Science has come to liberate the Bible from the clutches of the fundamentalists, the extremists, the suicide bombers, the sanctimonious militants who would tell us how to live and what to think. Science has come to peel away the layers of superstition and irrationalism that have encrusted the Bible. Science has come to restore the purity and benevolent power of this magnificent piece of literature we know as the Bible. And in the process, science will liberate all of humankind from the clutches of archaic and irrational thought and from the hatred and violence they engender.

"Ladies and gentlemen of the jury, your mission, your destiny, is to be part of that process of liberation. Your decision in favor of science will affirm the emergence of society from the dark ages. It is your duty as people of the modern world to bring in a verdict in favor of the defense."

Calabrese bowed slightly to the jury and returned to the

defense table. I thought he had done well. Throughout the trial, he had come back again and again to the argument of academic consensus, and this was the point he had emphasized in his closing. The faces of the jurors told me that it had been powerful and effective. I sighed. There was nothing more I could do. The trial was over. All that remained to be determined was the verdict.

The judge gave the jury final instructions and sent them off to deliberate. Calabrese's closing had been short compared to mine. It was still early in the afternoon. I hoped we could have a verdict later that day. Lavender and Marvin Williams went home to have dinner with their twins. The rest of us returned to my office in Manhattan.

I called my father to tell him that the case had gone to the jury, but that it would probably take a long time. He should not wait up for my call. I would call him first thing in the morning. He insisted I call right away.

June and I invited Margaret and Gerald to an early dinner in a midtown restaurant. There was plenty of time. Then we returned to the office to await the verdict. At my insistence, we did not talk about the case. There was no point to it. It would just jangle our nerves. There would be time to rehash the case after the verdict was returned.

The call came in at seven o'clock. We rushed to the courthouse. Calabrese came a few minutes after us.

The bailiff called the judge and brought in the jury. I tried to read their faces, but I could not.

"Members of the jury," said the judge, "have you reached a verdict?"

Jane Li, the forewoman, stood up.

"Yes, we have, your honor," she said.

She handed a folded sheet to the bailiff, who showed it to the judge and returned it to her.

"What say you?" said the judge.

"Your honor," she said, "in the matter of Williams versus

New York Board of Education, we find in favor of the plaintiff. She is to be reinstated and awarded the sum of four and a half million dollars."

I breathed a sigh of relief. Rabbi Gutmacher, smiling from ear to ear, came to shake my hand. Lavender was euphoric. She hugged everyone in sight. But I felt a letdown. It was strangely anticlimactic. Of course, I was also thrilled and pleased and gratified and all of that. But I sensed the adrenaline drain from my body and my soul, and I felt strangely empty.

I pulled out my phone and called my father.

"Tell me," he said before I even said hello.

"We won."

"Thank you, thank you, thank you. You did a good job. For our David. I'm proud of you, boychik."

I couldn't help but smile.

"I love you, Pop."

"I love you, too, boychik. Goodbye."

When I got off the phone, I saw Calabrese in conversation with Rabbi Gutmacher, then the two of them came over. Calabrese shook my hand.

"Congratulations, counselor," he said. "Well done."

"Thank you, Mr. Calabrese," I said. "It's very gracious of you."

"My clients would like to make an offer. As Rabbi Gutmacher's yeshivah is the owner of the award, as per previous agreement, the offer is extended to him, but we want you to hear it."

"Are the defendants offering a settlement after the verdict?"

"Yes, we are. You know, of course, that my clients are prepared to appeal the verdict. It may take years before Rabbi Gutmacher's yeshivah sees any money, if ever. In order to avoid the trouble and expense of a protracted appeals process, they're prepared to offer a settlement. Mrs. Williams will be reinstated, and the amount awarded by the jury will be reduced by half. Two million two hundred and fifty thousand dollars."

"You came up with this now?"

"My clients prepared the offer in case the verdict went against them. They want this to be over. We really should be speaking only to Rabbi Gutmacher, because he's the interested party. However, although you're not his yeshivah's attorney in this matter, he wishes to seek guidance from you. So here we are. The offer is on the table. What is your advice?"

I had wanted to forestall a settlement, because I needed a clear verdict in our favor. A settlement after the verdict to avoid the appeals process would not compromise our victory. Besides, I didn't want to risk the verdict being overturned on appeal.

"I think it's a good idea," I said. "Rabbi Gutmacher?"

"I agree," said the rabbi. "I just wanted to make sure you had no objections. You had the right, maybe not legally but morally."

"Excellent," said Calabrese. "I'll draw up the papers, and the rabbi can come to my office tomorrow. A cashier's check will be waiting."

Chapter Fifty-two

My father passed away during the evening. He didn't say good night to me. He said goodbye. I think he knew he wouldn't last through the night. He hung on to life until he heard the verdict, and then he could hold on no longer.

The funeral took place on Thursday. The service was well-attended. The eulogies were mercifully short. He was laid to rest near his parents and his wife in Deans, New Jersey. The family observed the Shivah mourning period together for two hours on Friday afternoon in Sylvia's house in Montclair. Afterward, my siblings were done, and I went home to observe the entire seven-day mourning period in my home in Manhattan.

Many of my friends and associates came to pay their respects. Lavender and Marvin Williams came and brought their twins. Rabbi Gutmacher came with some of the people I had met in Crown Heights. Even James Calabrese came by.

The post-trial articles were generally favorable. A new poll was encouraging. Among people who had followed the trial in detail online, sixty-two percent said they now had a more favorable opinion of the Bible. Twenty-three percent said they had a less favorable opinion. Nine percent said their opinion was unchanged. Six percent were undecided. I had not expected to score a knockout at the trial and instantly convince the entire world, but I had definitely succeeded in moving the needle. That was an important accomplishment. I had also succeeded in sowing doubt in the ideological basis of the American Identity Party. It was the best result I could have anticipated.

Perhaps the next step was to write a book of contemporary history about the Hesterville story that would include the bulk of the transcripts. I didn't think I could do it myself. It would need objectivity, which I did not have, but Jessica Davis could do it. It would help in her quest for the Pulitzer. I would have to discuss it with her and offer to help to the best of my ability. The battle was far from over.

On Monday morning, Morris Ackerman and Henry Cortez came from Hesterville. They had called my office to congratulate me on the verdict and learned that I was in mourning. They asked for my address, and my office gave it to them after clearing it with me.

"We're sorry for your loss," said Cortez. "We're not just saying. We really mean it."

"Your father was very old?" said Ackerman.

"He was. Ninety-three."

"Were you close with him?"

"I was."

"People think losing an old parent is not so bad," he said. "After all, they had a long life. They weren't gonna live forever anyway. But I know how you feel. My father passed away in his nineties, and believe me, it hurt real bad."

I nodded. "That's how I feel. It hurts real bad."

Cortez pulled his chair closer. "We came to pay our respects, but we also wanted to tell you something. They'll be erecting a large monument in front of the municipal building in Hesterville in memory of those who gave their lives on the Fourth of July for freedom and democracy. There'll be five names on the monument, listed in age order. Patricia Cole, Darius Washington, Lamar Biggs, David Goldfield, Kimberley Ann Adams. The first three died in front of the Shiloh Gospel Church, the last two in front of the Chabad House. We want to invite you to the ceremony."

I was touched. "I'll be glad to come."

"And we'd like you to be the featured speaker."

I hesitated for a long moment. I knew it would be painful, but I owed it to David and the others who'd given their lives on that day. A little pain wouldn't kill me.

"I'd be honored," I said.

Margaret came by in the afternoon and sat with me for a few hours. We chatted about this, that and the other. I didn't feel any of the old hostility.

"You know, I've been thinking really hard," she said, "trying to figure out why I've resented you all these years. Do you want to hear?"

"Of course, I do. It's important to me. Maybe I can fix it."

"You want to fix it? You blame yourself?" She shook her head. "It's not your fault."

"I don't understand."

"I realized that all of us live on two levels. We have micro lives, and we have macro lives. We have our own circumscribed private lives, and we're also part of a greater drama that's taking place on the large stage. Most of us conduct our lives only on the micro level, and we just get swept along on the macro level. But some people thrive on the macro level. People like you who want to change the world."

"Strange you should say that. Rabbi Gutmacher told me something a little similar just recently. I'll tell you about it some other time."

"I've seen this all my life, Dad. You went to Congress to change the world. You wrote your books to change the world. You took on this trial to change the world."

"No," I said. "I took it to get revenge."

She shook her head again. "You wanted to fix the world that killed our beloved David. You wanted to bring down the AIP."

"I don't fool myself about that. I don't think what I accomplished will bring down the AIP."

"Not by itself. But it'll help. I'm sure it'll help. You were performing on the macro level, as usual, and I think that's what I always resented about you. I know you were always there for me, but I felt that at the same time you were distant. And I resented it. I'm a micro person, and you're a macro person. We don't operate on the same wavelength."

"Does that matter? Can't we love each other anyway?"

"It shouldn't matter. I realize that now. I'm really proud of you, Dad. Whatever I said about blaming you for David's death was wrong, and I take it all back."

"Forget about it. You were in pain. I didn't take it seriously."

"Still, I shouldn't have said it. You know, Dad, David was like you. He didn't want to be limited to the micro level. He wanted his life to mean something important. And he was successful. His life was too short, but it was extraordinary. I thank you for that. We have to be close, Dad. All we have is each other. I love you, Dad."

She came over and hugged me, and I kissed her cheek.

"I love you, too, Margaret."

I was not convinced that Margaret's epiphany could instantly repair thirty years of damage in our complicated relationship. But it was certainly a start. Time would tell.

Acknowledgments

This book is dedicated to the memory of my good friend and colleague Rabbi Pinchas Stolper. He urged me to write it, helped me with the research and encouraged me at every step of the way; the evolution of the book over fifteen years is described on my website at www.rabbireinman.com. It saddens me that he has not lived to hold a copy in his hands. I will be forever grateful to him. I also want to thank Mrs. Cherna Moskowitz of Miami Beach, Florida, for her enthusiastic support for all Rabbi Stolper's projects.

My thanks go out to my wonderful agent Nancy Rosenfeld of AAA Books Unlimited, to my editor Dr. Susan Lipschutz, to my graphic artist Bracha Royde and to my wife, Zvia, my family and all my friends who read the manuscript and offered comments and criticism.

Most of all, I want to express my gratitude to the Almighty for everything He has done for me throughout my life. I hope this book will advance the quest for truth and bring honor to His holy Name.

The Hesterville Trial
The Full Transcript

Katherine Baker, presiding judge

Lavender Williams, plaintiff

Adrian Taylor, counsel for the plaintiff

Wesley Youngblood, Board of Education, defendants

James Calabrese, counsel for the defense

Williams v. Youngblood et al

Judge: Learned counsels for the plaintiff and the defense, ladies and gentlemen of the jury, before we begin the trial with opening statements, I want to make a few remarks regarding procedure. As you have surely surmised from the questions you were asked during *voir dire*, this trial will examine the authenticity of the Bible. Considering the complexity of the issues and the unusual nature of this trial, I will allow the attorneys broad latitude in the presentation of evidence and in the lines of questioning.

In addition, since a great deal of the expert testimony will be long and involved, I cannot expect the jury to remember it by the time cross-examination begins. I also don't want to have the court reporter read everything back to refresh your memories. It would take too much time. Therefore, I'll allow the attorneys to interrupt the testimony of an opposing witness at reasonable intervals, with my permission, for cross-examination and to present rebuttal testimony before the witness resumes his or her testimony. This will allow the jury to digest the evidence in smaller amounts. For the same reasons, the jurors will be provided with audio files and transcripts of the proceedings.

You are instructed not to speak to anyone about the proceedings, not even with your families. I see many members of the media here, and I'm sure the trial will receive a lot of publicity. Please do not read or view reports in the media. You are on your honor, ladies and gentlemen of the jury, to protect the integrity of this trial. If anyone tries to influence you, report it to me immediately.

One more thing, counsel for both sides feel it would be useful for each juror to have a Bible for reference. I agree. Bibles will be provided at the end of the day before you are dismissed.

Members of the jury, get ready for the long haul. Let's begin. Mr. Taylor, we are ready for your opening statement.

Opening Statement, Plaintiff

Mr. Taylor: Ladies and gentlemen of the jury, this is a civil lawsuit. My client, Lavender Williams, is a sixth-grade teacher. She was dismissed for using the Bible as a historical resource in her classroom. She is now suing for reinstatement and damages resulting from her wrongful termination. The facts of the case are clear. What is not clear is if her termination was indeed wrongful. Is the Bible disqualified from being a historical resource? Or can we glean significant information about the culture and history of ancient times, even if we disregard the supernatural parts?

The critical question is, when was the Bible written? Was it written at more or less the time it claims to have been written, say within fifty years or so? Or is it a mythological tale concocted about a thousand years later? The plaintiff will argue that its origins are in deep antiquity, and we will present expert witnesses supporting that view. Defense will argue the opposite and present its own expert witnesses. You, ladies and gentlemen of the jury, will have to weigh the evidence and decide which position is more reasonable.

This, my dear friends, is the true defendant in this trial. The holy Bible. I call it the holy Bible because it is definitely holy. Even its detractors, even the defendants and their counsel, would have to admit that the Bible is holy in the same way the Constitution of the United States is holy. It is holy because it has been revered and cherished by great numbers of people for thousands of years. No matter what anyone says about the Bible, it deserves our respect and reverence.

You have all been provided with copies of the Bible, and I suggest you take some time to familiarize yourself with it. It's a book of many facets. It begins with a long narrative, but it's much more than a story. The Bible is a book of law, of morals, of ethics, of poetry, of wisdom for living, a book that explores and delineates the relationship between man and his fellow man and the relationship between man and God. To call it a great literary masterpiece is a huge understatement. The Bible is in a class of its own in its ability to move, inspire, inform, instruct and touch the heart and the soul. There is nothing remotely like it in all the literature of the world, from ancient times to the present day. Nothing.

Ladies and gentlemen of the jury, this book has changed the face of the earth ... and it stands accused of fraud! This book is the cornerstone of Western civilization, the fountainhead of our morals and values, the champion of the sanctity of individual life and the inviolability of individual rights and liberties ... and it stands accused of fraud! This book has imbued human life with meaning, purpose and unlimited worth ... and it stands accused of fraud! Is it possible for a fake to come so close to the hearts and minds of billions of intelligent, thinking, caring people all over the world?

I think not. So much truth cannot possibly come from a lie.

My friends, in the course of this trial, you will be introduced to arcane subjects such as biblical scholarship, chronology, philology and archaeology. You will hear expert witnesses on both sides, and you will listen and evaluate. Don't let anyone tell you that you are not qualified to form opinions on subjects in which you are not experts.

Remember, the Bible is innocent until proven guilty. If counsel for the defense accuses the Bible of deliberate fraud and misrepresentation, he should back it up with incontrovertible evidence. And you will see, my dear jurors, that this is impossible.

I believe you will have no difficulty finding for the plaintiff.

Opening Statement, Defense

Mr. Calabrese:

Ladies and gentlemen of the jury, we all know there are tremendous stakes in this trial. Your verdict will be crucial to the future of free thought. Your unified voice will echo down the corridors of history long after we are all gone. Generations to come will remember your words, and they'll either praise you or berate you. The choice is yours. Their liberation is in your hands.

The American people believe in God; they want a relationship with the divine. They want spirituality in their homes. They want to be exalted and uplifted. In the Western world, people have achieved this for thousands of years through the great monotheistic religions – Judaism, Christianity and Islam. These religions are critical to our society. They provide us with moral teachings and social values that are indispensable to our private and public lives. No one denies this.

But at the same time, we have to realize that these religions come with serious baggage. These religions stem from the Bible, perhaps the most influential book in history. Yet the Bible tells a fanciful story about the birth of the Israelite people, the forerunners of the Jewish people today.

Most of us are familiar with these stories, at least to a certain extent. We were brought up on them. We thought they were true. This gave everything in the Bible powerful authority. Everything it said, whether reasonable or not, had to be accepted as the word of the living God.

However, modern science has held up the Bible to the light of reason and logic and exposed it as a fraud. Scholars have subjected the Bible to close analysis, and they've discovered that it was composed nearly a thousand years after it claims to have been written and that it was pieced together from a number of source documents. It's amazing how you can now look at a chapter or even a page of the Bible and clearly identify the different hands that wrote it.

Before we go on, I have to point out that I'm talking about the Old Testament, sometimes called the Hebrew Bible, the foundation of all the sacred books of the Western religions. This is the book, or rather set of books, we'll examine in this trial. We'll prove beyond a doubt that the Old Testament is a fraud. The scientific world has known this for over a century. It's a well-established fact. It's now time we enlightened the world.

Ladies and gentlemen of the jury, I want to take you on a journey into history to a faraway land and a distant time. I want to tell you about a group of nomads who lived in the hill country of the area now known as Palestine-Israel, in the district now known as the West Bank. The story begins over three thousand years ago and is extremely relevant to us here today.

The evidence will show that these nomads banded together to form a tribe and then a loose, informal nation known as the Israelites; that they built villages and turned to agriculture; that they had primitive religious beliefs; that these people established two adjacent kingdoms that were sometimes allies, sometimes enemies and always rivals; that their religion evolved into a monotheistic cult with a central temple in Jerusalem; that the northern kingdom was destroyed by the Assyrian Empire, that the southern kingdom aspired to rule over the remnants of its defunct cousin kingdom; that the priestly caste conspired to create a book that would give them virtual control over all the Israelites in both kingdoms.

This is how the Bible was born. It was the child of political and economic expediency, the product of a conspiracy by a group of people seeking a permanent advantage for themselves and their offspring. They did a great job. They fooled the people of their times, and they have continued to pull the wool over the eyes of humankind for thousands of years.

But evidence that surfaced in the last two centuries is overwhelming. Let me give you a little preview of this evidence. First, let's talk about the internal evidence. As you might expect, splicing together different documents is not an easy task if you want to pass them off on the public as an integrated document. Inevitably, a number of contradictions, redundancies, repetitions and anomalies will crop up in the text.

In the beginning, the editor or editors who pulled off this incredible deception got away with it. At least, that's how it appears. We don't have records of people objecting to the authenticity of the Bible until quite some time after it was formulated. But after a period of time, the inconsistencies began to catch the attention of intelligent people.

The rabbis of later generations, who grew up believing that the Bible was authentic, recognized many problems and attempted to resolve them by exegesis, interpretation and adding narrative elements to bridge the gaps. The rabbis were not prepared to admit that the religion in which they were so deeply invested was built on a deception. They could not even entertain the possibility. So, they strained their imaginations and came up with all sorts of solutions to these basic problems. Often, these solutions were quite ingenious, but they didn't satisfy everyone, especially not the pagans.

The writings of early Christian scholars, such as Origen and Jerome, contain responses to pagans that were calling into question the authenticity and antiquity of the Bible and denying that Moses had written it.

Then, for a long time, the questions went away. There was a strange silence. Why? Because the Christians conquered the pagan world, and anyone that dared speak against the Bible was put to death.

And thus, the Bible had gained the upper hand. The rabbis controlled the Jews. The priests controlled the Christians. The imams controlled the Muslims. There was no freedom of thought, no freedom of expression. The human intellect and the spirit of free inquiry were buried under an avalanche of piety.

But the questions couldn't be buried forever. They were right there in the text, sitting in plain view for anyone with an open mind to see. In the Middle Ages, some rabbis whispered that it appeared that the Bible was not entirely written by Moses. But they were afraid to speak out publicly in anything more than hints. Later, a number of Christian scholars and even a Spanish bishop took up the call. They didn't whisper, but they were not bold enough to face the truth head on. Some suggested that Moses had written the Bible but that editors had revised and expanded the text.

As we moved into the modern period, however, times were changing. The world was going through an intellectual revolution. People were no longer satisfied to accept on faith. The human mind in all its magnificent power was unleashed, and it was full of questions. The human mind wanted to know about the universe, about the natural world, about the relationship of humankind to the world. It put everything under the microscope of scientific investigation. It wanted to find its own answers and reach its own conclusions.

The Bible could no longer escape scrutiny under the bright light of reason. Great intellectual figures such as Thomas Hobbes and Benedict Spinoza concluded that Moses did not the author Bible, since it was clearly written long after its purported time. The floodgates opened. The Bible became fair game for scientific examination, and the results were inevitable.

Over the last two centuries, biblical scholarship has unlocked most of the mysteries of the authorship of the Bible. The pious fraud has been exposed. We can now identify the sources that thread through the Bible. We can pinpoint with amazing accuracy the time period when the sources were composed. We may even be able to determine the identity of the authors.

How was all this accomplished? By using scientific methods of analysis. Science has brought you cars and jets that give you the freedom to travel wherever you please. Science has brought you medicines and therapies that give you unprecedented freedom from sickness and disease.

Science has also brought you evidence of the true nature of the Bible and, by doing so, has set you free from the stranglehold of the religions of the ancient world.

You are now free to pick and choose. There are many worthy ideas in the Bible. There's much to be learned about ethics and morality from the Bible, just as there's much to be learned from Homer and Shakespeare. But you're not bound by any of the dogma or any of the rules and regulations if they fail the test of modernity. Biblical scholarship has set humankind free. And I will show you exactly how during the course of this historic trial.

Ladies and gentlemen of the jury, please bear with me for a few more minutes. We're almost done. I want to tell you about the final nail in the coffin of the ancient myth of the Bible.

Until this past century, the proof that the Bible is a pious fraud came from the internal evidence of the texts. Now it's our good fortune that a different branch of science has brought us confirmation.

Over the last century, the remains of ancient civilizations, buried for thousands of years, have been excavated and analyzed. The result has been a staggering mountain of information. The ground is yielding its deepest secrets and mysteries. We are today almost as familiar with ancient Egypt and Mesopotamia as we are with our own world.

Archaeology has proved that the Bible is nothing more than a fantasy. We have no more reason to believe there ever was an Abraham or a Moses than to believe in the Abominable Snowman. We have no more reason to believe there was ever a King Solomon than to believe there were a King Arthur and a Round Table of Knights. The hard evidence of the excavations has exposed the deception once and for all.

My dear jurors, the task before you is daunting, even frightening. It's fraught with emotion. Some of you will find it hard to accept the charges of fraud and misrepresentation leveled at the Bible. But the facts speak for themselves, and it's your responsibility to proclaim the truth as you see it.

Do not worry that you might deprive millions of people of the security and comforts of religion. You will not. The people that want to believe will continue to believe whatever they wish to believe. I assure you that religion will not die after you bring in your verdict.

Ladies and gentlemen of the jury, history is in your hands.

The Complaint

Judge: Let us proceed. Mr. Taylor?

Mr. Taylor: The plaintiff calls Lavender Williams.

• • •

Mr. Taylor: Mrs. Williams, what is your occupation?

Mrs. Williams: I teach sixth grade at Cushman Middle School in Bedford-Stuyvesant here in Brooklyn. At least, that's what I was doing until I was fired.

Mr. Taylor: Mrs. Williams, what exactly did you do that brought this on?

Mrs. Williams: I taught the children historical material that appears in the Bible.

Mr. Taylor: Did you bring Bibles into the classroom?

Mrs. Williams: No, but I assigned readings in the Bible. I assumed that most children had ready access to a Bible.

Mr. Taylor: What kind of material did you introduce to your classes?

Mrs. Williams: It was historical. The origins of the Israelites. The captivity in Egypt and the Exodus. I should point out that I didn't mention any miracles described in the Bible. Whether you believe those or not is a matter of faith, and I wasn't teaching faith in my classroom. I was teaching ancient history. I taught them about the conquest of Canaan, the establishment of the Kingdom of Israel under King David

	and King Solomon and the downward spiral until the eventual exile of the Israelites to Babylon.
Mr. Taylor:	And you never mentioned religion?
Mrs. Williams:	Only in the anthropological sense. I told them that the Israelites are especially important in history because they gave the world monotheism.
Mr. Taylor:	And this does not violate the separation of church and state?
Mrs. Williams:	Of course not. Religious beliefs and customs are important to the study of different societies. I wasn't telling the children what to believe or not believe. I never promoted religion as a personal faith.
Mr. Taylor:	Why did you think it was important to teach these things to them?
Mrs. Williams:	Because I wanted them to know the truth.
Mr. Taylor:	And you believe the Bible is historically accurate?
Mrs. Williams:	Yes.
Mr. Taylor:	Even though it tells miraculous stories?
Mrs. Williams:	We get a lot of historical information from ancient inscriptions, and most of them feature plenty of gods and miraculous tales. We don't chuck the historical stuff because we don't believe the religious stuff. I always felt the Bible deserved at least the same respect.
Mr. Taylor:	Now, Mrs. Williams, did you realize that teaching this material could lead to

<table>
<tr><td></td><td>problems for you?</td></tr>
<tr><td>Mrs. Williams:</td><td>Yes, I did.</td></tr>
<tr><td>Mr. Taylor:</td><td>So why did you feel it was so important to teach this material? Why risk the wrath of your principal?</td></tr>
<tr><td>Mrs. Williams:</td><td>I felt it was important for the children to know the Bible was a valid historical record. Especially the children in my school in Bedford-Stuyvesant.</td></tr>
<tr><td>Mr. Taylor:</td><td>Please explain.</td></tr>
<tr><td>Mrs. Williams:</td><td>Of course. The most stable social force in black society has always been our Christian religion. Jesus gave us comfort when we were slaves, and he continues to give us hope as we struggle for genuine equality in American society. Our faith is important to us. Most of our great leaders are clergymen, from Martin Luther King on down. The children hear all around them that the Bible is a myth, and their faith is shaken. That's a bad thing.</td></tr>
<tr><td>Mr. Taylor:</td><td>That's commendable, Mrs. Williams, but weren't you crossing the line into the area of religion?</td></tr>
<tr><td>Mrs. Williams:</td><td>No, I wasn't. I never talked to the children about their Christian faith. I never encouraged them to go to church or pray. I just taught them something that is true, something that is important for them to know. I taught them that the Bible is a valid historical record, as valid as anything else from ancient times. This is the opinion of many great scholars</td></tr>
</table>

and scientists. I don't think the school has the right to dismiss the Bible out of hand as a historical resource and send a message to the children that their religion is nonsense. It violates our freedom of religion and my right of free speech.

Mr. Taylor: But what if they could prove conclusively that the Bible is a myth?

Mrs. Williams: That would be different. But there is no way they could prove that conclusively. On the contrary, according to the scholarly books I've read, the evidence points the other way. The school has no right to suppress that point of view and give the children the impression that only religious fanatics accept the historicity of the Bible.

Mr. Taylor: I see. Very well, let's move on to the facts of the case. What is your principal's name?

Mrs. Williams: Wesley Youngblood.

Mr. Taylor: Is that Mr. Youngblood sitting over there?

Mrs. Williams: Yes, that's Mr. Youngblood.

Mr. Taylor: Did you explain your position to your principal clearly and logically, just as you explained it to the jury now?

Mrs. Williams: Yes, I did. In much greater detail.

Mr. Taylor: And what did he say?

Mrs. Williams: He wasn't interested. He just wanted me to stop. Period.

Mr. Taylor: And when you didn't?

Mrs. Williams: He fired me.

Mr. Taylor:	Did you have an administrative hearing at the Board of Education?
Mrs. Williams:	I did.
Mr. Taylor:	Did you explain yourself there?
Mrs. Williams:	I did. But it didn't do any good. They gave me an ultimatum. I could have my job back if I promised to stop. Otherwise, I was out.
Mr. Taylor:	So, what did you do?
Mrs. Williams:	I stood by my principles and refused.
Mr. Taylor:	Thank you, Mrs. Williams. I have no more questions.
Judge:	Your witness, Mr. Calabrese.
Mr. Calabrese:	No questions, your honor, but I would like to call a rebuttal witness at this time.
Judge:	Call your witness.
Mr. Calabrese:	The defense calls Wesley Youngblood.
Mr. Calabrese:	Can we have your full name and occupation, sir?
Mr. Youngblood:	My name is Wesley Youngblood. I'm the principal of the Cushman Middle School here in Brooklyn.
Mr. Calabrese:	Mr. Youngblood, is Mrs. Lavender Williams in your employ?
Mr. Youngblood:	She was. She taught sixth grade.
Mr. Calabrese:	And now she is no longer in your employ?
Mr. Youngblood:	She was fired for teaching the Bible to the children in her class.
Mr. Calabrese:	And why didn't you want her to teach them the Bible, Mr. Youngblood?

Mr. Youngblood: Because it is a violation of the separation of church and state.

Mr. Calabrese: Did you give her ample warning before you fired her?

Mr. Youngblood: I certainly did.

Mr. Calabrese: Did she try to justify what she was doing?

Mr. Youngblood: Yes. She said she was teaching history rather than religion.

Mr. Calabrese: And how did you respond to that?

Mr. Youngblood: I refused to get into a debate with her. I told her the Bible was not an acceptable historical resource for the classroom in a public school.

Mr. Calabrese: And what did she say?

Mr. Youngblood: She called me a house nigger.

Mr. Taylor: Objection! Irrelevant and highly prejudicial.

Judge: Sustained.

Mr. Calabrese: Thank you, Mr. Youngblood. There will be no further questions.

Judge: Do you wish to cross-examine, Mr. Taylor?

Mr. Taylor: Yes, your honor, I do. Mr. Youngblood, I objected to your telling the jury that Mrs. Williams called you a house nigger, and the judge sustained my objection. But the jury heard you. I might as well ask about that remark. Had she ever made such a remark to you before?

Mr. Youngblood: No, sir.

Mr. Taylor: Didn't this indicate that she felt strongly about what she was doing?

Mr. Calabrese: Objection. Calls for a conclusion on the part of the witness.

Judge: Sustained.

Mr. Taylor: Let me rephrase the question. Did you conclude in your own mind at the time that Mrs. Williams felt strongly about this issue?

Mr. Youngblood: Yes, I did.

Mr. Taylor: And yet you refused to discuss it with her.

Mr. Youngblood: We did discuss it.

Mr. Taylor: But didn't you just say that you refused to get into a debate with her?

Mr. Youngblood: Well, yes. But we did discuss that she should stop doing it.

Mr. Taylor: I see. By discuss you mean you issued your orders. You didn't really listen, did you? Didn't you think she had a right to be heard?

Mr. Youngblood: I listened to her.

Mr. Taylor: Yes, we know how you listened. Let's go on. How long had she been teaching about the Bible in her classroom when you ordered her to stop?

Mr. Youngblood: I'm not sure. I'd say a few months, maybe close to a year.

Mr. Taylor: You knew about it for a year and did nothing?

Mr. Youngblood: Well … I didn't do anything right away.

Mr. Taylor:	Why did you wait so long?
Mr. Youngblood:	It was not on top of my list. The Cushman Middle School is in a disadvantaged neighborhood. We deal with many problems on a daily basis. Other issues took priority. Her classroom was functioning. Other teachers were not doing nearly as well. I let it ride for a while.
Mr. Taylor:	A while being close to a year?
Mr. Youngblood:	I suppose.
Mr. Taylor:	What changed your mind, Mr. Youngblood? Have you solved all your other problems so that this was the only one that remained?
Mr. Youngblood:	I wish that were true. I decided to put a stop to it, because there were complaints.
Mr. Taylor:	Complaints? From whom?
Mr. Youngblood:	The American Conference on Educational Standards. They've been in the news lately because of their involvement in the fight against the Intelligent Design initiative. A.C.E.S. sent me a letter of complaint and said they would go to the attorney general's office if I didn't put a stop to it.
Mr. Taylor:	And so, you told Mrs. Williams to cease and desist?
Mr. Youngblood:	I did.
Mr. Taylor:	Mr. Youngblood, you've known her for a while, haven't you?
Mr. Youngblood:	Yes.

Mr. Taylor:	Has she ever struck you as a religious fanatic?
Mr. Youngblood:	No.
Mr. Taylor:	Thank you. No more questions.
Judge:	The court is adjourned. We will resume Monday morning at ten o'clock. Ladies and gentlemen of the jury, please remember my instructions. Get a good rest over the weekend.

Equipoise

Judge:	Mr. Taylor, please call you next witness.
Mr. Taylor:	Your honor, the plaintiff rests, but we reserve the right to introduce evidence at a later time if necessary.
Judge:	What is the meaning of this, Mr. Taylor? Doesn't the plaintiff intend to present on a case?
Mr. Taylor:	Absolutely, your honor. The plaintiff has just presented its entire case. We have proved that Mrs. Williams was dismissed for using the Bible as a historical resource. That has been firmly established. The defense has not disputed our contention. Therefore, we move for a directed verdict in our favor based on the principle of equipoise.
Judge:	Explain yourself, Mr. Taylor.
Mr. Taylor:	Your honor, according to the ruling of the Supreme Court in the case of *Schaffer v. Weast*, with Justice Sandra Day O'Connor writing for the majority, the general rule is that the burden of proof is on the party trying to change the status quo. If the evidence is in equipoise, meaning there is no clear indication to either side, the party calling for the maintenance of the status quo wins.
Judge:	I'm familiar with *Schaffer v. Weast*, counselor. How are you applying it here? As the plaintiff, aren't you the one seeking relief?

Mr. Taylor: We are, indeed, your honor. However, this case is not about whether or not Mrs. Williams was dismissed. That is not in dispute. It is whether the Bible is or is not an acceptable historical resource. That is the question before the jury. Regarding this question, which is the crux of the case, the status quo established for thousands of years in Western society is that the Bible is a reliable historical document. That status quo has never been officially changed in the New York City school system. Books published by certain members of the academic community do not represent a change in the status quo.

Therefore, the burden of proof falls on the defendants. They must prove that the status quo should not be allowed to stand. And if the evidence is considered in equipoise, the jury must find for the plaintiff. The plaintiff has proved she was fired for using the Bible as a historical resource and that her civil rights were violated. She should not be required to prove anything beyond that. If defense does not demonstrate that they did not violate her civil rights, plaintiff automatically wins.

Mr. Calabrese: Your honor, this argument is unexpected. The defense requests a brief recess to consider its merits.

Judge: You're not the only one taken by surprise, counselor. Court will adjourn until two o'clock, at which time I will rule on the motion by the plaintiff.

Judge: Before I issue my ruling on plaintiff's motion. I want to explain the principle of equipoise to the jury and the context of the Supreme Court ruling. The case of *Schaffer v. Weast* involved individualized education programs (IEP) that schools are required by statute to provide for children with disabilities. The Maryland public school system designed an IEP for Brian Schaffer, a child with learning disabilities. Brian's parents were unhappy with the IEP. They placed Brian in a private school, after which they initiated a due process administrative hearing challenging the IEP and seeking compensation for the cost of Brian's private education. Who had the burden of persuasion? The Supreme Court ruled that they did.

I've decided to allow the motion of the plaintiff. It is unreasonable to assume that an opinion that prevails in academic circles, but is not unanimous, constitutes a *de facto* change of the status quo. Since there is no official school policy specifically forbidding the use of the Bible as a historical resource, the plaintiff's use of the Bible as an extracurricular resource would be justified unless the defendants can prove that the Bible is not a legitimate historical resource.

The burden of proof, therefore, falls on the defendants. If the defendants present no case, I would be compelled to issue a directed verdict in favor of the plaintiff. The plaintiff would not be required to prove that the Bible is a legitimate historical resource. If the defendants do present a case, I will inform the jury that the burden of proof is on the defendants.

I am assuming that the defendants intend to present a case. Is that correct, Mr. Calabrese?

Mr. Calabrese: Of course, your honor.

Judge: As I explained, the burden of proof is on the defense. Are you prepared to begin now?

Mr. Calabrese: Yes, we are.

Judge: Then let us proceed. Please call your first witness.

Anachronisms

Mr. Calabrese: Can we have your full name, sir?

Dr. Clayton: Charles Ingersoll Clayton.

Mr. Calabrese: And what kind of doctor are you?

Dr. Clayton: I am a Doctor of Biblical Studies. I have been the Lindstrom Professor of Biblical Studies at Northwestern University for the last five years.

Mr. Calabrese: Dr. Clayton, could you give us a little background about biblical studies? How old is your field?

Dr. Clayton: Oh, I'd say it's become a full-fledged academic discipline in the last hundred and fifty years, but there was earlier movement in that direction.

Mr. Calabrese: Can you explain, Doctor? Hasn't the Bible been studied intensely for thousands of years? Wasn't every educated person in the Western world expected to have a thorough knowledge of the Bible?

Dr. Clayton: Certainly. But that is a different affair altogether. For thousands of years, hardly anyone questioned the authorship and authenticity of the Bible. Let's just talk about the Pentateuch, the first five books of the Bible, called the Five Books of Moses. Genesis, Exodus, Leviticus, Numbers and Deuteronomy. People simply accepted that Moses wrote these books of the Bible by God's command and everything in them was true. The efforts of scholars and educated people were to

	understand what the Bible was saying, to discern its divine messages.
Mr. Calabrese:	And that is not what you consider biblical studies?
Dr. Clayton:	Not at all. Biblical scholarship is a textual science concerned with determining the Bible's origin. Who wrote it? Why? When? How much in it, if anything, is historical? We're interested in the message only insofar as it helps determine the identity of the authors and their motivation. I see. And what do you mean by textual science?
Dr. Clayton:	Biblical scholarship conducts a critical analysis of the Biblical texts to determine the origins. We use the scientific method to analyze style, consistency, use of language and the like. What we do is generally called higher criticism.
Mr. Calabrese:	You mentioned that you try to determine the identity of the authors of the Pentateuch. Not author, but authors. In the plural. Are you saying that there was more than one author?
Dr. Clayton:	Without a doubt. Biblical criticism has determined that there were at least four authors and that an editor formed the first five books of the Bible by combining the writings of these authors.
Mr. Calabrese:	How interesting. You say this is certain?
Dr. Clayton:	Oh yes. It's an established fact, one of the great accomplishments of Western science. It ranks right up there with

	Darwin's theory of evolution. No intelligent person would dispute it.
Mr. Taylor:	Objection, your honor! This is offensive. Many millions of people would disagree with this witness, and I suspect that some of them might even be intelligent.
Judge:	Objection sustained. Strike it from the record.
Mr. Calabrese:	Let me rephrase the question. Is there a general feeling in the academic and scientific community that multiple authorship of the Bible is so clear that no intelligent person would dispute it?
Mr. Taylor:	Objection! Has the witness taken a poll?
Mr. Calabrese:	I withdraw the question. Doctor Clayton, you say the field of biblical scholarship seeks to determine who wrote the Bible, why and when. Why is it so important to determine the identity of the author or authors?
Dr. Clayton:	In order to gain a full understanding of any work, it's important to know the identity of the author, when he wrote it, the social conditions, his personal life, his motivations and prejudices. All these give us a true picture of what he's saying and why he's saying it. If we lack this information, we cannot gain a full understanding of the text. In high school and university classes, students are usually taught something about the author's life. It helps to know that Dostoevsky was a Russian of the Orthodox faith and that he

was an epileptic. If we want to understand the true meaning of the Bible, we need to know who wrote it, when and why.

Mr. Calabrese: Makes sense. I think that's beyond dispute. Why is it so clear to most biblical scholars that the Bible was not written by Moses?

Dr. Clayton: The Bible claims to have been written about thirteen hundred years before the common era. But many indications in the text itself and modern discoveries of archaeology place the time of authorship at a much later date. Some of these clues point to a perfect fit for these texts with conditions in the Israelite kingdoms some six or seven hundred years later.

Mr. Calabrese: How interesting.

Dr. Clayton: Believe me, it's fascinating. We call these anachronisms.

Mr. Calabrese: What are anachronisms?

Dr. Clayton: Anachronisms are statements of information that do not fit the times in which the Bible was supposedly written. For instance, an alleged eyewitness account of Napoleon's invasion of Russia in 1812 that describes Napoleon's arrival by helicopter at the siege of Moscow is obviously not authentic. There were no helicopters in Napoleon's time, so it could not have been written by an eyewitness. This is an anachronism. The Bible is full of anachronisms.

Mr. Calabrese: Could you share some anachronisms with

the court and the jury?

Dr. Clayton: Certainly. The most striking is the mention of camels in the time of the Patriarchs, which according to Biblical chronology was about 2000 B.C.E. The stories of the Patriarchs in Genesis are packed with camels, and yet we know that camels weren't domesticated until about 1100 B.C.E. Just to mention one instance, how could Abraham have sent his servant to find a wife for Isaac with a caravan of camels almost a thousand years earlier? It's like Napoleon flying in a helicopter. No, it's more like Julius Caesar flying in a helicopter.

Mr. Calabrese: So why would the Bible mention camels?

Dr. Clayton: It's obvious. Clearly, these stories were written at a much later time when there were plenty of camels. The writers, not having the benefits of modern archaeology, didn't know that camels were not in use at the time they were placing their story and that the characters should be using donkeys instead of camels.

Mr. Calabrese: For the record, can you give us a source for this information?

Dr. Clayton: I suggest *The Bible Unearthed* by Dr. Israel Finkelstein.

Mr. Calabrese: That is powerful evidence, Dr. Clayton. Are there any more anachronisms you can share with us?

Dr. Clayton: Certainly. History informs us that there were two small nations to the east of ancient Israel called Ammon and Moab. The first inkling we have of their existence is about 800 B.C.E. There is no archaeological trace of these kingdoms before then. Yet the Bible tells about encounters with them about 1400 B.C.E. Five hundred years before they emerge as nations! The Bible also gives them a history that goes back hundreds of years further. It's clear that the whole concoction was born in the imagination of the biblical writers. But they erred. They thought Ammon and Moab must have been in existence for thousands of years when, in fact, they were only in existence a few hundred.

Mr. Calabrese: And why would the biblical writers do something like that?

Dr. Clayton: Professor Finkelstein offers an explanation in his book.

Mr. Calabrese: Would you share it with us please?

Dr. Clayton: Certainly. But first I have to tell you the biblical story of the origin of these two nations.

Mr. Calabrese: Please tell us the story.

Dr. Clayton: Yes, the Bible tells about a nephew of Abraham by the name of Lot. Abraham and Lot travel to Canaan from Syria, but after they arrive, they part ways. They both have large flocks of sheep, and they need elbow room. Abraham goes to the hill country, and Lot settles in Sodom, the famous den of iniquity.

The Bible tells how God rains fire and brimstone on the city of Sodom and destroys it. Only Lot and his two daughters survive. They hide in a cave. Lot's daughters are convinced they're the only people left on earth, that when they die the human race will perish. They feel the burden of responsibility for the survival of humankind, but there are no men left to help them conceive.

Except for their father. So, they get their father drunk and have … uh … relations with him. One daughter gives birth to a son and names him Moab, which means 'from the father.' The other gives birth to a son and names him Ben Ami, 'son of my nation.' According to the Bible, the two nations of Moab and Ammon arose from these bastard children.

Mr. Calabrese:	I don't quite understand. Why would the biblical writers make up such a story?
Dr. Clayton:	They had a political agenda. At the time the Bible was written, Ammon and Moab were the regional rivals of the Israelite kingdom of Judah. The Judahites wanted to disparage them in the eyes of the world. They wanted to discredit them by portraying them as illegitimate offspring of incestuous unions. As Dr. Finkelstein points out, and I quote, 'No seventh century Judahite looking across the Dead Sea toward the rival kingdoms would have been able to suppress a smile of contempt at a story of such a disreputable ancestry.' That's in his book, and I think it is very

	well put.
Mr. Calabrese:	So that is why they made up these stories about Ammon and Moab?
Dr. Clayton:	Precisely. Because they wanted to ridicule them. But they didn't realize that way back then these nations simply didn't exist.
Mr. Calabrese:	This is powerful stuff, Dr. Clayton. Tell us more.
Dr. Clayton:	And then there are the Philistines, of course. Genesis reports that Isaac, the second Patriarch of the Israelites, had an encounter with Abimelech, the king of the Philistine city of Gerar. Abraham is also reported to have visited Gerar. As I mentioned, these encounters supposedly took place about 2000 B.C.E. The problem is that the Philistines didn't arrive in the region until about 1100 B.C.E.
Mr. Calabrese:	How do you know this?
Dr. Clayton:	It's really quite simple. The Philistines, also called the Peoples of the Sea, were raiders who came from the Aegean Sea area in southeastern Europe. They colonized the coast of the Mediterranean in what is now the Gaza Strip in about 1100 B.C.E. and built five cities. Gaza, Gath, Ashkelon, Ashdod and Ekron. We know this from ancient Egyptian records. Archaeologists have also identified Tel Haror northwest of Beersheba as Gerar, and excavations have shown that it was only an insignificant little village even

in 1100 B.C.E.. Once again, the biblical writer is tripped up by inadequate knowledge of the world about which he was writing. There were Philistines in the writer's time, so he assumes there were Philistines in the times of the Patriarchs. How was he to know that the Philistines didn't arrive until nearly a thousand years later?

Mr. Calabrese: It makes you think, doesn't it? Can you give the court specific citations about the Philistines in the Bible as well as some of the other anachronisms we discussed? You can give us chapter and verse.

Dr. Clayton: It's all here on this sheet I'm holding. Citation and source.

Mr. Calabrese: Permission to approach the witness. I'd like to submit this into evidence.

Judge: You may approach.

Mr. Calabrese: We have copies for the plaintiff and the jurors, your honor.

Judge: The bailiff will distribute them. You may proceed.

Mr. Calabrese: Dr. Clayton, you said that biblical scholars discovered anachronisms in the text and through archaeology. The anachronisms you mentioned – the camels, Ammon and Moab, the Philistines – are all based on the discoveries of archaeology. Can you tell us some of the anachronisms that arise from the text itself? But first, please explain what you mean by anachronisms from within the text.

Dr. Clayton: Of course. Upon a close reading, many statements in the text point to a later date of authorship. For instance, Genesis reports that four Mesopotamian kings captured Sodom and abducted Lot, Abraham's nephew, the same fellow that fathered children by his daughters. According to Genesis, Abraham mobilized his forces, pursued them until a place called Dan and rescued his nephew. As a matter of fact, there was no city called Dan at the time.

Mr. Calabrese: How do you know that?

Dr. Clayton: Because according to the Bible, Dan was Abraham's great-grandson. He was the patriarch of one of the Israelite tribes among whom Canaan was divided after the alleged Conquest. Dan's portion was in the northeastern corner. The Book of Judges reports that Dan tribesman attacked the city of Layish, wiped out its inhabitants and renamed it Dan. According to the Book of Joshua, the city was called Leshem before it was renamed Dan. This happened hundreds of years after Abraham's mythical raid and decades after Moses supposedly wrote the Bible in the desert. So why would he have called the place Dan? It's obvious the writer of these stories lived many years later and was quite familiar with the city of Dan.

Mr. Calabrese: Makes you think, doesn't it? Are there any more of these textual indications of a later authorship?

Dr. Clayton: Yes, indeed there are. Many.

Mr. Calabrese: The evidence seems quite overwhelming, Dr. Clayton. What conclusion do you draw?

Mr. Taylor: Objection, your honor. I believe the jurors would like to draw their own conclusions from the witness's testimony. They are intelligent people and perfectly capable of doing so on their own.

Mr. Calabrese: Your honor, Dr. Clayton is an expert witness. That's what expert witnesses do. They draw expert conclusions.

Judge: Objection overruled. The witness will answer the question.

Mr. Calabrese: Thank you, your honor. Dr. Clayton?

Dr. Clayton: I draw the only reasonable conclusion possible –

Mr. Taylor: Objection! We've been through this before.

Judge: Yes, we have, counselor. Objection sustained. Witness will refrain from making such incendiary statements.

Mr. Calabrese: Dr. Clayton, your conclusions.

Dr. Clayton: My conclusions. In my opinion, it is clear that the Bible was not written at the time it claims to have been written. Therefore ... in my opinion ... it has no historical value. The stories of the Bible, especially the Pentateuch, the Five Books of Moses, are foundational myths and legends, concocted many centuries after the alleged events supposedly took place.

	They were meant to give the emerging Israelite nation a unifying history and a sense of antiquity and stability.
Mr. Calabrese:	Thank you for your expert opinion. Now, the discovery of anachronisms doesn't solve the mystery of who wrote the Bible, does it?
Dr. Clayton:	No, it doesn't. But it's an important step forward. It establishes conclusively that the Bible was not written by Moses – if there ever was a Moses – but rather by someone who lived many centuries later. Now we can try to pin it down a little better by a close critical analysis of the text. If the Bible wasn't written when it claims to have been written, exactly when was it written? And who wrote it?
Mr. Calabrese:	Are you asking me? I don't know.
Dr. Clayton:	The questions were rhetorical. Biblical scholarship in the last one hundred and fifty years has discovered that the Bible is a composite of source documents. We've developed a set of ironclad criteria, and we can point with assurance at just about any passage, verse or verse fragment and identify the source document from which it was taken. This is called the Documentary Hypothesis.
Mr. Calabrese:	And this will help us discover who wrote the Bible and why?
Dr. Clayton:	It will. Since we have already established that it was not written at the time it claims to have been written but many years

<table>
<tr><td></td><td>later, we can view the Bible in the context of the political situation in Israel at the approximate time of its composition, and we can see that the various source documents serve the political goals of the different parties.</td></tr>
<tr><td>Mr. Calabrese:</td><td>Thank you for your testimony, Dr. Clayton.</td></tr>
<tr><td>Mr. Taylor:</td><td>Your honor, counsel for the defense has covered a lot of ground with this witness regarding alleged anachronisms. I'd like to cross-examine the witness on his testimony and present rebuttal witnesses.</td></tr>
<tr><td>Judge:</td><td>Motion granted. But the hour is late. Court is adjourned until tomorrow morning.</td></tr>
</table>

• • •

<table>
<tr><td>Mr. Taylor:</td><td>Dr. Clayton, you testified yesterday – and here I quote you verbatim from the transcript – 'since we have already established that it was not written at the time it claims to have been written but many years later, we can view the Bible in the context of the political situation in Israel at the approximate time of its composition.' You also said that we can see how the various source documents serve the political goals of the different parties. Am I quoting you correctly?</td></tr>
<tr><td>Dr. Clayton:</td><td>Yes.</td></tr>
<tr><td>Mr. Taylor:</td><td>In other words, the knowledge that the Bible was anachronistic lends impetus</td></tr>
</table>

to the reconstruction of the Hypothesis, about which we will soon hear testimony. Is that correct?

Dr. Clayton: Yes, it is.

Mr. Taylor: Thank you. Now, suppose we could demonstrate that there are no anachronisms. Suppose we could furthermore demonstrate that the Bible really is a document of great antiquity written at more or less the time it claims to have been written. What would that do to the Hypothesis?

Dr. Clayton: The Hypothesis is a proven fact, sir. The anachronisms are facts.

Mr. Taylor: If the Hypothesis is a fact, why is it only a hypothesis?

Dr. Clayton: It was a hypothesis originally, and the name has stuck. It's not important. The Hypothesis is a fact.

Mr. Taylor: Dr. Clayton, humor me. It's just a hypothetical. Suppose we could indeed demonstrate that the Bible is a document of great antiquity written at more or less the time it claims to have been written. What would that do to the Hypothesis the defense is about to present to the court? Would it basically demolish the Hypothesis?

Dr. Clayton: Well, I don't know if it would demolish it, but it might create a need for some... adjustments.

Mr. Taylor: I see. Adjustments. No doubt. Very well then, let's take a closer look at your alleged anachronisms. You mentioned camels, didn't you?

Dr. Clayton: Yes, I did. The Bible speaks about extensive use of camels in the Patriarchal age, which is about 2000 B.C.E., but archaeology has established that camels were not domesticated until close to 1100 B.C.E.

Mr. Taylor: And this is conclusive proof of anachronisms in the Bible?

Dr. Clayton: It is.

Mr. Taylor: Conclusive proof?

Dr. Clayton: Yes.

Mr. Taylor: Let's talk about this conclusive proof, Dr. Clayton. Have archaeologists excavated the entire ancient world?

Dr. Clayton: You mean every city, town and village?

Mr. Taylor: That's what I mean. Have they excavated all these?

Dr. Clayton: Of course not.

Mr. Taylor: How much have they excavated?

Dr. Clayton: I don't know. A small part.

Mr. Taylor: Ten percent?

Dr. Clayton: Less.

Mr. Taylor: One percent?

Dr. Clayton: Probably less.

Mr. Taylor: So, we don't really know what the other ninety-nine plus percent would reveal, do we?

Dr. Clayton: I suppose not. But we can project from

	the parts excavated.
Mr. Taylor:	I see. Projections. So it appears that your definite statement that there were no camels in use before 1100 B.C.E. is a projection based on less than one percent excavation. How can you know that we wouldn't find camels if we excavate some more?
Dr. Clayton:	It's a reasonable assumption.
Mr. Taylor:	I see. A projection based on an assumption. Are you saying that there is an assumption of conclusive proof based on a projection based on an assumption?
Dr. Clayton:	I'm saying there were no camels back then. It's a fact.
Mr. Taylor:	Let's move on. You testified yesterday that the mention of the nations of Ammon and Moab in the Five Books of Moses was an anachronism, because those nations did not exist yet. Is that correct?
Dr. Clayton:	Yes, it is.
Mr. Taylor:	And you quoted as your source a book called *The Bible Unearthed* by Dr. Israel Finkelstein. Is that correct?
Dr. Clayton:	Yes.
Mr. Taylor:	Now on page 40 of that book the author mentions another quite similar anachronism that you failed to mention. I have the book right here. Dr. Finkelstein writes about the biblical story of Esau and Jacob, the twin sons of Isaac and Rebecca. Esau, the elder, is a feral hunter,

while Jacob is a sensitive scholar. God tells Rebecca when she is pregnant, 'Two nations are in your womb, and two people, born of you, shall be divided; the one shall be stronger than the other, the elder shall serve the younger.' This bit of legend, Dr. Finkelstein argues, was concocted as legitimization of Israel's dominance over Edom, the nation supposedly founded by Esau, in late monarchic times. Am I correct?

Dr. Clayton: Basically.

Mr. Taylor: When the Bible tells about the encounter with the Kingdom of Edom shortly after the Exodus, the old rivalry is reignited. Am I correct?

Dr. Clayton: Basically.

Mr. Taylor: And then Finkelstein adds – and I quote – 'But Edom did not exist as a distinct political entity until a relatively late period. From the Assyrian source we know there were no real kings and no state in Edom until the late eighth century B.C.E. ... The archaeological evidence is also clear: the first large-scale wave of settlement in Edom ... may have started in the late eighth century but reached a peak only in the seventh and early sixth century B.C.E. Before then, the area was sparsely populated ... Thus, here too the stories of Esau and Jacob ... are skillfully fashioned as archaizing legends to reflect the rivalries of late monarchic times.' These are the words of Dr. Finkelstein, slight condensed. Do they sound familiar?

Dr. Clayton: Yes, they do.

Mr. Taylor: Why didn't you mention the anachronism of a non-existent Edom along with the anachronism of non-existent Ammon and Moab?

Dr. Clayton: Because I felt the case for Edom was a little weaker than the case for Ammon and Moab.

Mr. Taylor: Indeed? Isn't it true that there were developments after Dr. Finkelstein's book was published in 2001? Isn't it true that in 2005 an international team of American, Canadian, Jordanian and German archaeologists, headed by Dr. Thomas Levy, professor of archaeology at the University of California at San Diego, discovered that Edom existed hundreds of years earlier than previously believed?

Dr. Clayton: Yes.

Mr. Taylor: Isn't it true that they investigated an Edomite copper ore zone and found major copper production, massive fortifications and over a hundred building complexes going back into the second millennium B.C.E.?

Dr. Clayton: Yes.

Mr. Taylor: So, what happened to Dr. Finkelstein's projections?

Dr. Clayton: They were disproved. But they were legitimate at the time. He'd stepped right into the trap.

Mr. Taylor:	Which just goes to show you that even legitimate projections cannot be considered conclusive, doesn't it?
Dr. Clayton:	You can draw your own conclusions.
Mr. Taylor:	So can the jury. Let's move on. One of the most famous alleged anachronisms in the early days of the field of biblical criticism involved the Hittites, didn't it?
Dr. Clayton:	Yes, it did.
Mr. Taylor:	Please tell the court about that alleged anachronism, Dr. Clayton.
Dr. Clayton:	They thought there were no Hittites.
Mr. Taylor:	We need more details. Who thought there were no Hittites?
Dr. Clayton:	The scholars thought there were no Hittites.
Mr. Taylor:	I understand your reluctance to go into the whole story. I'll help you out, and all you have to do is confirm or deny. All right?
Dr. Clayton:	Go ahead.
Mr. Taylor:	The early Bible critics noticed that the Bible talks about a people called the Hittites, but history and the science of archaeology had absolutely no record of such people. Clear evidence, argued the Bible critics, that these were an imaginary people and that the Bible was a work of fiction. Isn't that true, Dr. Clayton?
Dr. Clayton:	But that was a hundred years ago.
Mr. Taylor:	And isn't it also true that an excavation

	about ninety miles east of Ankara, the capital of Turkey, revealed the city of Boghazkoy, the royal capital of the previously undiscovered Hittite Empire, which stretched across Turkey, Syria and Lebanon?
Dr. Clayton:	Yes.
Mr. Taylor:	Isn't it also true that archaeologists discovered in the royal archive of Boghazkoy over twenty-five thousand clay tablets covered in cuneiform writing, which added a mountain of information to what was already known?
Dr. Clayton:	Yes.
Mr. Taylor:	So tell me, if you knew that the absence of Hittites in the historical record one hundred years ago did not prove that this huge empire did not exist, if you knew that Dr. Finkelstein's conclusions about Edom had been disproved, why did you tell the court with such assurance that the mention of Ammon and Moab in the Bible is an anachronism?
Dr. Clayton:	I testified to the current thinking in the archaeological community.
Mr. Taylor:	Are you saying that you were not telling us a fact, but rather the prevalent current opinion in the archaeological community?
Dr. Clayton:	I was doing my best to give accurate information.
Mr. Taylor:	I'm sure you were. I think you made it clear. Let's move on. You gave us a motivation for the invention of ancient

	Ammon and Moab. Would you be so kind as to refresh our memories?

Dr. Clayton: I said, again relying on Dr. Finkelstein, that the Judahites wanted to delegitimize Ammon and Moab, who were their regional rivals, so they invented the legend that these two nations were descended from the incestuous union of Lot and his daughters after the destruction of Sodom.

Mr. Taylor: Tell me, who was the greatest hero in the history of the Israelite kingdoms both as a warrior and as a philosopher?

Dr. Clayton: I suppose one might say that it is ... King David.

Mr. Taylor: Exactly! King David, fearless leader, courageous warrior, poet, intellectual, the Sweet Singer of Israel. Who was his great-grandmother?

Dr. Clayton: I ...

Mr. Taylor: The court is waiting for your answer. Let me help you out. Wasn't King David's great-grandmother a Moabite convert named Ruth? Isn't that what we read in the Book of Ruth?

Dr. Clayton: Yes.

Mr. Taylor: So tell me, if the Bible was a collection of myths composed at a late date toward the end of the monarchy, as the defense claims, and if the writers composed the story of the Moabites' incestuous origins to besmirch the nation of Moab, why would they make the great King David a

	descendant of bastards? Doesn't that seem ludicrous to you?
Dr. Clayton:	If you put it that way, I suppose it is not very reasonable.
Mr. Taylor:	Thank you, Dr. Clayton. Let's move on. You said the mention of the city called Dan in the story of Abraham's pursuit of the Mesopotamian invaders is an anachronism.
Dr. Clayton:	I certainly did. At the time the Bible claims to have been written, it was called Layish, according to the Book of Joshua, or Leshem, according to the Book of Judges. Those books state quite explicitly that the city was renamed Dan years after the Conquest.
Mr. Taylor:	Yes, that is what you said. Let me ask you a question. Do you think the writers of the Bible were intelligent?
Dr. Clayton:	Certainly. Highly intelligent. The Bible is a masterpiece.
Mr. Taylor:	Was their purpose in writing the Bible to create myths and legends for the people or to convince them that this was historical truth?
Dr. Clayton:	Oh, there's no question they wanted the people to believe that all these things were true. Otherwise, how would they control them?
Mr. Taylor:	In fact, this is the very thrust of your testimony, that the fabrication of the Bible was the perpetration of a fraud by unnamed writers against the Israelite

	people and ultimately against the whole world, is it not?
Dr. Clayton:	It is.
Mr. Taylor:	Did these mysterious writers do a good job? Did they manage to pull the wool over the eyes of the people?
Dr. Clayton:	They most certainly did. They led the Jewish people to believe that God had given them the Law at Mount Sinai and that they were obligated to obey it. They did not realize that none of it was true.
Mr. Taylor:	So, does it make sense that these brilliant perpetrators of what must be the greatest hoax in history would do such a sloppy job? Why call a place Dan while writing Genesis when they must have known full well that the place was called either Layish or Leshem at the time and did not get the name Dan until hundreds of years later?
Dr. Clayton:	I don't know. Perhaps it was a slip up. Maybe the Books of Joshua and Judges had not yet been written.
Mr. Taylor:	Do you think they reviewed and proofread the texts before they released them?
Dr. Clayton:	I imagine they did.
Mr. Taylor:	And no one noticed the discrepancy?
Dr. Clayton:	I'm not responsible for what those people did. Maybe they were out partying the night before. People make mistakes.
Mr. Taylor:	Indeed, they do, Dr. Clayton. Even Dr. Finkelstein makes mistakes, as we have

	just seen. I'd venture to say that even you make mistakes sometimes, wouldn't you say?
Dr. Clayton:	People make mistakes.
Mr. Taylor:	Dr. Clayton, have you ever been to Albany?
Dr. Clayton:	Are you talking about Albany, New York, or Albany, Georgia?
Mr. Taylor:	Excellent question. Did you know that at least twenty-three states have cities named Albany? Wisconsin actually has two cities and one village named Albany.
Dr. Clayton:	I did not know that.
Mr. Taylor:	And did you know there are many other cities that have names identical to cities in other states?
Dr. Clayton:	Yes, I did know that.
Mr. Taylor:	Was it the same in the ancient world? Did cities share names?
Dr. Clayton:	Yes, I suppose. There were a number of cities named Alexandria or Antioch.
Mr. Taylor:	Are you aware that the names of the patriarchs and the tribes appear in ancient records?
Dr. Clayton:	Certainly. Ancient records mention people named Abram and Jacob and Asher and Zebulon and perhaps others I don't recall at the moment.
Mr. Taylor:	You are an expert in Semitic languages, aren't you?
Dr. Clayton:	I am.

Mr. Taylor: What does the name Dan mean?

Dr. Clayton: It is a variant on the word *din*, which means justice, quite common to most Semitic languages in ancient times.

Mr. Taylor: Then the name Dan could easily have been quite a common name, couldn't it?

Dr. Clayton: Yes, it could have been.

Mr. Taylor: And therefore, there could easily have been a number of cities named Dan, just as there are a number of cities named Albany and Alexandria and Antioch. Would you agree?

Dr. Clayton: I suppose.

Mr. Taylor: Now if Abraham was pursuing the Mesopotamian raiders, why would he stop at a certain city?

Dr. Clayton: Perhaps he got tired.

Mr. Taylor: Would it also be reasonable to assume that he stopped because the armies he was pursuing had crossed into their own country?

Dr. Clayton: Yes, that would make sense. It would be too dangerous to go further.

Mr. Taylor: So where was the border of the Mesopotamian kings?

Dr. Clayton: The Euphrates River.

Mr. Taylor: Would it be reasonable to assume that he gave chase until he reached a certain city which was near the Euphrates River?

Dr. Clayton: I suppose. Yes, it would be reasonable.

Mr. Taylor: This would place the city of Dan in

	northern Syria, quite far from the city called Layish, which was later renamed Dan as well. Would you agree?
Dr. Clayton:	I agree that if we place Dan all the way up there, it would have to be a different Dan from the one in the portion of Dan in Israel.
Mr. Taylor:	And do you also agree it would be quite reasonable to place the city of Dan at the end of Abraham's pursuit up there in Northern Syria?
Dr. Clayton:	I guess. I suppose I do.
Mr. Taylor:	So, can we kiss the anachronism of Dan goodbye?
Dr. Clayton:	Maybe, maybe not.
Mr. Taylor:	No more questions.

• • •

Judge:	Counsel for the plaintiff, you may call rebuttal witnesses.
Mr. Taylor:	The plaintiff calls Dr. Paulina Hernandez.
Mr. Taylor:	Dr. Hernandez, please describe to thecourt your field of expertise and your academic credentials.
Dr. Hernandez:	I'm a specialist in Semitic languages and in biblical linguistics. I'm a professor of biblical studies at the University of Southern California. For the current semester, I'm a visiting lecturer-in-residence at Harvard.
Mr. Taylor:	Impressive. Would you agree with Dr.

Clayton that scholars consider the Bible a work of fiction composed centuries after it claims to have been written?

Dr. Hernandez: Absolutely not. It's just one school of thought. I agree it has a considerable number of followers in academia, but there are numerous eminent scholars that disagree vehemently.

Mr. Taylor: Can you give us the name of a prominent scholar that opposes Dr. Clayton's views?

Dr. Hernandez: The most familiar name would be Dr. Kenneth Kitchen. He is one of the world's leading intellectuals. The breadth and depth of his scholarship is incredible. He is a prime authority on Egyptology, archaeology, Oriental history and ancient languages. He is fluent in cuneiform, hieroglyphics and hieratic script. More to the point, Dr. Kitchen's views on the Bible were set forth in two of his many books, an older one entitled *Ancient Orient, Old Testament* and a more recent one entitled *On the Reliability of the Old Testament*. He contends that the Bible is more or less as old as it claims to be.

Mr. Taylor: I don't understand, Dr. Hernandez. You say that Dr. Kitchen is such a towering intellectual figure, and yet he does not command the following of some of the lesser intellectual lights in the anti-Bible school of thought. Can you explain this phenomenon?

Dr. Hernandez: It's not so difficult to understand. The anti-Bible school, as you call it, is highly

	skilled at getting publicity. It packages itself as the liberal view and portrays Dr. Kitchen and the scholars that share his views, me included, as conservative and reactionary. Liberal is a good label in the academic community. Conservative is death. So, it's no wonder young doctoral students seek out the anti-Bible mentors.
Mr. Taylor:	Are you indeed conservative, Dr. Hernandez?
Dr. Hernandez:	I'm conservative in the sense that I'm not prepared to tear down the Bible on the basis of anomalies that can be readily explained. I'm conservative in the sense that I'm not prepared to tear down the Bible given the mass of evidence that supports its extreme antiquity.
Mr. Taylor:	Go on.
Dr. Hernandez:	In my opinion, biblical studies should be a search for the truth, a quest for the factual. Unfortunately, that's not always the case. It's fashionable these days to tear down the Bible. Therefore, it's also popular.
Mr. Taylor:	I see you care deeply about intellectual integrity in your field, Dr. Hernandez. Let me ask you a few specific questions. You heard Dr. Clayton testify that the mention of the city of Dan in Genesis is an anachronism. Are you familiar with that citation?
Dr. Hernandez:	Of course. It's in Genesis 14. The verse states, *vayirdof ad dan*, which means

	he gave chase until Dan. In other words, Abraham pursued the retreating Mesopotamian kings until the city of Dan.
Mr. Taylor:	Exactly. Thank you for the citation of the original Hebrew. Dr. Clayton pointed out that according to the Book of Joshua and the Book of Judges the city was named Layish or Leshem rather than Dan until years after the conquest. In your opinion, is this an anachronism? Does this seem to indicate that the text was written at a later time, or at the very least edited, by someone other than Moses?
Dr. Hernandez:	This is not a new observation. The Talmud offers Midrashic explanations, but there are a number of simple explanations. It's definitely not anachronistic.
Mr. Taylor:	How can you be so sure?
Dr. Hernandez:	A few reasons. First, as you pointed out yesterday during cross-examination, it would have been folly for a later writer to use a place name in the story of Abraham's pursuit that did not exist at the time. Such a writer would have had to be ignorant of the Book of Joshua. This is highly unlikely. The Bible is not a sloppy work. The Bible is meticulous with place names. When place names change, the Bible invariably reports them.
Mr. Taylor:	For instance.
Dr. Hernandez:	Let's name just a few that appear in the same episode of Abraham and the Mesopotamian kings. In Genesis 14:2,

'Bela, which is Zoar.' In Genesis 14:3, 'Emek Hasidim, which is the Salt Sea.' In Genesis 14:7, 'Ein Mishpat, which is Kadesh.' In Genesis 14:17. 'Emek Shaveh, which is Emek Hamelech.' The Bible writer should have written that Abraham 'gave chase until Dan, which is Layish.' The bald reference to Dan is completely out of place if it's not accurate.

Mr. Taylor: What about those simple explanations you mentioned before? Could you give us one or two?

Dr. Hernandez: Well, you already raised the simplest explanation yesterday during cross-examination. You pointed out that just as there is more than one Albany in the United States, there were probably more than one Dan in the ancient Levant. I think this is a reasonable and acceptable explanation. Again, as you pointed out, the Dan in the pursuit story is probably a city much further north, somewhere near the Euphrates River, the last point before crossing over into Mesopotamia.

Mr. Taylor: Can you give us another explanation?

Dr. Hernandez: There is also a rather brilliant explanation proposed by a scholar named Joshua Grinetz, but it gets into the intricacies of Biblical grammar. It is not one of the standard explanations, but it's quite clever.

Mr. Taylor: I'm not an expert in Hebrew grammar, but I think I could follow if you keep it fairly simple.

Dr. Hernandez: I'll do my best. Experts in the grammar of Biblical Hebrew are aware of a tendency to simplify clumsy constructions. Take the phrase 'that night.' The Hebrew should be *lailah hahu*, but often you'll find it condensed as *lailah hu*. The definite article is dropped even though this is not strictly grammatical. Here's another example. The phrase 'if you refuse' should be *im mema'ein atah*, but it appears as *im ma'ein atah*. The verbal prefix is dropped. And here's another. The phrase 'the heavens above' should be *hashamayim mimaal*, but it appears as *hashamayim mei'al*. Do you see what's happening here?

Mr. Taylor: I'm sure I will see as soon as you point it out.

Dr. Hernandez: In Hebrew, there are no capital letters and no vowels, only consonants of equal size. Vowels are indicated by vowel signs under or over the consonants. So, let's drop the vowels from the first two transliterated phrases and then look at them. It should jump out at you. The phrase *llh hh* becomes *llh h*. The phrase *m mmn th* becomes *m mn th*. Do you see it now?

Mr. Taylor: Yes. I think I do. Our honor, permission to approach. I'd like to hand the witness some equipment.

Judge: Permission granted.

Mr. Taylor: Please use this tablet, Dr. Hernandez. It's connected to the large screen over there. Please write these phrases. It will project on the screen.

Dr. Hernandez: Do you see it now?

Mr. Taylor: Yes, I think we all do. It seems that when you have three consecutive consonants one of them is dropped.

Dr. Hernandez: Precisely. Not always, but sometimes. It's actually the middle consonant that is dropped. In the first phrase, the middle Hebrew letter *heh*, or H in the English equivalent, is omitted. In the second phrase, the middle Hebrew letter *mem*, or M in the English equivalent, is omitted. In the third phrase as well.

Mr. Taylor: Interesting. So how does this relate to the question of Dan?

Dr. Hernandez: Well, as you pointed out, the logical location for the city of Dan would be in northern Syria near the Euphrates River. In fact, there actually was an important city right there called Didan or Didanus in ancient times. The name appears in ancient Sumerian inscriptions. King Shu-sin of the third dynasty of Ur mentions Didan on a victory wall, and the name also appears on the Gudea Statue. The prophet Isaiah mentions a people called the Didanites. The city where Abraham stopped his pursuit could have been this Didan, which was about as far as he could go without crossing into Mesopotamia.

Mr. Taylor: So why doesn't the Bible say he chased them until Didan?

Dr. Hernandez: Because that would be three consonants in a row. Here, let me show you. The

Hebrew phrase should have been *vayirdof ad didan*. We drop the vowels, and it becomes *vyrdf d ddn*. Do you see that? Three consecutive Hebrew letters *daled*, or D in the English equivalent. So, the Bible drops the middle consonant in the sequence, and the phrase becomes *vyrdf d dn*. It now reads as *vayirdof ad dan*, and he gave chase until Dan, but it is really saying that he gave chase until Didan. That is how an ancient reader would have understood it.

Mr. Taylor:	So, you are saying that if you read the verse in English translation, or if you are not familiar with biblical linguistics, you'd have no clue that the reference is to Didan rather than to Dan. Is that correct?
Dr. Hernandez:	It certainly is.
Mr. Taylor:	And the mention of the city of Dan is not an anachronism?
Dr. Hernandez:	It's not an anachronism any way you look at it. But according to this theory, it could be the exact opposite. It could be a strong confirmation of the antiquity of the Bible. Centuries after Moses the name Didan was no longer known in the ancient world. It was only recently rediscovered on Sumerian inscriptions by archaeologists. Anyone writing at a late date would not have known to mention Didan, and would not have been so foolish as to mention Dan, as I explained before. Something like this could only have been written in deep antiquity.

Mr. Taylor:	Excellent. Let's move on.
Mr. Calabrese:	Your honor, I would like to cross-examine the witness at this point.
Judge:	Go right ahead, counselor.

• • •

Mr. Calabrese:	Dr. Hernandez, you point out that in Biblical Hebrew when a consonant appears three consecutive times one of them is sometimes omitted. Is that correct?
Dr. Hernandez:	Yes, it is.
Mr. Calabrese:	And you suggest that the name Dan is actually Didan?
Dr. Hernandez:	It could be.
Mr. Calabrese:	Is the omission of one of three consecutive consonants similar to contractions in English? Like writing haven't instead of have not. Yes?
Dr. Hernandez:	That's a good comparison.
Mr. Calabrese:	If someone says haven't instead of have not, the meaning is still clear, is it not?
Dr. Hernandez:	Yes.
Mr. Calabrese:	In the examples you gave us of one consonant being dropped, does it cause confusion? Or is the meaning abundantly clear from the context?
Dr. Hernandez:	The meaning is clear.
Mr. Calabrese:	Are you saying, Dr. Hernandez, that the Bible would write Dan when it meant

	Didan? Are you saying the Bible would drop a consonant of a place name when doing so would obscure the name of the place?
Dr. Hernandez:	It might, but you raise a valid point. I would have to reconsider Dr. Grinetz's explanation. Even if it fails, however, there are plenty of good mainstream explanations.
Mr. Calabrese:	I see. When you say mainstream, you are referring to mainstream conservative thought, not the majority of biblical scholars. Correct?
Dr. Hernandez:	I'm referring to explanations that appear prominently in the literature.
Mr. Calabrese:	I understand. I have no more questions.
Judge:	Before the witness resumes her rebuttal testimony, we'll break for lunch. We'll reconvene at two o'clock in the afternoon.

• • •

Mr. Taylor:	Dr. Hernandez, thank you so much for sharing the views of Dr. Kenneth Kitchen with the court and the jury. As you pointed out, Dr. Kitchen is universally acknowledged as one of the greatest scholars of our times.
Dr. Hernandez:	It's an honor to represent his views to the court.
Mr. Taylor:	Indeed, it is. Let's move on. Dr. Clayton testified under cross-examination that archaeologists have uncovered a small

fraction of one percent of the ancient world, but that they're nonetheless justified in making generalizations based on what they find or do not find. Do you agree?

Dr. Hernandez: I do not agree. You can make cautious generalizations based on what you find, especially inscriptions and drawings, but you have to be wary of making broad generalizations based on what you don't find. Negative evidence is notoriously unreliable.

Mr. Taylor: I see. Dr. Clayton also testified, quoting from Dr. Finkelstein's book, that the Bible anachronistically mentions the use of camels in the Patriarchal age, which was about 2,000 B.C.E., although camels weren't domesticated until about 1100 B.C.E. Do you agree with that testimony?

Dr. Hernandez: I do not. This is an excellent example of the shortcomings of negative evidence. If you draw a conclusion from something you did not find, you stand a good chance of being proven wrong.

Mr. Taylor: Would you please explain?

Dr. Hernandez: The idea that there were no camels in the Patriarchal age originated with the late Dr. William Foxwell Albright, one of the preeminent giants in the field of archaeology. Finding hardly any traces of camel bones among the bones of other domesticated animals in archaeological digs until late in the second millennium B.C.E., he declared that the mention of camels in the Bible was an anachronism. But as it turns out, he was wrong.

Mr. Taylor: How so?

Dr. Hernandez: More recent discoveries in archaeology reveal plenty of evidence of the use of camels in the Patriarchal age and quite a bit earlier as well.

Mr. Taylor: Really? Could we have a few examples?

Dr. Hernandez: Sure. Dr. Kitchen brings evidence from ancient livestock registers listing 'sheep, cattle and camels' and from a Sumerian text from the city of Nippur dated around 2000 B.C.E. that mentions camel's milk. You would assume that milk comes from domesticated animals. You should try milking a wild animal. Not a good idea.

Mr. Taylor: Please go on.

Dr. Hernandez: There's more. Dr. Joseph Free describes an Egyptian clay camel head and a scene of camel riders on a terracotta tablet, both dated to pre-dynastic Egypt, about 3150 B.C.E. He also found camel artifacts from the first dynastic period, about 3000 B.C.E., the fourth dynastic period, about 2500 B.C.E., and the sixth dynastic period, about 2200 B.C.E. Shall I go on? There are more.

Mr. Taylor: No, I think that will be enough for now. Dr. Hernandez, maybe you can clear up a mystery for the court. Apparently, archaeologists from earlier generations assumed, based on the near absence of camel bones in archaeological digs, as you told us, that camels were not domesticated during the Patriarchal age. And yet, as time went on, plenty of evidence was discovered to support the use of camels during that time, as the Bible reports. So how do you explain the lack of camel bones?

Dr. Hernandez: Are you asking me to speculate?

Mr. Taylor: Yes, I am. Expert witnesses are allowed to speculate.

Dr. Hernandez: All right, I assume that camels in early times were not in such common use among the general population. They may have been a novelty, like royal elephants in India and the Far East. They may have been the luxury conveyance of the rich, like fancy Italian sports cars. You won't find the remains of too many Ferraris, Lamborghinis and Maseratis in your average neighborhood junkyards, would you?

Mr. Taylor: No, I don't think you would.

Dr. Hernandez: Now listen to this. The first mention of camels in the Bible is when Pharaoh gives Abraham a parting gift. What does he give him? Assorted livestock ... and camels! The first mention of camels is as part of a royal gift. And this was a truly royal gift. The ancient equivalent of a Rolls Royce. Abraham was probably the first on his block to have camels. These animals were a luxury form of transportation, but they were not commonly used by the people. That's why there are inscriptions and drawings but hardly any bones.

Mr. Taylor: Doesn't the Bible tell us that Abraham sent his servant Eliezer with ten laden camels to Harran to find a wife for Isaac?

Dr. Hernandez: Exactly. But when the sons of Jacob go to Egypt to buy food during a famine they travel on donkeys. No mention of camels. Abraham sent camels to Harran to impress the prospective in-laws. For their own transportation, his family used donkeys.

Mr. Taylor: Makes a lot of sense. Now, I'd like to talk about the Philistines. I'd like to explore one more issue with you. Dr. Clayton testified that the mention of Philistines in the time of Abraham and Isaac, who lived close to 2000 B.C.E., is anachronistic, because the Philistines did not appear in Israel until about 1100 B.C.E., almost a thousand years later. Do you agree with that argument?

Dr. Hernandez: I do not.

Mr. Taylor: All right. Let's go over this carefully. Is it true that the Philistines came to Israel about 1100 B.C.E.?

Dr. Hernandez: It is, and it isn't.

Mr. Taylor: I'm confused. Is it or isn't it?

Dr. Hernandez: Look, let's start from the beginning. We have inscriptions from the time of Ramses III, an Egyptian pharaoh from the twelfth century B.C.E., in which we get a vivid description of the invasion of the Philistines, also called the Sea

	Peoples. The Philistines were apparently a marauding people who migrated from the island of Crete, just south of Greece in the Mediterranean Sea, and settled on the southwestern coast of Israel.
Mr. Taylor:	Is it an established fact that the Philistines came from Crete?
Dr. Hernandez:	Yes. It's also confirmed by the Bible. The prophet Amos states in the name of God, 'Haven't I brought forth Israel from Egypt and the Philistines from Kaphtor?' One of the Hebrew names for the island of Crete is Kaphtor. The prophet Jeremiah states that 'God has destroyed the Philistines, the remnants of the isle of Kaphtor.' There seems to be no question that the Philistines came from Crete.
Mr. Taylor:	But when did they come?
Dr. Hernandez:	Aha! Good question. The Egyptian sources indicate they came in the twelfth century B.C.E. And once again the Bible seems to corroborate this.
Mr. Taylor:	Wait a minute, wait a minute. How can the Bible corroborate that the Philistines came in the twelfth century B.C.E. and at the same time talk about Philistines in the time of the Patriarchs many centuries earlier?
Dr. Hernandez:	The answer to this question will explain how some people mistakenly see an anachronism in the mention of the Philistines. Look, the Philistines are known to Biblical history as the

implacable enemies of Israel, the nemesis of Israel for centuries. The two nations fought many wars. Perhaps it would be more accurate to say that they were in a state of perpetual war.

Mr. Taylor: A hot and cold war.

Dr. Hernandez: Yes, that's a good description. Unending hostilities with periodic eruptions of fighting. These aggressive Philistines lived in a confederation of five garrison cities on the coast of Israel – Ashkelon, Ashdod, Gaza, Ekron and Gath – each ruled by a *seren*, a military commander. But strangely, there is no mention of any these five cities in the Five Books of Moses. We first hear mention of these cities in the Book of Joshua, which begins with the conquest of the Land of Canaan.

Mr. Taylor: But if the Philistines didn't arrive until the middle of the War of Conquest, why were they there in the time of Abraham and Isaac?

Dr. Hernandez: Those were not the same Philistines. Abraham goes to the Philistine city of Gerar, the site of the royal palace of King Abimelech. His son Isaac also goes to Gerar. A number of other cities are mentioned in the encounters between the Patriarchs and the Philistines. None of these cities is ever mentioned in connection with the coastal confederation of later years, nor are any of the cities of the coastal confederation mentioned in connection with the Patriarchs. The only city mentioned in the context of both is Beersheba.

Mr. Taylor: But how do you know that Gerar wasn't in the Philistine lands? Maybe it was a smaller town eventually eclipsed by the bigger cities.

Dr. Hernandez: Because the Bible places Gerar further south. The Book of Genesis states that 'Abraham traveled from there to the Negev and settled between Kadesh and Shur, and he lived in Gerar.' Kadesh is in the northern Sinai Desert. The Book of Genesis places Shur near Egypt, as does the Book of Exodus. We can safely assume that Gerar is somewhere in the northern Negev or the Sinai Peninsula.

Mr. Taylor: Who then were these Philistines? Where did they come from?

Dr. Hernandez: We should call them the Gerarites just to avoid confusion. They were different from the coastal Philistines. Gerar was a rather large country ruled by a king. The coastal Philistines, on the other hand, were a confederation of city states under military rule. The coastal Philistines were warriors. The Gerarites were shepherds and farmers. The Gerarites were reasonably friendly; they forged a covenant with Abraham and renewed it with Isaac. The coastal Philistines were belligerent. Their arrival in Israel was a disaster. It meant the loss of the fertile coastal plain for centuries. Constant warfare and strife. No hint of the possibility of rapprochement.

	Kill or be killed. These are not the same people as the Gerarites.
Mr. Taylor:	In a nutshell, the Bible differentiates between the Gerarite Philistines and the coastal Philistines. Is that correct?
Dr. Hernandez:	Yes. The Bible makes the distinction explicitly in the Book of Genesis. Listen to the words, 'And the Pathrusites and the Kasluchites, from where the Philistines emerged, and the Kaphtorites.' The Philistines that Genesis knows emerged from Kasluchia, or whatever that land was called. They are distinct from the Kaphtorites; they did not come from Crete.
Mr. Taylor:	Outstanding. You've really cleared up the mystery for the court. So let's get to the bottom line. Is the mention of Gerarites in the Patriarchal age an anachronism?
Dr. Hernandez:	Not at all. There is no anachronism. On the contrary, the references to the Philistines in the Bible are a powerful proof of its historical accuracy.
Mr. Taylor:	How so?
Dr. Hernandez:	Because, as I explained, the Bible clearly knows that the coastal Philistines arrived after the Conquest was already under way, which dovetails nicely with the information we have from Egyptian sources. Now, if the Bible were created many centuries later, how would the writers have known this information? Did they have access to ancient Egyptian

hieroglyphic inscriptions? That's more than a little absurd.

The Documentary Hypothesis

Judge:	Call your next witness, Mr. Calabrese.
Mr. Calabrese:	The defense calls Dr. Evan Winemaker.
Mr. Calabrese:	Can you give us your full name and occupation, sir?
Dr. Winemaker:	My name is Dr. Frederick Winemaker. I'm a professor of biblical studies at the University of Wisconsin.
Mr. Calabrese:	Dr. Winemaker, the court and jury have heard the Documentary Hypothesis mentioned a number of times during the course of the trial so far, but it hasn't really been explained. Could you enlighten us?
Dr. Winemaker:	Of course. The term Documentary Hypothesis is a bit heavy; it makes it sound more complicated than it really is. To state it as simply as possible, biblical scholarship has proven that the Bible was pieced together from a number of source documents.
Mr. Taylor:	Objection, your honor. It is not proven. Let the witness present his proof. Let counsel for the plaintiff cross-examine. Then the jury can decide whether or not it has been proven.
Judge:	Sustained.
Mr. Calabrese:	Dr. Winemaker, please rephrase your statement.
Dr. Winemaker:	Of course. The dominant view among biblical scholars is that the Bible was pieced together by an editor or editors

	from at least four different source documents. Biblical scholars have further identified the approximate historical period during which this work was done.
Mr. Taylor:	Objection! They haven't proven or identified anything. They've theorized, and they've surmised. Nothing more.
Judge:	Sustained. The witness will be more careful with his choice of words.
Dr. Winemaker:	I will, your honor. Although there are different opinions as to which source came after which, the consensus is that they all came from the same general historical period.
Mr. Calabrese:	When is that period?
Dr. Winemaker:	The middle of the first millennium B.C.E. Say between 700 B.C.E. and 400 B.C.E.
Mr. Calabrese:	What are the proofs for the existence of different source documents?
Dr. Winemaker:	There are a number of them. Each proof is a strong indicator on its own, but when taken all together, the conclusion is abundantly clear. We are looking at different works by different authors.
Mr. Calabrese:	Would you please explain?
Dr. Winemaker:	Let's begin with the most basic indicator, the appearance of numerous doublets in the Bible. The term doublet refers to the same story being told twice in the Bible. There are two different stories of the creation; two different stories of the forging of a covenant between God

and Abraham; two different stories of Abraham sending away Hagar, his Egyptian concubine; two different stories of the naming of Abraham's son Isaac; two different stories of Abraham presenting his wife Sarah to a foreign king as his sister; two different stories of Jacob making a journey to Syria; two different stories of God speaking to Jacob at Bethel; two different stories of Jacob's name being changed to Israel. This is just to mention a few. It is quite clear that these are two different sources presenting two different versions of the same story.

Mr. Calabrese: I see. What other proofs are there?

Dr. Winemaker: There's the crucial matter of the divine names. Investigators have discovered that sometimes the Bible identifies God as Elohim. We call that the E name. Sometimes God is identified by the Tetragrammaton, the name composed of the letters *yod*, *heh*, *vav* and *heh*. We call that the J name.

Mr. Calabrese: Why is that name called J when it starts with a *yod*, the Y sound?

Dr. Winemaker: Technically it should indeed be called the Y name. However, most of the early Biblical scholars were German, and in German the J has a Y sound. Anyway, as I was saying, the scholars identified the doublets I mentioned before, and they noticed that in most cases of doublets, one version used the E name and the other used the J name. This led them to conclude that there were two different source documents, the E source, which spoke of God as E, and the J source, which spoke of Him as J. This is strong proof that there were at least two sources.

Mr. Calabrese: You say at least two. Are there more?

Dr. Winemaker: There are. Based on linguistics, style and interest, scholars discerned a third source, which is the largest of all. It contains most of the legal matter of the Bible and is much concerned with matters relating to priests. Scholars called it the Priestly Codex, the P source for short. It is austere and dry. The P writer is concerned with legal matters and details, such as genealogies, statistics and measurements. He views God as a transcendent distant figure.

Mr. Calabrese: That's three. Are there more?

Dr. Winemaker: At least one more. Scholars discovered that the language, style and tone of Deuteronomy are markedly different from the rest of the Bible, indicating that it was composed by a fourth author. They called it the D source. So that's where we are. We have reached the point where we can point to any page in the Bible and identify one or more of the four basic sources.

Mr. Calabrese: Is there any evidence to support this view?

Dr. Winemaker: Oh yes, lots of it. Scholars have discovered contradictions among the source documents. For instance, in the two creation stories at the beginning of Genesis, we find the information contradictory. In the first story, the order of creation is plants, animals, humans, while in the second, the order is humans, plants, animals. In the first story, male and female are created together, while in the second story, the female is created much later. In the first story, the deity is distant and transcendent, while in the second story, the deity speaks to humans and walks in the Garden of Eden.

Mr. Calabrese: Interesting.

Dr. Winemaker: Then there is the story of the flood, in which the two accounts are woven together very tightly instead of being presented one after the other. The sources vary from verse to verse and sometimes both sources appear in the same verse. The editor did quite a job on that episode. But he was unsuccessful in removing all the contradictions between the two sources. The P source has the flood lasting a year, while the J source has it lasting forty days. The P source has Noah rescue one pair of each animal, while the J source has him rescue seven animals. P says that everything outside Noah's ark expired, while J says everything died. P is concerned with ages, dates and measurements. J is not. The P source pictures a transcendent, all-powerful God, while J describes a God that regrets having made mankind, that is aggrieved to His heart, that smells Noah's sacrifice. True, this is probably anthropomorphic but –

Mr. Calabrese: Excuse me for interrupting, Dr. Winemaker, but could you explain to the jury what you mean by anthropomorphic?

Dr. Winemaker: I apologize. Anthropomorphism means talking about God as if He were human to make it more understandable to people. To say that one sees God's hand in something does not mean that God has a hand; it is only a metaphor that helps bring the point across. The J writer uses anthropomorphisms. The P writer does not. All of this, in my opinion, proves conclusively that the Bible is a composite of four different source documents.

Mr. Calabrese: You also mention differences in language?

Dr. Winemaker: Oh, yes. I'll give you an example or two. All source documents agree that there were seven different pagan peoples in Israel, but the J source refers to them collectively as the Amorites, while E refers to them as Canaanites. The J source refers to Mount Sinai, while the E source refers to it as Horeb. The J source refers to the third of the patriarchs as Jacob even after his name is changed to Israel, while the E source calls him Israel.

Mr. Calabrese: Is there material in the Bible that doesn't come from these sources?

Dr. Winemaker: Yes, there's a fifth contributor. We call him R, for redactor, which means editor. Someone took all the source documents, cut them up and pieced them together into the mosaic known as the Bible. This editor did not disturb the original text for the most part. He wove the strands together expertly, made minor adjustments to smooth the connections and also added pieces of text to bridge the gaps.

Mr. Calabrese: How about pinpointing the sequence of the source documents and the approximate dates when they were composed?

Dr. Winemaker: Well, we know they weren't written at the same time. The J and E sources are the oldest, because they're unaware of material in the other sources. The general opinion is that the D source is next, and that the P source was composed last. For instance, the P source describes not only the three major festival of the year – the Feasts of Passover, Pentecost and Tabernacles – but also Rosh Hashanah, the Hebrew New Year, and Yom Kippur, the Day of Atonement. Deuteronomy describes the three festivals but makes no mention of Rosh Hashanah or Yom Kippur. Obviously, these observances were added later and unknown to the D writer. There's more.

Mr. Calabrese: Go on.

Dr. Winemaker: Scholars also established the sequence of the sources by the stages of development of the religion. German scholars of the nineteenth century discovered that just as there is an evolutionary process in the biological development of mankind, there is also an evolutionary process in its social and historical development. Religions evolve. They start off as nature-fertility religions, develop into spiritual-ethical religions and then become institutional-ritualistic-legal religions. The J and E sources reflect the primitive stage of the religion. The D source reflects the grand spiritual ideals of the major prophets of Israel during the late years of the monarchies. And the P source reflects the priestly ritualistic stage when the priests and rabbis gained power after the monarchies fell and the Israelites were driven into exile in Babylon. The P source was probably written after they returned to Israel.

Mr. Calabrese: When would that be?

Dr. Winemaker: About 500 B.C.E. or later.

Mr. Calabrese: You mentioned monarchies. Plural. Could you tell the jury just a little something about the monarchies? Keep in mind that we're not academics, so just tell us what we need to know.

Dr. Winemaker: I'll be brief. The later books of the Bible say there was a United Kingdom of Israel under David and Solomon, and that after Solomon died the kingdom split into the northern kingdom, called Israel, and the southern kingdom, called Judah. The two kingdoms were rivals and occasionally warred with each other. This is generally accepted as accurate. Centuries later, the northern kingdom was destroyed by the Assyrians. The southern kingdom lasted for over a hundred years more, then it was destroyed by the Babylonians. The people were exiled. They returned about a hundred years later. The rebuilt Israel was not ruled by a king but, to all intents and purposes, by the High Priest of the Temple in Jerusalem. The monarchy became a theocracy. Am I going into too much detail?

Mr. Calabrese: You're at the limit, I think. So where were these sources composed?

Dr. Winemaker: Scholars believe the E source came from Israel and the J source from Judah.

Mr. Calabrese: How can they tell?

Dr. Winemaker: You can tell by the things the sources say and the things that concern them. For instance, in the J source, Jacob on his deathbed bequeaths the rights of the firstborn to Judah and tells him that his father's sons will bow down to him. In the deathbed scene in the E source, however, Jacob gives Joseph the double share which is the right of the firstborn. You see what is happening. The J source supports the claim to power of Judah, which is supposedly descended from the Judah of the Biblical story, while the E source supports the northern kingdom, which traces its roots to the Joseph described in the Bible. There are many more examples such as these.

Mr. Calabrese: So, you're saying that the J and E sources were composed during the time the Kingdom of Israel and the Kingdom of

Judah were rivals.

Dr. Winemaker: That is correct.

Mr. Calabrese: And Deuteronomy, the D source? When was it composed?

Dr. Winemaker: After the fall of Israel, there were periods of religious reform in Judah when the kings tried to eradicate idol worship. One of these was King Josiah. In the eighteenth year of his reign, the year 622 B.C.E., the Bible reports that a scroll of the Law was found in the Temple. A scribe read it to Josiah, and he immediately tore his clothing in anguish. After the prophetess Hulda validated the authenticity of the scroll, Josiah had the scroll read in public and campaigned to cleanse the land of idolatry and destroy all private altars so that sacrifices could be brought only in the Temple in Jerusalem. The book Josiah discovered was Deuteronomy, in which Moses exhorts the people against idolatry or sacrificing to God on private altars rather than in the Temple. Scholars are convinced the book was written shortly before its supposed discovery for the express purpose of overcoming the pagan cults and strengthening the power of the central priesthood in Jerusalem.

Mr. Calabrese: How do they know that the book is not older?

Dr. Winemaker: Because the earlier prophets such as Samuel, and kings, such as Saul, David and Solomon, all sacrificed on private altars, and it was not held against them. Obviously, the laws requiring the centralization of the sacrifices were not yet known. Therefore, we conclude that Deuteronomy was composed much later. It was made to look as if it came from Moses, but of course, it did not. Although it may have been written with good intentions, scholars nonetheless refer to it as a pious fraud.

Mr. Calabrese: And the P source was written even later?

Dr. Winemaker: Yes. It was written after the return of the Israelites from Babylon over a hundred years later.

Mr. Calabrese: And when were these source documents woven together to form the book we know as the Bible?

Dr. Winemaker: Some time after that. There is quite a bit of speculation about when the editor lived and who he was, but we have no definitive information about it. Only some rather interesting theories.

Mr. Calabrese: You've really given us a lot of information here, Dr. Winemaker. Thank you. Before I let you go, I want to summarize for the benefit of the jury. Correct me if I make a mistake.

Dr. Winemaker: By all means, go ahead.

Mr. Calabrese: You have told us that scholars have discerned four different strands in the part of the Bible called the Five Books of Moses – the E, J, D and P sources. They are identified by repetitions of the same material, contradictions, the tendency to use different divine names and differences in style, interest and religious outlook. Scholars have further determined that the E document was composed in the Kingdom of Israel, while the J and D documents were composed in the Kingdom of Judah. The P document was composed after the fall of the monarchy and the return of the Israelites from exile. You also pinpointed the appearance of the D document as 622 B.C.E. All these documents were composed many hundreds of years after the events described in the Five Books of Moses supposedly took place, and therefore, the Bible – this pious fraud, as you called it – is not a valid historical source.

Dr. Winemaker: That is exactly correct.

Mr. Calabrese: Thank you, Dr. Winemaker. I have no more questions.

• • •

Mr. Taylor: Dr. Winemaker, you called the Bible a pious fraud. Strong words. Fighting words. You can't say something like thatunless you're prepared to back it up.

Dr. Winemaker: I believe I've backed it up.

Mr. Taylor: Have you backed it up with evidence or with assumptions?

Dr. Winemaker: Solid evidence, sir.

Mr. Taylor: We'll see. Let's begin. Dr. Winemaker, in the entire history of the world, has there ever been a case of another book – any book – that was put together in this way? I mean, we know that some ransom notes are made this way. Some kidnappers snip a couple of words from one magazine and a couple of words from another and send it to the family. But has there ever been a single recorded case of an editor taking four different books, cutting them up with a pair of scissors into big and little pieces, pasting them together into one book, publishing this mishmash as a unified book written by a single author?

Dr. Winemaker: Well, it's not so –

Mr. Taylor: Yes or no?

Dr. Winemaker: No.

Mr. Taylor: You say that there are four source documents.

Dr. Winemaker: I do.

Mr. Taylor: Isn't it true that recent scholars have identified many more source documents?

Dr. Winemaker: Yes, it's true.

Mr. Taylor: As many as fifteen or twenty?

Dr. Winemaker: Perhaps. But that's just speculation.

Mr. Taylor: You don't subscribe to those views?

Dr. Winemaker: No, I do not.

Mr. Taylor: It seems absurd that editors spliced the Bible together from over a dozen sources, wouldn't you say?

Dr. Winemaker: It's a little far-fetched.

Mr. Taylor: But four documents is not far-fetched?

	Do you expect the jury to believe that the only book ever put together in this bizarre way became the most widely read, admired and beloved book in the history of the world?
Dr. Winemaker:	Well, as I –
Mr. Taylor:	A yes or no answer, please.
Dr. Winemaker:	Yes, sir. I do.
Mr. Taylor:	Dr. Winemaker, this pious hoax pulled off by an unidentified editor, how could such a thing have happened? How did he fool everyone?
Dr. Winemaker:	I really don't know. My field of expertise is the biblical text, not social conditions at the time it was introduced.
Mr. Taylor:	I see. Well, let me ask this question another way. If you'd been living in the land of Israel at the time the Bible was introduced, do you think you'd have accepted the Bible as genuine?
Mr. Calabrese:	Objection. The question calls for speculation on the part of the witness.
Mr. Taylor:	Your honor, aren't expert witnesses allowed to speculate?
Mr. Calabrese:	Counsel is not asking this expert witness to speculate within his field of expertise. He is asking for personal speculation. How is the witness supposed to know what he would have done or believed under those circumstances?
Mr. Taylor:	Your honor, I suggest that, if the witness claims the Bible was put together as

he contends, the likelihood of public acceptance is relevant to his thesis. He should not be allowed to disregard that issue. Furthermore, the point of my question is to establish bias on the part of the witness.

Mr. Calabrese: Is counsel suggesting that Dr. Winemaker is anti-Semitic or anti-Christian?

Mr. Taylor: Not at all. I have no doubt that Dr. Winemaker is a fine, upstanding person of goodwill, a seeker of truth. However, I believe he has a bias against people of the ancient world. I believe he considers them less intelligent and less sophisticated than people of modern times. My question is meant to determine if he considers the ancients equals or inferiors.

Judge: Mr. Calabrese?

Mr. Calabrese: I still think the question is unfair. If he had been in the pagan world, he might have been a polytheist, but now he knows better.

Judge: Mr. Taylor?

Mr. Taylor: Mr. Calabrese's point about polytheism is well-taken. Nonetheless, my question is not ideological. I just want to know if, in his opinion, the alleged editors could have pulled the wool over his eyes. Or to use another metaphor, could they have sold him a pig in a poke? Does he think he's a more evolved human being?

Judge: I'll allow it. Objection overruled. The witness will answer the question.

Mr. Taylor:	Dr. Winemaker, do you want the court reporter to read the question back to you?
Dr. Winemaker:	I remember the question.
Mr. Taylor:	And? Would you have accepted the Bible as genuine?
Dr. Winemaker:	I think … I would have seen through it.
Mr. Taylor:	Here we have ancient Israel, a country of several million people, or at least several hundred thousand, and all of them fell for the hoax. Were they boors?
Dr. Winemaker:	I really don't know. Anything is possible.
Mr. Taylor:	Do you think the authors and editors of the Bible were talented?
Dr. Winemaker:	Yes, of course.
Mr. Taylor:	Could a society of boors produce such people?
Dr. Winemaker:	I suppose.
Mr. Taylor:	Could a society of boors produce Shakespeare?
Dr. Winemaker:	Perhaps not.
Mr. Taylor:	I understand. Time to stop beating a dead horse. Dr. Winemaker, is there a shred of external evidence that corroborates the existence of different source documents, assorted writers and unidentified editors? Is there a single inscription in any ancient archive or on a stone or a piece of pottery that even hints at such a possibility?
Dr. Winemaker:	None has been discovered yet.
Mr. Taylor:	I see. So, we've established that, as of now, the theory is not supported by a single

shred of external evidence, that it rests entirely on a reading of the text. Let us now examine your reading of the text. I would like to begin with two of the criteria you mentioned. Interest and style. Let's talk about interest first. You stated that P is concerned with legal matters and dry details, such as genealogies, statistics and exact measurements, while J and E are more focused on narratives. This indicates that there are different writers at work here. Is that correct?

Dr. Winemaker: Basically.

Mr. Taylor: Now, if the Bible is intending to tell the story of the development of the Israelite people, their encounter with God and the code of laws He gave them, wouldn't you expect the interests to vary? Is there any reason why the Bible has to behave only as a novel or a history book?

Dr. Winemaker: It's not normal for a book to be so varied.

Mr. Taylor: Let me put it to you another way. If you were writing a biography of Albert Einstein, would it be reasonable for you to devote twenty or thirty pages to a general description of the theory of relativity?

Dr. Winemaker: I suppose it would.

Mr. Taylor: Now if Albert Einstein was descended from Maimonides, the great Jewish philosopher of medieval Spain, would you include that information in your biography?

Dr. Winemaker: Probably.

Mr. Taylor: And if you had birth records and other genealogical information that traced Einstein's lineage to Maimonides, would you include them in the book?

Dr. Winemaker: I would imagine so.

Mr. Taylor: So would a professor who came across your biography of Einstein be justified in assuming that it was written by three different people because part of it was a story, part of it was physics and part of it was genealogy?

Dr. Winemaker: It's not the same.

Mr. Taylor: Just answer the question, sir. Would he be justified in making such an assumption about your biography of Einstein?

Dr. Winemaker: No.

Mr. Taylor: You claim that the styles are different. I believe you said that the P writer was austere and dry. The implication being that the E and J writers are warmer. Is that correct?

Dr. Winemaker: Yes.

Mr. Taylor: Let's go back to your biography of Einstein. You have chapters on his early life, his struggles, his triumphs, his family. And you have chapters on the theory of relativity and his genealogy. Would your styles of writing be different in these chapters? Would you be warm and even passionate in the narratives and dry in relating the scientific information and the genealogies? A yes or no answer, please.

Dr. Winemaker: Yes.

Mr. Taylor: So listen to this. You decide to create a measuring stick called interest and perceive different documents simply on the basis of different subject matter. Then you discover that the different documents have different styles! You have confirmation of your theory! Don't you think this is circular reasoning?

Dr. Winemaker: I do not.

Mr. Taylor: During your testimony, you implied that your case was overwhelming. Do you still contend that interest and style are reliable criteria for establishing that the Bible was written by different writers?

Dr. Winemaker: They may be weaker than some of the other ways.

Mr. Taylor: Are prophetic visions one of the ways you differentiate E from J?

Dr. Winemaker: Yes. In J, God reveals Himself to people in corporeal form and speaks to them directly while they are wide awake. In E, God speaks to people through dreams and visions by night.

Mr. Taylor: I refer you to Genesis 15:1, which reads as follows, 'After these things, the word of J came to Abram in a vision.' Here we have a vision and the J name is used. How do you explain this?

Dr. Winemaker: It's a mistake. The word vision should not be there. It's a scribal error that fell into the text during the copying and recopying.

Mr. Taylor:	How do you know it's an error?
Dr. Winemaker:	It has been proved by earlier scholars. I couldn't tell you exactly.
Mr. Taylor:	Does the name Hermann Gunkel mean anything to you?
Dr. Winemaker:	Yes. He was a great biblical scholar.
Mr. Taylor:	How did he prove that the word vision was a scribal error and should be removed? Should I refresh your memory?
Dr. Winemaker:	Please do.
Mr. Taylor:	Here is Gunkel quoted by Dr. Umberto Cassuto in *The Documentary Hypothesis*, and I quote, 'Gunkel justifies the textual emendation on the ground that theophanies in dreams and visions are characteristic of E.' I'd like to explain for the benefit of the jury that theophanies are visions of God. Gunkel claims that theophanies are characteristic of the E writer. Have I refreshed your memory?
Dr. Winemaker:	You have.
Mr. Taylor:	Let me understand this. You create a rule for differentiating between documents by the mention of visions, and when you find a mention that is out of place according to your thinking, you just change the text. Is that intellectually honest? Doesn't it occur to you that you may be wrong?
Mr. Calabrese:	Objection, your honor. Counsel is badgering the witness.
Mr. Taylor:	I withdraw the question. Dr. Winemaker, I refer you to Genesis 26:24, and I

quote, 'And J appeared to him that night and said, I am the God of your father Abraham ...' Here is another case of a vision in the night that appears in a J document. What do you do with this one?

Dr. Winemaker: The verse is deleted.

Mr. Taylor: The entire verse?

Dr. Winemaker: Yes.

Mr. Taylor: Why?

Dr. Winemaker: Because it's out of place.

Mr. Taylor: How did it wander there in the first place? Scribal error? Did a scribe copying the Old Testament scrolls happen to include by accident an entire verse of twenty-two words plucked out of thin air?

Dr. Winemaker: I can't explain it.

Mr. Taylor: Very well, let's go to doublets. I won't belabor the jury by taking you through all the ones you cited. Let's talk about only a few of them. You mentioned two stories of God forging a covenant with Abraham. Yes?

Dr. Winemaker: Yes. The first is J. The second is E.

Mr. Taylor: Are the two identical?

Dr. Winemaker: Almost.

Mr. Taylor: Isn't it a fact that the second covenant features two important new elements, Abram's name being changed to Abraham and the introduction of the covenant of circumcision?

Dr. Winemaker: That's true.

Mr. Taylor:	Are you telling me that the J writer never knew that Abram's name was changed to Abraham and that he continued calling him Abram?
Dr. Winemaker:	Of course not. I'm sure he was also aware of the change. He just never describes the actual act of changing it.
Mr. Taylor:	How about circumcision? I believe you said the J writer was from Judah. Were the people in Judah circumcised?
Dr. Winemaker:	Perhaps not. The J writer doesn't mention the custom.
Mr. Taylor:	But isn't circumcision a major element of Judaism?
Dr. Winemaker:	It is.
Mr. Taylor:	It's universally practiced by observant Jews and by most non-observant Jews as well, is it not?
Dr. Winemaker:	It is.
Mr. Taylor:	Are you saying that it was only practiced in the northern kingdom but not in the kingdom of Judah?
Dr. Winemaker:	Perhaps circumcision was practiced in Judah, only the J writer didn't mention it in his document.
Mr. Taylor:	Is it reasonable that the J writer would fail to mention the very mark of an Israelite, the sign of the eternal covenant with God?
Dr. Winemaker:	I don't know. Perhaps he did. Perhaps the editor removed it.
Mr. Taylor:	Why would the editor remove it? Because

	it was redundant since E had already written about it?
Dr. Winemaker:	Perhaps.
Mr. Taylor:	So why didn't the editor remove all the other apparent redundancies you claim to have found in the Bible?
Dr. Winemaker:	I don't know.
Mr. Taylor:	You mentioned two different stories of Jacob making a journey to Syria after he cleverly appropriates his brother Esau's birthright. Yes?
Dr. Winemaker:	Yes.
Mr. Taylor:	I refer you to Genesis 28:7-12, and I quote, 'And Jacob listened to his father and to his mother, and he went to Paddan Aram. And Esau saw that his father Isaac disapproved of the daughters of Canaan. And Esau went to Ishmael and took Mahalath the daughter of Ishmael the son of Abraham, the sister of Nebaioth, as his wife. And Jacob left Beersheba and went to Harran ... And he came upon the place and stayed there all night, because the sun had set ... And he dreamed, and behold, there was a ladder set upon the earth with its top reaching into the heavens ... and behold, angels of E were ascending and descending on it.' It's a little condensed, but that's the gist of it. So where is the doublet? Is it the first mention that Jacob went to Paddan Aram?
Dr. Winemaker:	Yes.
Mr. Taylor:	When the Bible goes on to say that he

went to Harran, which is a city in the province of Paddan Aram, and tells the story of his experiences on the journey, that is a doublet?

Dr. Winemaker: Yes.

Mr. Taylor: Amazing. So, the first is a J story, and the second is an E story?

Dr. Winemaker: Yes. You see yourself that the E name is used.

Mr. Taylor: So we read in this E story that Jacob went to sleep and had a fantastic dream. Then he got up in the morning, and I quote again, 'And Jacob awoke from his sleep, and he said, Surely J is in this place, and I didn't know it.' Hey, this sounds like a J document. Can you imagine? Jacob fell asleep in an E story but woke up in a J story. He must have been disoriented.

Dr. Winemaker: Very amusing. I admit there are exceptions to the rule. But most of the time, the J name does not appear in E.

Mr. Taylor: If you don't mind my asking, why don't you just snip out that J name and say it was a scribal error?

Dr. Winemaker: I've never heard that it was a scribal error.

Mr. Taylor: Dr. Winemaker, let me present to you a modern-day doublet that will puzzle future historians. They will read two stories that were not identical in all their details but took place at about the same time and were quite similar. An American president named George W. Bush put together a coalition to fight a Persian Gulf war against Iraq, whose president was a man named Saddam Hussein. One story is said to have taken place in 1991. The other is said to have taken place in 2002. Are these two stories a doublet? Are they really one and the same story told by different writers?

Dr. Winemaker: Of course not. Many of the details differ. For one, the first president is George H. W. Bush and the second is George W. Bush.

Mr. Taylor: Perhaps the extra H is a scribal error.

Dr. Winemaker: Touché. They differ in numerous details. One took place in 1991 and the other in 2002. One was triggered by the Iraqi occupation of Kuwait and the other by the destruction of the Twin Towers in New York. And many others.

Mr. Taylor: I see. One of the doublets you identified is the two stories of Abraham sending away his concubine Hagar. But aren't there important differences? One story takes place soon after Abraham takes the concubine into his house because his wife Sarah cannot conceive. Hagar quickly conceives and becomes insubordinate to her mistress Sarah. Abraham sends her away, but when she submits to her mistress, he takes her back. The second story takes place some twenty years later. Similar to 1991 and 2002, isn't it? Hagar's son Ishmael is already a young man. Sarah has given birth to Isaac thirteen years after Hagar has Ishmael. Young

Isaac is growing up under the malevolent influence of Ishmael, and Abraham sends Hagar and Ishmael away for good. Have I told the stories correctly?

Dr. Winemaker: Yes, you have.

Mr. Taylor: And don't you think these are important differences? Do you still think they should be considered a doublet?

Dr. Winemaker: Perhaps if you examine every little piece, you can explain it away, but when you take it all together ...

Mr. Taylor: It's all right. Let's move on. Let's talk about the most basic of your criteria, which is the variation of the divine names. The E name denotes one writer, and the J name denotes another. In fact, according to what I heard you say, they lived in two different kingdoms. Yes?

Dr. Winemaker: That is correct.

Mr. Taylor: Very well, let me read to you a passage from I Samuel 4-6. I have printed it out in condensed form and made copies for the benefit of the court and the jury. Do you see what I have done here, Dr. Winemaker? The divine names in bold and color so that they stand out when you look at the passage in total. Now let me read this passage to you. I will now begin the quotation. And the elders of Israel said, 'Why has **J** smitten us today before the Philistines? Let us fetch us the ark of the covenant of **J** from Shiloh.' The people sent to Shiloh and they brought from there the ark of the covenant of **J** ... And there were the sons of Eli with the ark of the covenant of **E** ... And it happened when the ark of the covenant of **J** came into the encampment ... And the Philistines ... knew that the ark of **J** had come into the encampment. And the Philistines were frightened, for they said, '**E** has come into the encampment ...' And the ark of **E** was taken ... And the Philistines took the ark of **E** ... to the Temple of Dagon ... Behold, Dagon had fallen onto the ground before the ark of **J** ... And the ark of **J** was in the fields of Philistia seven months ... That is the end of the quotation. Did you notice, Dr. Winemaker, that the writer of the Book of Samuel alternates back and forth, back and forth, back and forth between the J and the E names. Would you say that this passage was spliced together from two different source documents?

Dr. Winemaker: No, I wouldn't.

Mr. Taylor: Of course not. It would be absurd. So, don't we see here that the Bible uses the divine names interchangeably?

Dr. Winemaker: In this passage, it apparently does.

Mr. Taylor: After all that we talked about this afternoon, are you still as convinced as ever that the evidence for different source documents is strong?

Dr. Winemaker: Absolutely.

Mr. Taylor: But why?

Dr. Winemaker: Because that is the academic consensus.

Mr. Taylor: Isn't this exactly what this trial is about – whether academic fundamentalism and the truth are one and the same thing?

Mr. Calabrese: Objection, your honor. Is counsel asking a question or is he making his closing arguments to the jury?

Mr. Taylor: Never mind. I withdraw the question. I'm prepared to call my rebuttal witness. Thank you, Dr. Winemaker. I have no more questions.

• • •

Mr. Taylor: Dr. Halliday, what are your academic credentials?

Dr. Halliday: I teach biblical studies and ancient Semitic languages at Yale.

Mr. Taylor: Were you present in the court when Dr. Winemaker gave his testimony?

Dr. Halliday: I was.

Mr. Taylor: I'd like you to comment on some statements he made. Let's start with the issue of doublets. Dr. Winemaker told the court that the two divergent accounts of the creation story represent a doublet. Do you agree?

Dr. Halliday: I do not. This literary form is common in ancient Near Eastern inscriptions, which begin with a general statement and then zero in on specific aspects. Many inscriptions from Urartu, for instance, begin with a paragraph that describes a military victory achieved by the chariots of the god Haldi, followed by a description of the same victory achieved by the king. Does that mean we should separate the inscription into the H source for Haldi and the K source for the king?

Mr. Taylor: Obviously not.

Dr. Halliday: In Genesis as well, the account starts with a description of creation in the broadest terms, and then it reviews the creation in closer focus. The minor duplications are meaningless. You see, the Germanic style of telling a story is linear, in a straight line. The Hebrew style – in fact, the prevalent style in the ancient Near East – was to tell a story in a sort of spiral, circling in on the story in ever narrowing circles.

Mr. Taylor: Interesting. How about the difference in the order of creation? Why does the first account speak of plants, animals and humans as the order of creation and the second as humans, plants, animals?

Dr. Halliday: That's easily explained. The first account gives the chronological order of creation. The second gives the order of importance, which begins with humans, of course, followed by plants, which provide food for the humans. Animals are last, since humans were forbidden to eat meat at this point.

Mr. Taylor: And why does the first story say that 'male and female were created,' which implies that they were created together, while the second story tells of the woman being

	created after the man?
Dr. Halliday:	Here again, we see the distinction between general and specific. In the first story, which is general, we're given the bare fact that man and woman were both created on the same day. In the more specific story, we spiral in on the details and discover that they were created in sequence. All the discrepancies can easily be resolved in this way. Moreover ...
Mr. Taylor:	Yes, Dr. Halliday?
Dr. Halliday:	Well, in the first place, it seems unreasonable that this hypothetical editor splicing together these strips of parchment would begin his work with two contradictory creation stories. This hypothetical editor must have considered them complementary, so why should we think otherwise?
Mr. Taylor:	Indeed. Basically, you're saying, 'What was this guy thinking by starting his book with two contradictory stories back-to-back? Did he think no one would catch on?' Is that correct?
Dr. Halliday:	Well, yes. But I'm looking at it from a more scholarly angle. If the alleged editor, for whatever reason, considered them complementary, how can we use that as proof that there are two contradictory sources?
Mr. Taylor:	Thank you. Let's move on to the flood story. Again, we're told this is a doublet, and a rather unusual one. Dr. Winemaker

claims that the two strands were woven together so tightly that they appear to be one story. Nonetheless, he is able to discern different authors in different verses and even in different parts of the same verse. Do you agree with this reading?

Dr. Halliday: Not at all. First of all, I do not accept that an editor spliced together a single verse from fragments taken from diverse sources. This is inconceivable to me.

Mr. Taylor: I understand.

Dr. Halliday: As for the differences between the two stories, they are mostly linguistic, such as the expressing the demise of a creature as 'expired' or 'died,' and other similar differences. However, this strict limit on linguistic variations is a nineteenth century Germanic prejudice. Perhaps German literature works that way, but ancient Near Eastern literature does not. They preferred what is known as elegant variation. Had these German scholars been familiar with ancient inscriptions and literature, they could not have missed the constant and deliberate variation of language. Once a word is used, the authors are slow to use it again. The Pentateuch and the Books of the Prophets follow this pattern closely. I can give you hundreds of examples. In my opinion, it would be preposterous to chop up the text wherever two different words are used for the same idea. Why, even in my English

	writing classes, I was discouraged from using the same word over and over again.
Mr. Taylor:	Weren't we all?
Dr. Halliday:	Let me give you an example. Genesis 25:8. 'Abraham expired, and he died in a good old age, old and full of years, and he was gathered in to his people.' The critics say that the first part that speaks about Abraham expiring and the second half of the verse are from the P source, while the rest is from the J source. Doesn't this seem ludicrous? Why would an editor cut the verses into little pieces and splice them together so that Abraham passes away twice in this verse, once by expiration and again by death?
Mr. Taylor:	Why, indeed. How about the apparent contradictions between the two strands? One story speaks of Noah selecting seven each of every pure animal, while the other speaks of two animals. One story tells of a year-and-ten-day duration for the flood, while the other speaks of Noah opening the window of the ark at the end of forty days. I know we could analyze this passage all day, Dr. Halliday, but for the sake of the jury, we won't belabor the point. Just explain these two seeming discrepancies.
Dr. Halliday:	There are no discrepancies. The Bible states that the animals entered the ark *shnayim shnayim.* The word *shnayim* means two, but in this context, it means a pair. The animals entered the ark by pairs.

That's all it means. As for the duration of the flood, when the Bible says that Noah opened the window at the end of forty days, it means at the end of forty days after the receding waters uncovered the mountaintops, which is exactly what we are told in the previous verse. Again, I have to point out an obvious problem. How could an editor in his right mind splice together two accounts that openly contradict each other from verse to verse? These same critics say that the splicing job was brilliant. But to deliberately join contradictory verses? Does this show brilliance or folly?

Mr. Taylor: I can't argue with that. How about one story telling that Noah sends out a raven to find dry land and the other that he sent out a dove? Is this duplication?

Dr. Halliday: Not as it appears in the text. First, he sends out a raven, but the raven just hovers near the ark. Then he sends out a dove, which flies away and comes back with no sign of dry land. Seven days later, he sends out the dove again, and it comes back with an olive branch in its beak. There is no problem with the story as it stands. No contradiction.

Mr. Taylor: Dr. Halliday, do you have any indications that the Noah story is one unified text and not two different accounts spliced together?

Dr. Halliday: Actually, there are indications from outside sources. Those nineteenth century

German scholars, picking apart the Noah story and pasting it together according to their schemes, didn't know that excavations in Mesopotamia would yield cuneiform tablets that contradicted them.

Mr. Taylor: Really, how so?

Dr. Halliday: The Epic of Gilgamesh appears on Tablet XI and also features a flood story. Many elements are identical to the Noah flood story. A man named Utnapishtim is told to build a ship and seal it with pitch. He's given the exact measurements. These supposedly correspond to the alleged P source in the Noah story. He sends out both a raven and a dove. This corresponds to both the alleged J and the P sources. His ship lands on a mountaintop. This corresponds to the alleged P source. He brings a sacrifice. This corresponds to the alleged J source.

Mr. Taylor: What is going on here?

Dr. Halliday: Confusing, isn't it? The Gilgamesh Epic predates the Bible by at least a thousand years, almost two thousand years according to the Hypothesis. That author of the Epic didn't have a copy of the Bible in front of him. So how come he tells a story that seems to be a combination of two sources?

Mr. Taylor: Maybe the writers of the Bible copied the story from him?

Dr. Halliday: Really? You mean the J writer took some elements and the P writer took others?

	Did these two hypothetical writers get together to discuss how to split up the Gilgamesh story, you take this, and I'll take that?
Mr. Taylor:	It does seem absurd. All right, let's move on. Let's talk about the divine names. Is there a problem with the Bible sometimes using the E name and sometimes the J name?
Dr. Halliday:	None at all. In fact, other divine names are also used. Should we designate sources for those as well? It's elegant variation. Anyway, if you have even the most basic knowledge of ancient inscriptions, you would see that different names are used all the time in the same account. For instance, the Berlin Stela –
Mr. Taylor:	Excuse me, Dr. Halliday, but could you tell us what a stela is?
Dr. Halliday:	Of course. It's a stone slab or a pillar carved or inscribed to commemorate an event or a person. This particular stela is an Egyptian stone that uses five different names for the god Osiris. In addition to Osiris, we read Wennofer, Khent-amentiu, Neb Abydos and Nuter. No one in his right mind would suggest that these revealed the hands of O, W, K, NA and N writers. The same phenomenon of multiple divine names occurs in Mesopotamian, Canaanite, Hurrian and Hittite inscriptions. The use of multiple divine names should not ring any alarm bells.

Mr. Taylor:	Are there any guidelines for when the one is used or the other?
Dr. Halliday:	Different ideas have been advanced. The Midrashic solution is that the E name is used when God is manifesting the attribute of strict justice, while the J name is used to indicate the attribute of merciful judgment. Also, Dr. Cassuto has quite an elaborate set of rules that seem to work well, the central rule being that the J name, which is specific, is used when God is relating to the Israelites, while the E name is used when God is relating to all the nations of the world. Do you want me to elaborate on this?
Mr. Taylor:	No, we get the idea. Let's go on. Dr. Winemaker perceived P as different from D, because Deuteronomy mentions the three annual festivals – Passover, Pentecost and Tabernacles – but makes no mention of Rosh Hashanah or Yom Kippur, while Leviticus mentions the three festivals plus Rosh Hashanah and Yom Kippur. From this observation, he drew the conclusion that D did not know about Rosh Hashanah and Yom Kippur and that P was written much later. Is this a valid observation?
Dr. Halliday:	Not in the slightest. You have to look at the two passages in context. What comes before the mention of the three festivals in Deuteronomy? The commandments to give charity to the beggar and to an indentured servant who was emancipated.

Then it says that during the three festivals you should invite widows, orphans and other poor people to feast at your table and share the bounty that God granted you. It is an extension of the commandment to aid the disadvantaged. Rosh Hashanah and Yom Kippur, however, are solemn rather than festive occasions. You're not really expected to invite poor people to your house on Yom Kippur to fast and repent with you. In Leviticus, however, the topic is the ritual priestly service, which applies equally to the festivals and to Rosh Hashanah and Yom Kippur. There is no discrepancy.

Mr. Taylor: I see. Yes, that is clear. All right, one final point. Dr. Winemaker seemed to believe that religions develop by an evolutionary process, and therefore, he felt compelled to view the alleged sources as representing the different stages of the development of Judaism. What is your opinion?

Dr. Halliday: Again, we come into contact with nineteenth century German thinking that refuses to be dislodged from the academic community. According to Friedrich Hegel, everything proceeds slowly toward higher stages of development, primitive to advanced. There are no radical changes. But history has shown us otherwise, especially the history of the ancient world. Three times Egypt rises, falls dramatically and rises again – after the Old, Middle and New Kingdoms. In Mesopotamia, we witness the successive flowering in full-

	blown form of Sumerian, Babylonian and Assyrian civilizations. We find evidence of drastic change in all aspects of civilization – political, social, economic and religious.
Mr. Taylor:	So the historical argument is not valid?
Dr. Halliday:	It is not.
Mr. Taylor:	Do you see any signs of erosion in the support for the Hypothesis in the academic community?
Dr. Halliday:	Actually, I do see some movement away from it. It's encouraging.
Mr. Taylor:	Let's sum up. Is there reason to doubt the Bible was written by one author at more or less the time it claims to have been written?
Dr. Halliday:	None.
Mr. Taylor:	I have no further questions. Thank you very much, Dr. Halliday.
Judge:	Mr. Calabrese, do you wish to cross-examine?
Mr. Calabrese:	Yes, your honor. I do.
Judge:	Do you need much time? If you do, we'll take a break now. If not, we'll just push through and then adjourn for the day.
Mr. Calabrese:	I don't need that much time, your honor.
Judge:	Very well. Go ahead and cross-examine.

• • •

| **Mr. Calabrese:** | Dr. Halliday, who do you think wrote the Bible? |

Dr. Halliday: I'm convinced it was written by one author in deep antiquity, because it reflects the ancient world in the second millennium B.C.E.

Mr. Calabrese: Do you think Moses wrote it?

Dr. Halliday: That's as good a choice as any. The Bible says Moses wrote it, and I have no scientific reason to doubt it.

Mr. Calabrese: Dr. Halliday, you had all sorts of explanations for the anomalies in the text that lead scholars to the conclusion that the Bible is a composite of different source documents. But how do you explain that the criteria seem to coincide? You will find that the E source uses the E name and is also consistent in the language it uses, its attitudes, its interests. And the same consistency goes for the other sources. How do you explain that?

Dr. Halliday: If I were a physicist testing a theory, I'd only consider it proved if it worked all the time. I would reject it if it only worked most of the time. Most is just not good enough. As a scientist investigating the Bible, I demand the same standards. I have no patience for theories like the Hypothesis that have so many exceptions and emendations of the text when it violates the rules imposed on it. I do not approve of explaining all those exceptions as scribal errors or editorial changes. That is not sound scholarship.

Mr. Calabrese: Dr. Halliday, are your views representative of the views of most scholars in the field of biblical studies?

Dr. Halliday: No, but there are –

Mr. Calabrese: Are you accusing the majority of scholars in your field of unsound scholarship?

Dr. Halliday: It is not their scholarship that is unsound, it is the assumptions –

Mr. Calabrese: Dr. Halliday, please give me just a yes or no answer.

Dr. Halliday: If truth were determined by a majority vote, we'd all be Chinese.

Mr. Calabrese: You're saying that most biblical scholars are mistaken?

Dr. Halliday: I am.

Mr. Calabrese: I have no more questions for this witness.

Mr. Taylor: Your honor, I have one more witness in rebuttal of Dr. Winemaker's testimony.

Judge: Please call your witness.

Mr. Taylor: The plaintiff calls Dr. Sadhu Singh.

• • •

Mr. Taylor: Can we have your full name and occupation, sir?

Dr. Singh: My name is Sadhu Singh. He spoke in heavily accented English. I'm Professor of Statistical Mathematics at Massachusetts Institute of Technology in Boston.

Mr. Taylor: Are you aware of a statistical study of the authorship of the Bible?

Dr. Singh: I am. A group of scientists at the Technion Institute in Haifa, Israel, headed by

	Yehuda Radday and Haim Shore, did a statistical analysis of the Old Testament. It was published as *Genesis: An Authorship Study*.
Mr. Taylor:	Can you give us a brief synopsis of their work?
Dr. Singh:	The scientists involved applied objective scientific and mathematical methods to linguistic studies. They analyzed each word in the sample and recorded the absolute forms of nouns and verbs, word length, numbers and gender, prepositional prefixes, position in the verse. Samples were drawn from fairly homogenous texts. No poetry or legal material was used, so they were checking for the authorship of the supposed E and J sources. Instead of saying that the two sounded alike or different from each other, as many scholars have done, they limited themselves to objective criteria.
Mr. Taylor:	Who were the scientists participating? Were they secular? Religious? Were they all Israelis? Europeans?
Dr. Singh:	All kinds. One religious man, mostly seculars. Some Israelis. A German. Dr. David Noel Freedman, Professor of Religious Studies at the University of Michigan, a respected biblical scholar, wrote the preface.
Mr. Taylor:	And what were the results of the study?
Dr. Singh:	The evidence was overwhelming that J and E were written by the same author.

	The similarities were substantially greater than the internal similarities of the works of Kant and Goethe, which had internal similarity of twenty-two percent and eight percent respectively. The internal similarity percentage of the J and E documents was eighty-two percent. Stunning.
Mr. Taylor:	Do you agree with the results, Dr. Singh?
Dr. Singh:	It is hard to disagree. The mathematics is brilliant.
Mr. Taylor:	On the basis of the mathematical analysis, are you convinced that J and E are one and the same document?
Dr. Singh:	Absolutely.
Mr. Taylor:	Thank you, Dr. Singh.

• • •

Mr. Calabrese:	Dr. Singh, are you a religious man?
Dr. Singh:	I am a religious Sikh. I have no interest in the Bible whatsoever. It means nothing to me one way or the other.
Mr. Calabrese:	This is a bit of a radical study, isn't it? An unconventional approach?
Dr. Singh:	Yes.
Mr. Calabrese:	The study was published about four decades ago, yes?
Dr. Singh:	Yes.
Mr. Calabrese:	Has it gained wide acceptance in the academic community?

Dr. Singh: No. But –

Mr. Calabrese: A simple no is enough, Dr. Singh. Thank you. No more questions.

Judge: You may call your next witness, Mr. Calabrese.

Mr. Calabrese: The defense calls Dr. Jamison Potemkin.

Biblical Archaeology

Mr. Calabrese: Good morning, sir. Please state your name and occupation.

Dr. Potemkin: Dr. Jamison Edward Potemkin. I'm professor of biblical archaeology at the University of Rhode Island.

Mr. Calabrese: Dr. Potemkin, I understand that archaeology can be a technical and arcane field. Is that not so?

Dr. Potemkin: It can be for amateurs. For the true archaeologist, all the minutiae are exceedingly interesting.

Mr. Calabrese: No doubt. Most of us here in this courtroom are just amateurs, so I'll ask you to couch your answers in layman's terms.

Dr. Potemkin: I'll do my best.

Mr. Calabrese: Very well. Based on your knowledge of biblical archaeology, would you say the Bible is a reliable historical source?

Dr. Potemkin: When you say the Bible, you're covering an exceedingly long period, from the creation story until the destruction of the Jerusalem Temple in 586 B.C.E. and beyond. Your question has to be more specific.

Mr. Calabrese: That's fine. I'll ask specific questions. Before we go on to talk about archaeology, however, two quick points about chronology. First, the Bible states that Pharaoh Shishak went up against

Jerusalem in the fifth year of the reign of King Rehoboam, son of King Solomon. In what year did Shishak conduct his campaign against the Kingdom of Judah?

Dr. Potemkin: It was 925 B.C.E.

Mr. Calabrese: That means that Solomon died in 930 B.C.E. Is that consistent with the conventional chronology?

Dr. Potemkin: Yes, it is.

Mr. Calabrese: Does anyone in the academic community question the conventional chronology as you've explained it to this court?

Dr. Potemkin: No, sir. It's universally accepted.

Mr. Calabrese: Thank you. Now let's go on to more serious issues –

Mr. Taylor: Counsel has introduced new testimony. I'd like to cross-examine.

Judge: Go ahead, counselor.

• • •

Mr. Taylor: Dr. Potemkin, how do we know that Shishak invaded Judah in 925 B.C.E.?

Dr. Potemkin: It's an established fact.

Mr. Taylor: But how was it established? Isn't it true, that this is one of the points of synchronicity by which Egyptian chronology is established? Isn't the date for Shishak's campaign derived from the conventional chronology of Israel and Judah rather than the other way around?

Dr. Potemkin: Yes.

Mr. Taylor:	All of ancient chronology is a muddle, isn't it?
Mr. Calabrese:	Objection, your honor.
Mr. Taylor:	I withdraw the question. You can continue, Mr. Calabrese.

• • •

Mr. Calabrese:	Dr. Potemkin, you were making a distinction between different parts of the Bible. Please continue with the point you were making.
Dr. Potemkin:	I was saying that ... Look, if we limit ourselves to Israelite history and start with the Patriarchs, the Bible covers a period of well over a thousand years. Some radical minimalists deny all Israelite history, saying it was all invented during the Hellenistic period under the Greeks. I do not subscribe to that school of thought. Nor do most moderate archaeologists.
Mr. Calabrese:	All right.
Dr. Potemkin:	As we come closer to the modern era, we find corroboration of the biblical account from extra-biblical sources. Aramean, Moabite and Assyrian inscriptions mention Israelite kings. We have coins, seals and other remnants of what we call the material culture.
Mr. Calabrese:	From excavations?
Dr. Potemkin:	Yes, of course. But as you go back further, there is practically no outside corroboration of the Biblical account.

There was a time when archaeologists believed archaeology would confirm the biblical story. In recent generations, however, we've come to the conclusion that archaeology supports the view that the early accounts of the Bible are pure fiction.

Mr. Calabrese: You mean there was no Israel in ancient times?

Dr. Potemkin: We know there was an Israel in 1207 B.C.E. The famous Merneptah Stela mentioned an Israel in the Judean hills.

Mr. Calabrese: And what is the Merneptah Stela?

Dr. Potemkin: It's a large stone monument commissioned by Pharaoh Merneptah. The monument is densely inscribed with Merneptah's glorious military victories. On the stela, Israel is identified as a people rather than a state, so this was probably at the very beginning of its development as a nation. Other than that, we hear nothing about Israel in the Egyptian record. There is no mention of the settlement of a patriarchal Israelite family in Egypt.

Mr. Calabrese: I see.

Dr. Potemkin: It's also preposterous that an Israelite named Joseph would become the second most powerful person in Egypt. There is absolutely no mention of the bondage of Israelites in Egypt. There's no record of an Exodus. There's no record of many travels and encampments in the desert for forty years.

Mr. Calabrese: How about the War of Conquest under Joshua?

Dr. Potemkin: There's no record of a military conquest of Canaan. No record of a wide-scale destruction of Canaanite cities. No Israelite inscriptions from this period confirming any of the Bible's claims. In fact, we've never found any Israelite inscriptions, although we've found inscriptions from just about every nation in the area; it certainly shows the lack of sophistication of any Israelite kingdoms that may have existed in ancient times.

Mr. Calabrese: It does make you think, doesn't it? Go on.

Dr. Potemkin: Yes, where was I? Ah, yes. The Bible reports that the Israelites besieged and destroyed the city of Jericho, but the archaeological record, according to the prestigious archaeologist Dame Kathleen Kenyon, shows that Jericho was not inhabited at that time. That discovery was the last nail in the coffin of the maximalists such as William Albright and his school.

Mr. Calabrese: You've made many provocative points, Dr. Potemkin. I'd like to review them one by one, if you please. You say it's unlikely that an Israelite such as Joseph would rise to a position of supreme power in Egypt.

Dr. Potemkin: Pure fantasy. Romantic fiction.

Mr. Calabrese: And you say there's no record of Israelites enslaved in Egypt?

Dr. Potemkin: According to the Bible, Israelites in large numbers, perhaps hundreds of thousands, were enslaved in Egypt. Now, the Egyptians kept meticulous records. They left huge archives that include records of government affairs, military records and business. One would expect that the enslavement of hundreds of thousands of people would be recorded. But it isn't. Not a trace of their being there, not a trace of their escape into the desert.

Mr. Calabrese: And you said something about no records of their encampments.

Dr. Potemkin: That's right. According to the Bible, the Israelites camped at forty-two places in the desert before entering Canaan. We found no trace of such an encampment anywhere. You might argue that we can't be sure of the exact locations of these camps. Two of the places, however, can be identified with reasonable assurance – Kadesh Barne'a and Etzion Geber. Yet in neither of these has a single thirteenth century pottery sherd been found.

Mr. Calabrese: And the Biblical story of the conquest of Canaan?

Dr. Potemkin: The archaeological record shows there was no violent conquest. The Canaanite city of Hazor was destroyed. That's true. But there's no record of thirteenth century destruction for the other cities recorded as conquered in the Book of Joshua. As for the colorful story of the siege of Jericho and the sounding of the ram's horn that brought its walls tumbling down, there's no archaeological record of habitation in Jericho at that time.

Mr. Calabrese: Tell me, Dr. Potemkin, is there a record of an increase of population in Canaan during the thirteenth century?

Dr. Potemkin: Yes, there was apparently a significant increase in population, mostly in the Judean hill country. But even so, the population was nowhere near the hundreds of thousands reported by the Bible. According to archaeological data, the population of Canaan in the thirteenth century B.C.E. was approximately 45,000 in 250 sites. By the eight century B.C.E., the total population of Judah and Israel was about 160,000 in 500 sites.

Mr. Calabrese: Not very great numbers indeed. Obviously, the Bible's figures cannot be taken seriously. But nonetheless, as you have said, there was undeniably a significant population increase in these lands in the thirteenth century. How do you account for that increase?

Dr. Potemkin: There are different opinions among archaeologists. All agree there was an influx of a different population group, because the luxury implements and fine ceramic pottery of the sophisticated Canaanite cities were replaced by rough and primitive implements and ceramics.

Mr. Calabrese: Who were these new people?

Dr. Potemkin: The German scholar Albrecht Alt suggests

that the new arrivals were the result of peaceful infiltration of peoples from surrounding areas. George Mendenhall suggests there was a peasant revolt in the Canaanite cities. This theory was dismissed, because no archaeological evidence supports it. Israel Finkelstein suggests they are the result of the resedentarization of nomads.

Mr. Calabrese: The what? Please explain.

Dr. Potemkin: Of course. Dr. Finkelstein suggested that, because of difficult times, many city people abandoned urban life and became nomadic shepherds. Then, in the thirteenth century, they decided to settle down again to a sedentary life. Thus, we find a sudden increase in population. Nomads do not register in the archaeological record, but cities, towns and villages do. I subscribe to this point of view. The Israelites were originally Canaanites.

Mr. Calabrese: Interesting. One more question. The Bible reports that King David and King Solomon ruled over a large and glorious kingdom. Does archaeology support or contradict this view?

Dr. Potemkin: The Bible reports that King Solomon rebuilt the northern cities of Megiddo, Hazor and Gezer. In all these places, archaeologists uncovered monumental palace remains. They also had characteristic city gates that had three chambers on each side. These came

	to be identified as the Solomonic architectural style.
Mr. Calabrese:	Was that corroboration?
Dr. Potemkin:	It didn't turn out that way. At first, there was some excitement, as many thought they'd found corroboration for the Bible. But it was a false alarm. The sites were tested with carbon-14 dating, and it was discovered that the ruins were over a century younger, well after the time of David and Solomon. It appears that Israel under David and Solomon was at best a backward mountain kingdom.
Mr. Calabrese:	Please sum up for us, Dr. Potemkin.
Dr. Potemkin:	Archaeology has demonstrated that Israel began modestly in the hill country of Judah and did not reach the level of a respectable regional kingdom until late in its history. The Bible is a fantasy.
Mr. Calabrese:	Thank you, Dr. Potemkin. No more questions. Your turn, counselor.

• • •

Mr. Taylor:	Dr. Potemkin, you've made a blanket statement that there was no significant Israelite presence in Egypt. Your basis for this sweeping generalization is that there's no record of it. Would you consider this negative evidence?
Dr. Potemkin:	I suppose.
Mr. Taylor:	Isn't it a rule in archaeology and in general that absence of evidence is not

	evidence of absence? Isn't it generally assumed that negative evidence only proves that you have not found anything but that you very well may?
Dr. Potemkin:	This is true. Nonetheless, you would expect to see some record.
Mr. Taylor:	Where would you expect to find such records?
Dr. Potemkin:	On papyrus rolls from Egyptian archives.
Mr. Taylor:	And since the Israelites were in the Nile Delta, isn't that where you would expect to find such records? Like in Heliopolis or Pi-Ramesses?
Dr. Potemkin:	Yes.
Mr. Taylor:	Now we know that such archives existed from tomb records in the dry sands of Saqqara, isn't that so?
Dr. Potemkin:	Yes.
Mr. Taylor:	What happened to those archives?
Dr. Potemkin:	They have not survived.
Mr. Taylor:	Why not? Because the climate is wet, and the ground is muddy.
Mr. Taylor:	I see. How many papyri from these archives have survived? None.
Mr. Taylor:	Nothing? Not even a scrap?
Dr. Potemkin:	Not even a scrap.
Mr. Taylor:	So, there could have been volumes of records of Israelites in those archives that disintegrated in the heat and the mud.

	Isn't that so?
Dr. Potemkin:	Who knows what was in those archives? There could have been anything. But just because the archives were destroyed doesn't prove that there were Israelites mentioned there. If the biblical narrative is true, you would expect to see some record somewhere. Just something. Anything.
Mr. Taylor:	Are there records for Semitic people infiltrating Egypt in times of drought and famine, as the Bible recounts?
Dr. Potemkin:	Yes.
Mr. Taylor:	Do Egyptian inscriptions identify different Semitic groups?
Dr. Potemkin:	No, they're all called Semites.
Mr. Taylor:	And there are inscriptions in the tomb of the vizier of Thutmose III of Semites making bricks, aren't there?
Dr. Potemkin:	Yes. But they're described as prisoners of war.
Mr. Taylor:	But don't we have a basis for Egyptians using captive Semites for forced labor? Doesn't the Bible speak of an *erub rab*, a mixed multitude, joining the Israelites in the Exodus? Couldn't these have been other captive Semitic peoples as well as disgruntled Egyptians?
Dr. Potemkin:	Anything could be. We don't believe it.
Mr. Taylor:	Dr. Potemkin, this court is not interested in your beliefs. We're looking for facts. And you've given us hardly any facts. You

say the Joseph story is romantic fiction, that it would have been impossible for a Semite to rise to such power in Egypt. Is that correct?

Dr. Potemkin: Yes, that is correct.

Mr. Taylor: How about Aper-El, vizier to Amenhotep III and Akhenaten? Wasn't he a Semite?

Dr. Potemkin: Maybe. His name would indicate he was.

Mr. Taylor: So, if Aper-El could be vizier, why couldn't Joseph? In fact, didn't Jaroslav Cerny observe that during the Ramesside era it became quite common for men of foreign origin to serve in high office at court?

Dr. Potemkin: It's unclear. Anyway, the Joseph story supposedly took place before the Ramesside era.

Mr. Taylor: Let's move on to Solomon's construction projects in Megiddo, Hazor and Gezer. You say these projects are dated more than a century after King Solomon. When did King Solomon live?

Dr. Potemkin: In the late tenth century B.C.E. That is almost 1000 B.C.E.

Mr. Taylor: How do you know that?

Dr. Potemkin: We can date it back from the destruction of the Temple he built. According to the Book of Kings, the Temple stood for four hundred years. Since it was destroyed in 586 B.C.E., it must have been built around 990 B.C.E. Those palaces in Megiddo, Hazor and Gezer were built in the mid-

	800s B.C.E.
Mr. Taylor:	I see. You're using the conventional chronology. But if you follow the Talmudic chronology – that the Temple was destroyed in 420 B.C.E. – everything falls into place neatly, doesn't it? The Exodus and Conquest take place exactly when the Bible claims they took place, and Solomon's construction projects take place exactly when the Bible says they took place. Isn't that so?
Dr. Potemkin:	What do you want me to say? I think that chronology is wrong.
Mr. Taylor:	All right. Let's talk about the significant increase in population in Canaan in the thirteenth century. If the Bible is fiction, how did the Bible writers, supposedly writing seven hundred years later, know exactly when to place the Israelite influx into Canaan so that it would coincide with a sudden and rapid growth in population? Were they archaeologists?
Dr. Potemkin:	I have no answer to that question. Perhaps they had a tradition.
Mr. Taylor:	A tradition? They remembered nothing factual about their history, but they knew exactly when they arrived. Tell me, was there anything unusual about the remains from these thirteenth century Israelite habitations?
Dr. Potemkin:	What do you mean? Their pottery and implements were relatively primitive, as I mentioned before.

Mr. Taylor: Was there anything unusual about their eating habits? You know ... about the kind of meat they ate?

Dr. Potemkin: Oh, yes, of course. No pig bones were found in these settlements.

Mr. Taylor: Were pig bones found in the habitations of the Canaanites, the Philistines and the other peoples of the area?

Dr. Potemkin: Yes, many pig bones.

Mr. Taylor: But no pig bones in the Israelite habitations?

Dr. Potemkin: None.

Mr. Taylor: How do you explain that?

Dr. Potemkin: We have no explanation for it. It's a mystery.

Mr. Taylor: Isn't it a strange coincidence that the Bible forbids pig meat? Could that have been the reason for the absence of pig bones?

Dr. Potemkin: It couldn't have been, because the Bible did not exist at the time. The Israelites probably decided not to eat pigs and then wrote it into the Bible.

Mr. Taylor: Why would they do such a thing? Pigs are a good source of meat. They're also easy to feed, because they'll eat anything. Why would a people struggling to eke out a livelihood deprive themselves of pig meat? Is there any other instance of a people deciding not to eat pig meat?

Dr. Potemkin: I know of no other instance, and I cannot speak for the motivation of the early Israelites. They may have felt that

	abstaining from pig meat would make them stand out among their neighbors. Who knows? They may have considered abstinence from pig meat a sign of distinction.
Mr. Taylor:	That is your thesis?
Dr. Potemkin:	I do not have a thesis. As I said before, it's a mystery.
Mr. Taylor:	I see. I have no more questions for this witness, your honor. I'd like to call my next rebuttal witness.

• • •

Mr. Taylor:	Please state your name and occupation, sir.
Dr. Webster:	My name is Dr. Kyle Webster. I'm professor of archaeology and ancient Near Eastern history at the University of Pennsylvania.
Mr. Taylor:	Dr. Webster, let's start with the Joseph story. Is it plausible?
Dr. Webster:	Oh, yes. Eminently plausible. There are numerous indications of its authenticity. Scholars with specialized training in Egyptology have long recognized the powerful Egyptian elements of the story. I refer you to Dr. Kenneth Kitchen, one of the greatest scholars in the world, head and shoulders above everyone else in Egyptology and comparative Near Eastern studies. Specifically, I recommend his latest book, *On the Reliability of the Old*

	Testament. It is totally authoritative.
Mr. Taylor:	Any others?
Dr. Webster:	Many. I would also recommend Dr. James K. Hoffmeier's *Israel in Egypt,* an excellent piece of scholarship. Dr. Alan R. Schulman, quoted by Hoffmeier, claims that the writer of the Joseph story must have had an exceedingly intimate knowledge of Egyptian life, literature and culture.
Mr. Taylor:	Can you give us details of this intimate knowledge?
Dr. Webster:	There are many. I'll try not to overload you. First, there's the average price of slaves. At the time of the Joseph story, it was indeed twenty shekels, as the Bible reports, but then it rose sharply. It's highly unlikely that later writers could guess the price of a slave centuries before.
Mr. Taylor:	And the price of slaves at that time was discovered in the archaeological record?
Dr. Webster:	It was.
Mr. Taylor:	Would you consider that archaeological evidence for the early authorship of the Bible?
Dr. Webster:	Most certainly. It's irrefutable evidence. At least for the Joseph story. There's more.
Mr. Taylor:	Go on. Illuminate us.
Dr. Webster:	When Joseph was purchased by Potiphar, the Bible states that he was appointed 'over the house.' This expression – 'over the house' – is found on ancient papyri as

a phrase referring to domestic servants. Then the Bible supplies names – Potiphar, Potiphera, Asnath, Tzafnath-paane'ah – all genuine Egyptian names. Potiphera, whose name incorporates the name of the Egyptian sun god, is described as the priest of On, which was the cult center of the sun god at exactly the time the Joseph story purportedly took place. The word *hartumim*, meaning dream interpreters or magicians, is an ancient Egyptian word. There are also many other linguistic connections. And of course, there is the use of the name Pharaoh.

Mr. Taylor: What about the name Pharaoh?

Dr. Webster: Scholars are frustrated that the Bible does not mention the name of the Pharaoh of the enslavement or the Exodus, as the Bible does in the Books of the Prophets where we read about Pharaoh Necho or Hofra or Shishak. But not in the Books of Genesis and Exodus. Why the omission?

Mr. Taylor: Why, indeed?

Dr. Webster: There's a good reason. Pharaoh means 'the great house' in Egyptian. It wasn't used as a title for the king until the middle of the second millennium B.C.E., about 1450 B.C.E. For the next five hundred years or so, the king was known just by the name Pharaoh without the addition of a personal name. Afterward, the personal name began to be added. If the Books of Genesis and Exodus were written during these five hundred years, they would not

	have identified an Egyptian king by any name other than Pharaoh, which was the accepted Egyptian custom.
Mr. Taylor:	Interesting. Anything else?
Dr. Webster:	There is the investiture ceremony when Joseph is appointed to high office. The Bible states that Joseph was arrayed in fine linen, a golden chain was placed on his neck, and he was transported in the royal chariot. Once again, we know from ancient inscriptions that this is an accurate description of the ceremony. A writer composing a story hundreds of years later could not have known any of this.
Mr. Taylor:	I see.
Dr. Webster:	And listen to this detail! Joseph was also given the royal signet ring during this ceremony. You would expect the ring to be placed *al yado*, on his hand, or on his finger to be more specific. But the Bible says it was placed *biyado*, in his hand. Since when do you place a ring in someone's hand? Strange, isn't it? But lo and behold, if you look at Plate XXXVIII, Figure 45, in Kitchen's book, that is exactly what you see. They are placing the ring into the hand of the person being invested with high office.
Mr. Taylor:	Fascinating.
Dr. Webster:	You already mentioned during your cross-examination of Dr. Potemkin that Semites did indeed reach high office in Egypt.

	That's an important piece of evidence, because how would a later writer have known such a thing? There is much more evidence. Would you like me to go on?
Mr. Taylor:	I think you have made a powerful case for the authenticity of the Joseph story, Dr. Webster. Let's move on to the Exodus.
Dr. Webster:	As you pointed out during cross-examination, the archives in the Nile Delta have not survived, but we do have a lot of indirect evidence for the presence of the Israelites in Egypt and the Exodus, some of which you have already covered yesterday during your cross-examination. Take for instance the Bible's statement that the Israelites asked for permission to go into the desert to worship their God. Strange request, wouldn't you say? Yet there is plenty of evidence that it was customary for laborers in Egypt to be given time off for religious observances. How would someone writing centuries later know this?
Mr. Taylor:	How, indeed?
Dr. Webster:	I would also like to point out an interesting piece of information. The Bible says that the Israelites turned back at Pi-ha-hiroth and encamped before Migdol. Scholars always wondered about the etymology of Pi-ha-hiroth, which they thought was an Egyptian term, like Pithom or Pi-Ramesses. But it turns out that it isn't. There have long been hints that Egypt was protected by a frontier

canal, which ran north to south. Satellite imaging has confirmed the existence of this ancient canal. Pi-ha-hiroth is a Semitic term for the mouth of the canal. The Israelites had to turn back because their progress was blocked by the canal.

Mr. Taylor: Fascinating. All right, let's talk about the desert travels of the Israelites. Dr. Potemkin seemed to feel that there should have been some trace left over, at least a few broken pieces of pottery. How come there is no trace of any habitation at any of those places at that time?

Dr. Webster: Well, Dr. Potemkin should not have been expecting to find traces of pottery. People on the move, even if they're traveling at a leisurely pace, are not likely to bring along heavy ceramic pottery. You only go shopping for ceramics after you settle down. As long as you're on the road, you make do with leatherwork or skins. You see?

Mr. Taylor: I do.

Dr. Webster: Kitchen points out that there was a major Egyptian mining site at Serabit el-Khadim in the Sinai at about that time, and there must have been a lot of traffic back and forth with periodic stopping places, yet no trace has ever been found. You wouldn't expect to find traces of desert travelers after three thousand years. From recent experience, we know that all traces of nomadic encampments usually disappear after about fifty years.

Mr. Taylor: So you're not disturbed by the absence of evidence of habitation at these sites?

Dr. Webster: Not at all. On the contrary, I believe the absence of habitation is actually strong proof to the authenticity of the desert itinerary.

Mr. Taylor: Really? How is that?

Dr. Webster: Look, it's common sense. The Israelites traveling through the desert would not have encamped at a spot already occupied by other people. They needed empty, uninhabited spots. That's obvious. Now if archaeologists had found that some of these purported sites of encampment had houses and pottery at the time, it would really raise questions about the itinerary. But as it is, everything works out perfectly. All forty-two camp sites were uninhabited at the time, so the Israelites had room to encamp. Now, could a writer living hundreds of years later have guessed that every single one of the forty-two places he picked out of a hat would be uninhabited back then, especially since some of them were inhabited during his own time?

Mr. Taylor: Let me understand this. Are you saying that the mention of forty-two uninhabited places is actually proof of the antiquity of the Bible?

Dr. Webster: Exactly.

Mr. Taylor: How about the lack of evidence of the destruction of the Canaanite cities mentioned in the Conquest list of the

Book of Joshua?

Dr. Webster: The Bible does not say they were destroyed but that they were smitten. Smitten, does not mean destroyed. Why would they destroy the Canaanite cities? They weren't some foreign invaders who would burn, pillage and go back home. They were invaders, immigrants. They intended to live in this land. Moses had promised them they would live in houses other people had built. They weren't about to destroy their future homes. That's why the Conquest took so long. They couldn't just attack and destroy. They had to fight house to house, door to door, so that they wouldn't destroy the valuable property. Only a couple of cities, such as Hazor, had to be destroyed to break the resistance.

Mr. Taylor: How about there being no signs of habitation in Jericho at that time?

Dr. Webster: According to archaeological evidence, Jericho was destroyed by fire about 1550 B.C.E. and then was uninhabited for two hundred years. As Dr. Kitchen explains, when a new city is built on the ruins of the old, the ruins are preserved. But when the site is left uninhabited, the remains are destroyed by erosion and by scavenging for building materials. During these two hundred years, erosion wiped out almost all traces of the old Jericho. What we know of the old settlement is based on a few fragments. Then the city was resettled in 1350 B.C.E. When the

Israelites destroyed the city again about a hundred years later, they made a taboo against rebuilding the city. As a result, it was uninhabited for another four hundred years. During that time, erosion and scavengers erased every trace of the city, as expected.

Mr. Taylor: Let's talk about the increase in population in Canaan during the thirteenth century B.C.E. What do you think of Dr. Potemkin's theory that the early Israelites were local Canaanites?

Dr. Webster: The archaeological evidence is clear that this is when the Israelites arrived on the scene. The archeological evidence also shows they were different from the indigenous population. Different implements and ceramics. Different architectural styles. Different dietary customs. Twist it as hard as you wish, you cannot make a reasonable case for them coming out of the local woodwork.

Mr. Taylor: What do you mean by architectural styles?

Dr. Webster: Their villages were oval, patterned after desert encampments.

Mr. Taylor: What does this prove? Why couldn't they have been nomads who were settling down, as Finkelstein claims?

Dr. Webster: Because this theory is unsound. Dr. William Dever takes it to pieces in *Who Were the Early Israelites and Where Did They Come from?* He points out that Finkelstein himself admits that nomads in Palestine in all periods up until the present comprise no more than ten to fifteen percent of the population. Yet during the thirteenth century B.C.E., the population of the hill country of Judah tripled. If all the nomads settled down and became farmers and villagers, you still wouldn't come close to accounting for the tremendous increase in population. If you don't accept the historical authenticity of the Bible, it's an insoluble mystery.

Mr. Taylor: Dr. Webster, I would like to talk to you about population. Yesterday, Dr. Potemkin testified, based once again on Finkelstein, that the population of the hill country of Judah in the thirteenth century was about 45,000 and that there were about 160,000 people in Judah in the eighth century. Do you agree?

Dr. Webster: No, I most emphatically do not. Let's just look at extra-biblical sources. According to the Sennaherib Stela, King Sennaherib of Assyria claimed to have exiled over two hundred thousand people from Judah to Assyria. According to Finkelstein, that's more than the total number of people who lived in Judah during that time. Not only does he disregard the information in the Bible, he also disregards the ancient inscription record.

Mr. Taylor: Well, Finkelstein didn't just make up those figures, did he? How did he arrive at those figures? Where did he go wrong?

Dr. Webster: Finkelstein arrives at his figures by using something called the Population Density Coefficient. It sounds complicated, but it's not. They measure the population density in modern-day settlements that feature primitive conditions without the benefits of modern technology. Life hasn't changed so much for these people in the last few thousand years. The population density in Jerusalem in 1918, as in Aleppo and Tripoli, was 51 people per dunam, which is about a quarter of an acre. But Finkelstein uses the figure of 25 people per dunam. Dr. Isaac Maitlis, an Israeli archaeologist, disputes these figures in *Excavating the Bible*. He bases his projections on population density figures for the Jewish Quarter of Jerusalem in 1870, which was 157 people per dunam, six times Finkelstein's number.

Mr. Taylor: Do you have any population density data a little further back in time than the last couple of centuries?

Dr. Webster: We most definitely have. The Book of Nehemiah lists 2,872 heads of households returning to Jerusalem from exile in Babylon. If we use the conservative figure of four people per family, that means about 12,000 people. The archaeological data show that Jerusalem at the time measured about 120 dunams, which give us a density of about 100 people per dunam. I suggest we work with the conservative figure of 100 people per dunam for ancient Israel and Judah.

Mr. Taylor: Can we use this to get an idea of the total population?

Dr. Webster: We can. I'll make a long story short. Archaeological studies have shown that in ancient times between three and seven percent of a country's population lived in cities, settlements that measure fifty dunams or more. This means that about ninety-five percent of the population lived in small villages in the countryside. Let's say it's only ninety percent, just to be on the safe side.

Mr. Taylor: You're saying that ancient societies were rural. Only ten percent urban. Correct?

Dr. Webster: Correct. According to Dr. Yigal Shilo, there were sixty settlements of fifty dunams or more west of the Jordan River during the time of the Kingdoms of Israel and Judah. At the density coefficient of one hundred per dunam, that means that each of these settlements had at least five thousand, for a total urban population of at least three hundred thousand people. Since cities held only ten percent of the population, that means a total population of at least three million people and probably more, not even counting the settlements east of the Jordan River.

Mr. Taylor: And this is in keeping with the figures in the Bible?

Dr. Webster: Very much so. It also fits perfectly with the information on the inscriptions of the Sennaherib Stela in Assyria.

Mr. Taylor:	This is illuminating. Perhaps you can help us clear up another matter as well. Yesterday, Dr. Potemkin testified that there are no inscriptions on stelae and monuments in Israel and Judah such as are found in all the neighboring countries. He said that this raised questions about the sophistication of these kingdoms. Can you enlighten us about this matter?
Dr. Webster:	My pleasure. You know, archaeologists love inscriptions. As much as you can potter about in the pottery, you're really just groping in the dark. But inscriptions! Ah, what a pleasure. Names! Places! Stories! The ancient world opens up. But in Israel ... no inscriptions. The problem is not that we haven't found any yet. Apparently, no Jewish kings, not even Herod the Great, who lived in 30 B.C.E., left stone inscriptions. If not for Josephus, we wouldn't know who built Caesarea.
Mr. Taylor:	Why didn't they leave inscriptions?
Dr. Webster:	The Bible mentions two individuals who erected monuments in their own honor – Saul and Absalom. The Bible looks askance at both of these. You have to understand the Biblical culture of ancient Israel, their world view. The ancient Israelite kings ascribed their successes to God and considered raising monuments to their own glorification presumptuous. This attitude of royal humility became so ingrained in the Israelite culture that no kings, not even the idolatrous

ones, dared raise monuments to their own glorification.

Mr. Taylor: Extraordinary. The Bible actually demands humility of the king, doesn't it?

Dr. Webster: It certainly does. The Bible forbids the king to take too many wives, accumulate too much money or have too many horses. And it commands him to carry a scroll of the Law with him at all times.

Mr. Taylor: One last question, Dr, Webster. I believe you have information about an ancient record of the Israelites in Egypt. Please tell the court about it.

Dr. Webster: Well, it's not as if I dug up an inscription no one else knows about. It is just a new reading – which I believe is correct – of the famous Merneptah Stela, erected in 1207 B.C.E. It's also known as the Israel Stele, because it is the earliest known mention of Israel outside of the Bible.

Mr. Taylor: Are you going to read us the text?

Dr. Webster: Not all of it. Most of the inscription describes the victory of Merneptah, the Egyptian king, over the Libyans. At the end of the inscription there is a poem. It reads as follows:

The princes are prostrate,
saying, 'Mercy!'
Not one raises his head among the
Nine Bows.
Desolation is for Tehenu; Hatti
is pacified;
Plundered is Canaan with every evil;

Carried off is Ashkelon; seized upon is Gezer;

Yanoam is made as that which does not exist;

Israel is laid waste; his seed is not;

Hurru is become a widow for Egypt!

All lands together, they are pacified.

Here is a picture of the stela.

You can see that it's covered with a lot of text. It's a long victory poem. The part I just read is the last part of the poem. It is famous. Archaeologists assume that the Israel referenced here is in the hill country of Judah and that it was at an exceedingly early stage of development.

Mr. Taylor: Why do they think that?

Dr. Webster: Well, you see, in Egyptian hieroglyphic writing, names are generally followed by determinative symbols. The three-hill symbol indicates a city-state. A man and a woman followed by three slashes indicate a people. He pointed to an image projected on the screen. This is the symbol for a state or a city-state.

And this is the symbol for a people.

The three lines indicate the plural. It was used for a tribe or a clan. Many men and women but no state.

All the place names mentioned in this poem are followed by the three-hill symbol for a city-state, except for Israel, which is followed by the determinative symbol for a people. Archaeologists infer that the Israelites had just begun settling into the hill country of Judah and were not yet organized into a real state with a central government and governmental institutions. The Egyptians, therefore, considered them only a people and not yet a state.

Mr. Taylor: How do they explain Merneptah's claim that 'Israel is laid waste; his seed is not'? This seems pretty drastic, and we know it wasn't true.

Dr. Webster: The archaeologists aren't concerned by this. Pharaohs have been known to stretch the truth and make fanciful claims to glorify themselves.

Mr. Taylor: And you disagree with this interpretation?

Dr. Webster: I do. I have several issues with this reading. First of all, why tell a lie that is bound to be exposed right away? Israel lay on the well-traveled route from Egypt to Mesopotamia. People were bound to see plenty of Israelites running about, quite undestroyed. What profit was there for Merneptah in such a flagrant lie? All he had to say was that Israel was vanquished or defeated. Why say they were wiped out, that 'his seed is not'?

Mr. Taylor: Valid point.

Dr. Webster: There's more. Which would be a greater threat, a city-state or a tribal people? Common sense would say that a city-state with an organized government and an army would be of greater concern to the Egyptians. Therefore, it would seem that of all the places mentioned in the poem, the least threat would come from Israel, the only tribal people among all those city-states. And yet . . . and yet

. . . Merneptah reserves his harshest language for Israel. His seed is not! Tehenu, which is the Egyptian name for Libya, is desolate. Hatti, which is the Hittite kingdom, is pacified. Canaan is plundered. But Israel? His seed is not! It doesn't make sense. Moreover, why does an insignificant nomadic people deserve mention on Merneptah's glory monument in the first place?

Mr. Taylor: So how do you explain it, Dr. Webster?

Dr. Webster: I think the key to the poem is the last line. *All lands together, they are pacified.* Merneptah ascended the throne of Egypt as an elderly man. I think he was in his sixties. He didn't have time to do all these things mentioned in the poem. In the entire text of the stela before the concluding poem, Merneptah only talks about his victory over Libya. Do you know why? Because that's all he did. The rest of the victories took place over a period of time, maybe a century, and were accomplished by his predecessors. Merneptah's great accomplishment was to defeat Libya and remove the final thorn in Egypt's side so that 'all the lands together are pacified.' He put the finishing touch to the list that appears in the poem.

Mr. Taylor: So how does that explain the harsh language about Israel?

Dr. Webster: It explains it perfectly. All the other names were external threats to Egypt, states and city-states on the periphery of the Egyptian empire. But Israel was an internal threat to Egypt. They were a populous group inside the borders of Egypt that aroused fear in the hearts of the Egyptian monarchy, so much fear that they had to enslave them. They threatened Egypt as a people, not as a city-state. After the plagues, however you understand them, one of Merneptah's predecessors on the Egyptian throne drove the Israelites out of Egypt and crowed to the world that he had removed a great internal threat. So Merneptah boasted that Israel was laid waste, driven out of Egypt, and that his seed is not, that not a single one remained within the borders of Egypt. And that was the truth. Voila, archaeological proof of the Exodus!

Mr. Taylor: Interesting, Dr. Webster. Thank you. No more questions. Your turn.

• • •

Mr. Calabrese: Dr. Webster, have you adequately explained why there's no trace of Jericho? Do you expect us to believe that a whole city with massive walls could vanish without a trace?

Dr. Webster: You can believe what you choose, sir. Four hundred years is a long time. It is perfectly reasonable to believe that erosion removed a good part of the traces. You also have to understand that people scavenge the stones and bricks of abandoned ruins, which are right there for the taking, to use in their homes and buildings. After hundreds of years of exposure, every stone and brick would have been removed by people in the area. As for the scraps left over, erosion would easily take care of it.

Mr. Calabrese: I will not debate the point with you. But it must certainly seem a far-fetched scenario to any reasonable person. Let's talk about population.

Dr. Webster: By all means.

Mr. Calabrese: According to your ... ah ... calculations, you arrive at a population in the millions in ancient Israel. How could the land support so many people?

Dr. Webster: Where's the problem? According to a census taken by the Roman Empire, eight million people lived in ancient Israel in the first century B.C.E. They were eating well and living a fairly decent life.

Mr. Calabrese: But seven or eight centuries earlier?

Dr. Webster: Customs didn't change so fast in agriculture in the ancient world. If the land could support eight million people in Roman times, it could support three million people in deep antiquity.

Mr. Calabrese: Let's talk about the Merneptah stela. Your reading of it is kind of cute. Does your interpretation appear in the literature?

Dr. Webster: No. I mean, not yet. But it will when my book is published.

Mr. Calabrese: I see. And when will that be?

Dr. Webster:	Sooner rather than later.
Mr. Calabrese:	But the publication of your book is not imminent.
Dr. Webster:	It is not.
Mr. Calabrese:	Dr. Webster, what is the consensus in the academic community? Are your views shared by the mainstream?
Dr. Webster:	They're shared by many academics.
Mr. Calabrese:	I understand. I have no more questions for this witness, your honor.
Judge:	Mr. Taylor, do you have any more rebuttal witnesses?
Mr. Taylor:	I do. One more. The plaintiff calls Dr. Allen Graves.

• • •

Mr. Taylor:	Can we have your full name and occupation, sir?
Dr. Graves:	Allen Pinkerton Graves. I am Professor of Ancient Oriental Studies at McMaster University in Toronto, Ontario. That's in Canada.
Mr. Taylor:	Dr. Graves, how old is the field of Ancient Oriental Studies?
Dr. Graves:	Oh, I'd say about a hundred years old.
Mr. Taylor:	Is the field of biblical studies older?
Dr. Graves:	Yes, quite a bit. The hypotheses of the Bible critics were fairly full-blown when ancient Oriental studies were still in their infancy. They knew little about the life

and customs of the ancient world.

Mr. Taylor: Did this lack of knowledge influence their perception of the Bible?

Dr. Graves: Without a doubt. You see, the more we learn about the ancient world in the second millennium before the common era, the more we realize we're looking at the world of the Old Testament. The spirit, the customs, the way of life, the feel of the times, they all point straight at the Old Testament. I'd venture to say that much of the dry information we have derived from other sources comes to vivid life in the Old Testament. Yes, without a doubt the Old Testament has the resounding ring of truth.

Mr. Taylor: I would like you to explain to the jury how this lack of knowledge of the ancient world affected the development of biblical studies.

Dr. Graves: Well, you see, the early biblical scholars were working in a vacuum, so to speak. They found anomalies in the Bible, and according to their nineteenth-century German perception of literature, they concluded that they were looking at an anachronistic amalgam of different source documents spliced together centuries after the fact. Wherever they found inconsistencies with their theories or text that seemed to make no sense, they made emendations. They deleted text. They changed words. They saw scribal errors. They took liberties with the text, because they didn't know any better. They didn't recognize the literary style and standards of the Patriarchal era. They didn't understand the language in the context of the other languages of the time, because they knew nothing about them.

Mr. Taylor: And this is all wrong?

Dr. Graves: It's not just wrong, it's scandalous. They showed no respect for the ancient texts. He pulled an index card from his pocket. This is the certification at the end of an Egyptian funeral papyrus from about 1400 B.C.E., quoted in Cerny's *Paper and Books in Ancient Egypt*. '[The document] is completed from its beginning to its end, having been copied, revised, compared and verified sign by sign.' See the meticulous care with which Egyptian scribes prepared a simple funerary papyrus. Do you think Hebrew scribes were less careful with the preparation of their sacred literature? Is it conceivable that they put together the Bible without copying, revising and comparing it letter by letter? Horsefeathers!

Mr. Taylor: But when the flow of information from ancient Oriental studies increased, why didn't these biblical scholars abandon their earlier theories?

Dr. Graves: Because they were accustomed to their ingenious reconstructions. They were mentally conditioned in one direction. As you phrased it during your cross-examination of Dr. Winemaker, many of them became academic fundamentalists. They saw only one pathway, and they followed it blindly. But you'll be happy to hear that in recent years the old discredited preconceptions are slowly crumbling into the ash heap, where they belong.

Mr. Taylor: Do you think the study of the ancient Near East corroborates the historicity of the Bible?

Dr. Graves: I do. William Albright wrote in *Archaeology and the Religion of Israel* that 'the Mosaic tradition is so consistent ... so congruent with our independent knowledge of the religious development of the Near East in the late second millennium B.C.E. that only hypercritical pseudo-rationalism can reject its essential historicity.'

Mr. Taylor: Those are strong words.

Dr. Graves: And more recently, Dr. Henri Blocher wrote in *Révélation des Origines: Le Début de la Genése* that 'the critics, when they judge the internal phenomena [of the Bible], project into it their customs as modern Western readers and neglect all we know today of the writing customs of biblical times. The taste for repetition, the structure of a global statement, repeated with development, the replacement of a word by its synonyms, especially the change of a divine name in a text (e.g., the names of Osiris on the Ikhernofret stele) are well-attested characteristics of ancient

Middle Eastern texts ... The biblical text, as it is, agrees with the literary canons of its time.'

Mr. Taylor: Can you give us a few examples?

Dr. Graves: Glad to. I'm going to give you examples of obscure features of the ancient world during the early parts of the second millennium B.C.E., features that would not be known to people living hundreds of years later unless they were archaeologists. And there were no archaeologists in the ancient world.

Mr. Taylor: Go ahead.

Dr. Graves: Take the customs of inheritance, for instance. In the Book of Genesis, we find a number of curious customs unfamiliar to modern readers, which must have been equally unfamiliar to readers of the Bible in the middle of the first millennium B.C.E., the time the Bible was allegedly produced. First, we read in Genesis how the childless Abraham laments that his servant Eliezer will inherit his wealth if he has no sons. Strange. Why should his servant inherit rather than nephews? Well, behold, we find on cuneiform tablets unearthed in Mesopotamia at Ur and especially at Nuzi – discovered in 1925, and as of now, we have more than 5,000 of those tablets – that it was the custom during the Patriarchal age for childless couples to designate their servants as their heirs.

Mr. Taylor: Remarkable. What else?

Dr. Graves: We find among the customs of that period that a childless wife could produce an heir by proxy, so to speak, by giving her handmaiden to her husband. Indeed, that is what Sarah did. She gave Hagar to Abraham, and the son born, Ishmael, became Abraham's heir. But when Isaac was born to Sarah, he immediately replaced the handmaiden's son as Abraham's heir. This again was the ancient custom of those times. The customs further dictated that when a son was born to the principal wife the handmaiden and her son should be allowed to remain in the household and not sent away. Understandably, we find Abraham distressed that Sarah wanted him to expel Hagar and Ishmael; only a divine command could make him accept the expulsion.

Mr. Taylor: Go on.

Dr. Graves: Then we have Esau, Jacob's older brother, who sells his birthright for a bowl of soup. Selling a birthright? Who ever heard of such a thing? Yet this is exactly what Tupkitilla of Nuzi did. He sold his birthright for three sheep. A bit of a better deal than Esau got, wouldn't you say? But we find no other record of anyone selling a birthright, not in the legal codes and not in the chronicles. You can't make up stuff like this.

Mr. Taylor: Makes you think, doesn't it?

Dr. Graves: The realism of the Patriarchal narratives is extraordinary. Let's move on to property taxes. After Sarah dies, Abraham attempts to buy the Cave of the Machpelah in Hebron for an ancestral burial ground. The owner is a Hittite named Ephron. All Abraham needs is the cave, but in the end, we find that he buys the entire field in which the cave is located. Why should he buy the whole field if he has no need for it? Eh?

Mr. Taylor: I give up. Why?

Dr. Graves: Because there is a Hittite law that if the owner of a property sells only part of his field, he remains liable for the taxes on the entire field, even the part that no longer belongs to him. But if he sells the whole property, the new owner pays the taxes. Ephron didn't want to sell off only the cave, because he would have had to continue paying taxes on it. He knew he had Abraham over the barrel. Abraham's dead wife was lying there, waiting to be buried. Abraham was under pressure, so Ephron forced him to buy the entire field. It makes perfect sense once you know Hittite law, but those nineteenth-century German scholars didn't even believe there had ever been a Hittite people. They had no idea that in the next century a vast Hittite Empire would be discovered.

Mr. Taylor: Really interesting. What else do you have for us?

Dr. Graves: The *lex talionis*.

Mr. Taylor: The *lex talionis*? What is that?

Dr. Graves: It's Latin for the law of retaliation. Let me backtrack a little bit. In the Book of Exodus, we are told that if an ox gores and kills someone the ox's owner must pay a stiff fine. Then we are told that 'if it should gore a son or gore a daughter, the same rules apply.' What's the point? Why should there be a difference between an ox goring a boy or goring a girl?

Mr. Taylor: All right, tell us.

Dr. Graves: It's a clear challenge to the Code of Hammurabi.

Mr. Taylor: Who was Hammurabi?

Dr. Graves: He was a great Babylonian king who lived from about 1810-1750 B.C.E. He formulated a code of laws that was not discovered until the twentieth century. The code consisted of two hundred and eighty-two laws, most of which survive on cuneiform tablets. Listen to these. Laws 209-210. 'If a man strikes a free-born woman so that she loses her unborn child, he shall pay ten shekels for her loss. If the woman dies, his daughter shall be put to death.' Laws 229-230. 'If a builder builds a house for someone, and does not construct it properly, and the house he built collapses and kills its owner, the builder shall be put to death. If it kills the son of the owner, the son of that builder shall be put to death.' There's your *lex talionis*, your law of retaliation. You kill a woman, your daughter is put to death. You kill someone's son, your son is put to death. So, the Bible rejects these laws. No way. No matter if the ox gores a son or a daughter, the owner is assessed a fine. His son or daughter is not put to death.

Mr. Taylor: This is interesting. Are you saying that the Bible must have been aware of the Code of Hammurabi?

Dr. Graves: That's exactly what I'm saying. The Code of Hammurabi was in effect during the second millennium B.C.E., and the Bible goes out of its way to contradict it. But by the first millennium, the Code was no longer in effect in Mesopotamia. By the middle of the first millennium B.C.E., most people had never even heard of the Code of Hammurabi, and surely, no one at all was familiar with its laws. So how could these alleged late composers of the Bible write about an ox goring a son or a daughter when they probably never even heard of the Code of Hammurabi? And even if by some miracle they had knowledge of Hammurabi's laws, why would these alleged late writers compose laws to contradict obsolete and forgotten laws?

Mr. Taylor: Why, indeed. Could you sum up for us, Dr. Graves?

Dr. Graves: With pleasure. You see, the more we learn about the ancient Near East, the more we see how perfectly the Bible fits into that setting – in the customs, the laws, the lifestyles, the treaties and covenants, the language, the historical picture. The

	Old Testament transports us back to the second millennium B.C.E., and the times and societies come alive before our eyes. For scholars in my field, and even for laypeople, it is an incredibly exciting journey of discovery. In my opinion, the Bible is one the most priceless historical treasures in existence.
Mr. Taylor:	Thank you, Dr. Graves. No more questions.
Judge:	Mr. Calabrese, Do you wish to cross-examine?
Mr. Calabrese:	Yes, your honor.

• • •

Mr. Calabrese:	Just a quick point. You quoted Dr. Henri Blocher's opinion that the Bible conforms to the literary canons of its time. Does Dr. Blocher teach in a university?
Dr. Graves:	He is a professor at Wheaton College in the Boston area.
Mr. Calabrese:	Biblical studies or archaeology or ancient Oriental studies?
Dr. Graves:	He's a professor of theology.
Mr. Calabrese:	Theology? Is Wheaton a Christian college?
Dr. Graves:	Yes, it is.
Mr. Calabrese:	And you accept his opinion as objective and unbiased?
Dr. Graves:	Of course, I do. I don't discriminate against religious scholars. I evaluate their work on its own merits, and Dr. Blocher's

work is excellent.

Mr. Calabrese: No doubt. I have no more questions for this witness.

Plaintiff's Closing Statement

Mr. Taylor: Good morning, ladies and gentlemen of the jury. I want to tell you a story about a famous Egyptian boy king named Tutankhamun, popularly known as King Tut. Tutankhamun lived about three and a half thousand years ago. But the story I'm about to tell you is not about his life. It's about his death.

At first, the Egyptian pharaohs were entombed in the pyramids; the pyramids are mausoleums. The tombs of the pharaohs were filled with works of art, gold, precious stones and all manner of magnificent treasures meant to accompany them into the hereafter. But after graverobbers started looting the tombs, they buried the kings in a bleak and remote desert in southern Egypt, known as the Valley of the Kings. The tombs were dug into the mountainsides and concealed. Even if the graverobbers could make their way to this valley, they would not find the tombs. And indeed, they didn't.

Tutankhamun's multi-chamber tomb surpassed all other tombs in magnificence and funerary treasures. The king's mummified body was laid to rest in the main chamber in a golden sarcophagus – that's a coffin – with a stunning golden death mask attached to his face. Tutankhamun's tomb was legendary, but its location was unknown.

Early in the twentieth century, British archaeologists discovered the tomb after years of search and excavation. Over a period of ten years, they removed five thousand precious artifacts and shipped them off to Cairo. They also moved the sarcophagus to Cairo and displayed it in a museum. They opened the sarcophagus, removed Tutankhamun's death mask and studied his mummified body.

This was considered one of the greatest discoveries in the history of archaeology. Over the years, exhibitions of artifacts from the tomb toured the museums of the world, and millions came to view them. You can catch one of these traveling exhibitions if you look out for them, and you can even check out Tutankhamun's body if you visit Cairo.

So, let me ask you a question. How are these archaeologists different from the graverobbers? What gave them the right to disturb the rest of the dead? What gave them the right to take the body of the dead king out of his grave and put it into a museum? Is there a statute of limitations on the sanctity of the grave? Are the dead fair game after thousands of years?

So, they'll say they do it in the interest of science rather than for greed. What science? Did disturbing the grave of Tutankhamun help them save lives? Did it help them find cures for diseases? Did it help them relieve poverty? Of course not. It only increased our knowledge of the culture and history of ancient Egypt. So, if archaeologists were studying American history in the eighteenth century, would it be acceptable to dig up George Washington and check out his wooden teeth? Is academic curiosity about ancient times a valid excuse for violating the sanctity of the grave?

Would you want your body dug up? Maybe, you'd be okay with it if it helped save lives. But in the interests of learning about the culture of the twenty-first century? I don't think you'd want your grave disturbed for that. The dead deserve the sanctity of the grave. Why then was it acceptable, even exciting, to dig up Tutankhamun and put him into a museum?

Now, don't get me wrong. I'm in favor of archaeological studies of ancient ruins that teach us about ancient civilizations. But with boundaries! Why can ancient graves be disturbed? Makes you think, doesn't it?

Let me tell you what I believe. Modern academics do not relate to Tutankhamun as a person but as an ancient artifact. The passage of time has dehumanized the ancients in the modern mind. Certainly, the people of the ancient world – at least some of them – were brilliant and talented and creative, but they were not Us. They were an earlier version of Us, an earlier stage in the evolution of civilized humankind. They were our ancestors, our antecedents, but they were not Us, and they do not deserve the respect we extend to full-fledged fellow human beings.

Counsel for the defendants would have you believe that the Bible, one of the greatest literary masterpieces in history, was a pious fraud spliced together from different source documents in an extremely sloppy manner. To mention just one example, one of his proofs is that the Bible begins with two contradictory creation stories. But why would these hypothetical splicers have done such a thing? Why not include just one? Didn't it occur to these hypothetical splicers that people would find that strange?

If you recall, I asked Dr. Winemaker if he would have been taken in by the hoax, and he said that he would have seen through it. But he still insists that the ancients would not have seen through it. Do you know why? Because they were not Us. If they are not Us, we can acknowledge their talent and brilliance in putting together a masterpiece such as the Bible, and we can still cluck our tongues at their bumbling clumsiness. You really couldn't expect much more from the unfinished prototypes of the model that would one day become Us.

But you, the members of the jury, know that this is not true. During jury selection, one of you said that – and I quote – the ancients were more intelligent, because although they were lacking our technology and knowledge, they had the opportunity to think about life and things. They didn't watch television, and their phones weren't ringing all the time.

The literature of the ancients is sophisticated and complex. They were just as intelligent and as shrewd as we are. They were Us living in deep antiquity. You couldn't pull the wool over their eyes so easily. The style of the Bible is unfamiliar to us, but as we have shown, it accurately reflects the literary style of its time. And as we have also shown, the contents of the Bible reflect the customs of the second millennium B.C.E., customs that were forgotten by the first millennium B.C.E. and remained forgotten until they were discovered by archaeologists in the last two centuries. The Bible could not have been written nearly a thousand years after it claims to have been written. It comes to us intact from deep antiquity, and as such, it is as reliable a source of history as Merneptah's stela.

Ladies and gentlemen of the jury, I didn't take this case because I'm a religious man. On the contrary, God and religion played hardly any role in my life. I accepted the academic orthodoxy that the Bible is myth without giving it much thought. It didn't matter to me.

Why did I take this case? Because, as some of you may know, my beloved grandson, my only grandchild, was murdered in Hesterville by thugs from the American Identity Party, the party that justifies race wars by claiming that the Bible is a fraud and that its moral teachings are irrelevant. They view people as intelligent animals and believe that survival is the only morality. I took this case because I wanted to strike a blow against the ideological foundation of their movement.

If you recall, at the beginning of the trial I claimed equipoise, and the judge ruled in my favor. That means that the burden of proof regarding the historicity of the Bible is on the defendants. The Bible has been accepted as historical by billions of people for thousands of years, and if the defendants claimed it was unhistorical, they would have to prove it. I felt I could weaken their case enough to get a favorable verdict based on equipoise.

But as I dove into a deep study of the Bible and the academic literature, I discovered that the evidence in favor of the Bible was extraordinarily strong, far better than the evidence against it, and I hope I have presented the evidence to you clearly.

But if the evidence for the Bible is so strong, you might ask, why is there so much opposition to the Bible in the academic community? The answer is that it stems from German scholars in the nineteenth century who wanted to free Germanic society from the shackles of the Bible. A strong strain of anti-Semitism and anti-Christianity runs through the writings of Wellhausen, the father of the Documentary Hypothesis.

But how could he extricate people from the grips of the Bible, which was so deeply ingrained in their hearts and minds? The Bible had to be exposed as a hoax. The authorship had to be moved up about a thousand years so that its historicity could be discredited. Because if the Bible were written when it claims to have been written, it would be hard to argue that there was never an encounter with the divine, that the Ten Commandments and the Golden Rule had no validity.

Under the cloak of academic scholarship, they dissected the Bible and added layer upon layer of unsupported speculation. With the passage of time, those unsupported speculations became academic orthodoxy and were accepted as fact. Biblical studies in universities used the manufactured facts as the starting point of their teaching. Students were not invited to question the underlying assumptions. Rather, they pored over the biblical text in search of ever more source documents until the Bible was rendered a ridiculous patchwork of scraps and pieces. It didn't matter that no other book was ever produced this way. The Bible had to be relegated to myth.

But I believe we've demonstrated, ladies and gentlemen of the jury, that the Bible is not a work of fiction but a work of magnificent history of the highest importance. Whether or not you choose to believe the miracle stories, the basic historicity of the Bible cannot be denied, just as the historicity of the Merneptah stela cannot be denied, despite its miracle stories.

Ladies and gentlemen of the jury, this trial is not about the separation between church and state. Our society permits people to believe whatever they wish about God, even nothing at all. Mrs. Williams was not teaching religion in her classroom. She was teaching the history of the ancient world, which is wonderfully preserved in the Bible.

The school board has no list of approved supplementary texts that can be used in the classroom. Teachers can bring in any history book of their choice, many of which are much less reliable than the Bible. Mrs. Williams chose to use the Bible, and she was fired. Her civil rights were violated. I hope you will agree that the defendants are guilty as charged.

Thank you, and God bless you.

Judge:	We've reached the lunch hour. Mr. Calabrese, are you ready to make your closing arguments after we break for lunch?
Mr. Calabrese:	I'm ready, your honor.

Defense's Closing Statement

Mr. Calabrese: In a short time, you'll be making the most important decision of your lives, outside of your personal affairs. You'll go down in the annals of history. You have a tremendous responsibility, and I implore you to vote with your heads rather than with your hearts.

You have listened to countless hours of expert testimony about whether or not the Bible is a reliable historical record or a beautiful collection of inspiring myths and legends. I'm sure you'll be relieved to hear that I don't intend to review all the material today. The proofs we've presented are just the tip of a vast iceberg of evidence that the Bible is a brilliant creation of writers and editors living many centuries after it claims to have been written.

No one has disputed in this trial that the overwhelming majority of biblical scholars in the world have reached this conclusion after studying the Bible intensively. They have analyzed every verse, every phrase, every word. Faced with the overwhelming mass of evidence, they have reached the inevitable conclusion – that the Bible was composed in the middle of the first millennium B.C.E., many centuries after it claims to have been written. The references are all from the later period. The historical context is the later period. The style of the language and the vocabulary are from the later period. As you have seen, the evidence from the text itself is crystal clear. And then we have the archaeological evidence, which only corroborates the conclusion the scholars have already reached.

I cannot expect you to become Bible experts in such a brief period of time when the experts have toiled for many years. But I can expect you to get a sense of the mountain of evidence that exists on the authorship of the Bible. You should recognize that a consensus exists among Bible scholars, not on every piece of the evidence, but certainly on the overall conviction that the Bible – specifically, the Five Books of Moses – was not written in the second millennium B.C.E. In fact, the consensus among scholars is that there never was a Moses, nor an Abraham, nor an Isaac, nor a Jacob, nor a Joseph. These are all mythical figures, larger than life, the stuff of legend, the products of the creative genius of the composers of the Bible. Such is the verdict of science.

At one time, humankind lived in a world governed by superstition and magical thinking, when faith ruled supreme and reason was disdained. But we've progressed since then. We've become enlightened. The human intellect has been liberated. Reason now rules supreme. Who among you is ready to sacrifice your reason to faith? I venture to say that not one of you would do so. Your presence on this jury is an affirmation of the rule of reason. You are here to make a rational evaluation of the facts, not to promote some spiritual ideal or irrational faith.

My friends, he continued, the science of biblical studies does not reject the Bible, nor am I asking you to do anything of the sort. The science of biblical studies rescues the Bible from the prison of ignorance, obscurantism and blind faith and allows its pure light to shine forth and illuminate the world. Do we have to believe that great novels such as Stendhal's *The Red and the Black* and Maugham's *Of Human Bondage* are true stories in order to appreciate their insights into the inner crevices of the soul? Don't we recognize literature as one of the highest forms of creative art? We should also recognize the Bible as one of the greatest masterpieces of literature in the history of the world. Nothing less. Nothing more.

To restrict the Bible to the narrow confines of a true story is to rob it of its universal power. It's not important to insist that Abraham and Moses existed; it's important to recognize the ideals they represent. We need to embrace the messages of compassion, social responsibility, liberty and justice found in the Bible; they're the enduring truth. If all of humankind were to embrace these ideals, this world in which we live would be a far better place. But it's ridiculous to confuse the Bible's legends and myths with history. Too many people have done so over the centuries and brought untold tragedy and misery on the world.

Science has come to liberate the Bible from the clutches of the fundamentalists, the extremists, the suicide bombers, the sanctimonious militants who would tell us how to live and what to think. Science has come to peel away the layers of superstition and irrationalism that have encrusted the Bible. Science has come to restore the purity and benevolent power of this magnificent piece of literature we know as the Bible. And in the process, science will liberate all of humankind from the clutches of archaic and irrational thought and from the hatred and violence they engender.

Ladies and gentlemen of the jury, your mission, your destiny, is to be part of that process of liberation. Your decision in favor of science will affirm the emergence of society from the dark ages. It is your duty as people of the modern world to bring in a verdict in favor of the defense.

The Verdict

Judge:	Members of the jury, have you reached a verdict?
Forewoman:	Yes, we have, your honor.
Judge:	What say you?
Forewoman:	Your honor, in the matter of *Williams v. Youngblood et al*, we find in favor of the plaintiff. She is to be reinstated and awarded the sum of four and a half million dollars.

Bibliography

Albright, William, *Archaeology and the Religion of Israel*

Blocher, Henri, *Révélation des Origines: Le Début de la Genése*

Cassuto, Umberto, *The Documentary Hypothesis*; *La Questione della Genesi*

Dever, William, *Who Were the Early Israelites and Where Did They Come From?*

Hoffmeier, James, *Israel in Egypt*; *Ancient Israel in Sinai*

Kitchen, Kenneth, *Ancient Orient, Old Testament*; *On the Reliability of the Old Testament*

Maitlis Isaac, *Excavating the Bible*

Yehuda Radday and Haim Shorr, *Genesis: An Authorship Study*

www.ingramcontent.com/pod-product-compliance
Lightning Source LLC
Chambersburg PA
CBHW071550120726
48009CB00007B/249/J